# Black Man's
# America

# Black Man's America

## Simeon Booker

Prentice-Hall, Inc.
Englewood Cliffs, N.J.

To

My wife Thelma, and
our next generation—
Theresa, Simeon, Jr.
and James.

# Acknowledgments

John H. Johnson, my publisher for the past ten years who provided me with the opportunity for experience on the civil rights front line and whose help and co-operation made the book possible; Dr. Philip M. Hauser, Dept. of Sociology, University of Chicago, for advice and use of material from his book, "Population Perspectives." Arthur M. Brandel, a freelance writer, for editorial assistance; Dr. Samuel D. Proctor, President of A and T College, Greensboro, N.C. for many hours of discussion; Pat Munroe, Washington correspondent, *Editor and Publisher*; Arthur Chapin, special assistant to the Secretary of Labor; Dr. Booker T. McGraw, a housing specialist; Theodore Brown, a Harvard labor fellow; Louis Lyons, former Curator, Nieman Foundation, Harvard University; Prof. Lewis W. Jones, Fisk University sociologist, and Harry Bass, of the Department of Agriculture. Special appreciation to my own staff: Miss E. Fannie Granton, a faithful assistant who served as my ablest critic, and Miss Mary Dean, the office girl friday.

# Contents

# ★ ★ ★ 1 Reverse Integration

On Mother's Day, 1961, I sat in the rear of a bus traveling from Atlanta to Birmingham—a Negro reporter covering the first Freedom Ride. I had been riding buses for more than a week, observing what happened to a group of whites and blacks venturing on a hazardous and risky mission—the attempt to integrate bus facilities in the heart of the Nation's most bigoted area.

I watched police arrest a Negro for trying to get his shoes shined in Charlotte, North Carolina; I heard a white man tell how he was beaten to the ground because he accompanied a Negro into a white waiting room; I talked to another Negro, who had been chased from a town by a possible lynch mob because he had entered the white waiting room. But next came the crucial test in two of the country's most backward states—Alabama and Mississippi.

When the bus, one of two carrying Freedom Riders on this stretch of Dixie, stopped in Anniston, Alabama, a small city just over the state line, I reviewed the strategy. Two testers—a Negro and a white—sat in the forward section. The observer, a white woman, was to get off the bus when either of the testing pair tried to use accommodations in the various bus stations. If an arrest occurred (the Negro for using white facilities or the white for using the Negro "john"), the observer would send word to the New York office of the Congress of Racial Equality (CORE). At the moment, she winked and handed me a copy of a newspaper on which she had scrawled, "It's touch and go."

Seven white passengers boarded the bus; one of the Freedom Riders (a college professor from Detroit) got off to get some food.

The new passengers appeared to be white toughs—shirts open at the collar, hair unkempt, crude talkers. My seatmate, a photographer, whispered, "You think we're all right?" I nodded. Powerless to do anything, what else could I do? I recalled what the Reverend Martin Luther King, Jr., hero of the Montgomery bus strike, had told me the previous night in Atlanta: "I've gotten word you won't reach Birmingham. They're going to waylay you." I thought of my wife and three kids in Washington—but fear never produced progress.

As the bus driver started the motor, one of the Freedom Riders blurted out that a passenger was missing—the professor who went for food. The bus driver got out and went back into the station; the missing passenger, meanwhile, showed up with a bag of sandwiches. (Seemingly by sleight of hand every member of the Freedom Ride team received a sandwich without the rest of the passengers becoming aware of the teamwork or identifying any as members of the team.)

When the bus driver returned, his face was drawn and ashen. He announced: "A Greyhound bus which left here a few minutes ago is in flames, set afire by a mob. There is no information yet on injuries or deaths. We are going to get this bus to Birmingham. I cannot do it as long as Negroes sit in the front section."

The news jarred me. I wanted to shout and run. I felt desperate, but almost simultaneously came a glimmer of strength. I wondered whether those Freedom Riders were alive, whether they had been beaten and thrown back into the burning bus.

"All right, let's move!" I heard the driver order. I knew he had spoken to two Negroes sitting in the front section. They sat there —not calmly, I'm sure—but they didn't move. The driver sidled from the bus, and the explosion went off!

The toughs took over. They started to beat the Negroes and drag them from their seats. As the white Freedom Riders objected, the fighting spread throughout the bus.

Here I sat at the ringside of what might be the horrible end of the Freedom Riders and even myself. I punched a small hole in a newspaper and pretended to read. I watched the beatings, heard the wallops, saw blood fly through the air. Parts of the bread and meat from the sandwiches, smeared with blood, were scattered everywhere.

The Freedom Riders were piled like pancakes in the aisle dividing the whites and Negroes. The toughs sat on the hand rests; one flashed a pistol. The driver returned and began the trek to Birmingham—not on the scheduled run, I heard him say, but by an alternate route. I halfway expected the driver to be forced to turn into a lonely road, where the bus would be burned—just like the other one.

"Aw, you goddam nigger lovers," a thug howled when the professor fell off the pile of victims and tried to get to his feet, his face a mass of blood, cuts and hair. "Get on back with the niggers."

I peered through the hole in the newspaper and tried to identify one of the thugs, so that I could give a description to the FBI. I got the picture, framed it and tried to keep it, but all white folks looked alike to me at that moment.

Jim Peck, the white man who had spent hours telling me how he quit Harvard to join the cause, stumbled to his feet and was slammed into a seat, his head hitting the window. He was bleeding profusely, but no one was allowed to go near him.

Although a veteran at covering civil-rights assignments, I felt sick inside and weak. If relief doesn't come, injury does. During the two-hour ride I recalled other experiences.

I remembered the day in Chicago when Emmett Till's body arrived at the funeral home and how I stood by his mother as they opened the cheap pine box. I saw the rope about his neck, and I saw the top of his skull fall off and the brains scramble out. I felt his mother fold up right down to the floor. Later, while covering the trial of the boy's accused murderers, I was rammed in the ribs by a sheriff. When I waited until the end of the trail to hear the verdict, most of the other Negroes called me crazy and sped for their nearest settlement.

At Little Rock, circulating in the center of the mob which surrounded Central High School, I was spit upon and chased. I watched the mob turn over cars and a telephone booth with a Negro inside.

I've seen racial explosions in many states and have tramped miles through the Deep South, disguised in overalls and slouch hat, sleeping by day and moving by night, often avoiding highways. I've had to comfort hysterical widows and grief-stricken children.

To make the time go faster I tried to think of something humorous. There was the Howard University student. For days as the Freedom Riders wended their way through Virginia and the Carolinas, he complained that he wasn't arrested and didn't make headlines. In South Carolina he was rewarded. Explaining how he was attacked as he entered a white waiting room, he said: "The guy was a little feller. He didn't know a thing about boxing. He showed me where he was going to hit. I could have beaten him with one finger, but he knocked me all over the place. This is the last Freedom Ride I want." Then I thought of Mandy, the star witness in the Emmett Till case. After the trial, when the whites went scotfree, a group had to bundle up Mandy and take her out of the state for her protection. She had violated protocol by testifying against a white man. We were sitting in a Mississippi home while Mandy was dressing. Suddenly there was a roar followed by a series of grunts and groans, then a piercing scream. Grabbing guns, we left the room and dashed toward the back of the house, fearing some invaders were trying to kidnap Mandy. It wasn't that way at all —even though one man excitedly fired a shot into the air. Mandy had gotten her head trapped in a corset and was wrestling on the floor trying to wriggle out of it.

A strange calm seemed to settle over the bus as it rumbled into the downtown streets of Birmingham. The toughs took seats, the beaten passengers had revived enough to sit straight and wipe blood from their faces. Outside, men huddled on the street and in the terminal.

As the bus rolled into the terminal, there was no rush to get off —not by the whites in front or the Negroes (and the few so-called nigger lovers) in the back. The emptying of the bus was slow and orderly. It had to be. Some of the Freedom Riders were so badly mauled they could hardly walk. I hesitated, toying with my bag, and was almost the last to get off.

As my foot touched the ground, I saw trouble ahead. The beaten and groggy Freedom Riders slowly plodded toward the white waiting room in what might have been regarded as the most foolhardy step of all. In any event, what transpired immediately afterward set a new record in violence.

As I slipped around the bus, I heard a wild roar emanate from a corridor. Turning, I saw white crusader James Peck, already badly beaten, being crushed to the floor by a huge crowd. A white photographer sank straight downward from the blows. A Negro who was attacked proclaimed his innocence. A Negro woman screamed, "Lord, help us!" Fighting erupted everywhere. As I proceeded beyond the bus, I passed groups of whites racing toward the terminal. They didn't bother me.

I hailed a cab (the only Negro one on the street) and told the driver to rush me to a minister's home, our stopover, so that I could alert the local Negroes to go down to the terminal and pick up the stranded Riders, who were being chased all over the downtown area—without police interference. Once at the minister's home, I called the New York office of CORE and my home in Washington. Then I sat down; the awful tension began to drain away.

After a brief respite, I returned to the terminal area and found Peck, blood-covered and slumped on a wooden chair on a sidewalk. No doctor was available anywhere in Birmingham. Fearing further harm, Peck didn't want to go to a hospital but finally police came and forced him to; he received 56 stitches in his head. I was asked to obtain treatment for a young Morehouse College student who had received a deep gash in his head. With a Negro nurse I went to the home or office of several Negro doctors, but each refused to treat him. Finally, the nurse sewed his wound.

Later that evening, I watched the Riders from the other bus troop into the minister's home. All were black with soot and coughing. They had been rescued by a caravan of 15 autos driven by gun-toting Negroes, after state police refused to help them get out of Anniston.

Racial hatred, the damnable and terrible cancer in our American life, had illustrated its malignancy throughout events of the day. That evening and many times since, reliving the tragedy, I have trembled and struggled to free my mind of the discouraging outlook for race relations. The deteriorating racial picture escapes too many Americans. Violence, lawlessness and hoodlumism still have a part in our life. Far too long I have witnessed brutality by mobs, gangs and hoodlums in many southern and some northern states.

On Thanksgiving Day, 1962, my two sons, friends and I sat in the huge new municipal stadium in Washington. The attraction was the annual schoolboy football classic, which pitted the Catholic school champions, St. John's, against the public school champions, Eastern High. The St. John's team was predominantly white; the Eastern team all Negro. Some 50,000 fans, of which approximately 42,000 were Negro, were on hand for the contest. Everything seemed fine. There were the cheer leaders, the bands, the enthusiastic students. It was an ideal Turkey Day event in the nation's capital, model of school integration for the entire country.

The shock came after the game—a race riot in which my own people were the main offenders. I couldn't sleep that night, so vivid were the scenes of Negroes chasing and beating white men, women and children. When the daily papers obscured what had happened at the game and arguments flared in my downtown office building the next morning, I was faced with the challenge of whether I, a reporter, should disclose what I had seen and how I thought the riot had been triggered? Should I, a Negro who long has known the wrath of violence, blame my own people? Should I give to Southern members of Congress the opportunity to use such an occurrence in opposing school integration?

I wrote a letter detailing what I'd seen, describing to the best of my knowledge the chronological order of events, and pinpointing a few basic causes. Then I shoved the letter into a desk drawer and tried to forget. A Negro colonel called me and described how his son tried to help a neighbor's boy who had gone to the game with him and was also beaten savagely. "Just because this kid is white," said the colonel, "these boys mauled him." A Pentagon secretary told how she came upon a white woman crying in the parking lot after the game. The woman's daughter was stretched across the back seat of their car badly bruised and beaten. The daughter and a girl friend she had taken to the game had been separated by an unruly gang.

More calls came. But still I asked myself: Can I, a Negro, afford to buck the tide of racial nationalism? Many times in the past, I have been aware of the heavy penalty paid by others. Sensitivity to criticism probably has a historical background, but through the years it has grown. Today, a Negro who criticizes for any reason the stand of some of his leaders or a condition of his people may be hoisted to the gallows and hung—mentally, morally and socially. The designation "Uncle Tom" is as strongly abhorred as the term "nigger" is detested. In the Negro-white relationship, there is no middle ground, no reason, no compromise. Either you go along, or you are trampled. This is the psychology of the mob or the thundering herd but, unfortunately, it is the spirit which has kept alive the flame of freedom for Negroes. It has smothered our moderates, our conservatives, our compromisers.

Several close friends mentioned the possibility of my being ostracized or causing difficulties for my publishing firm. They indicated that certain elements would be unable to understand what I was trying to do—bare the problem and get community action to alleviate it. "You must think of your image," one friend told me, "This can harm you. You might be condemned and written off as sold out to the white folks." When a prominent physician pursued this line of reasoning, I replied, "I'm a reporter. Would you give inferior service to a patient because of his color?" One Negro told me, "They've been beating us for years. It's time we give them some of their own medicine." Another Negro said, "Forget it, man.

A week from now, it'll pass over. Why make this a big deal?" But a few Negroes advised, "Have courage. Don't be second-rate. No job is done without brickbats."

Man has few opportunities to prove the value of his upbringing, his education and his integrity. Color is no factor in this test. My letter, mailed to the three daily newspapers in Washington, D.C., read:

Thursday was a Black Thanksgiving. Along with another adult and seven youngsters, I attended the stadium high school football game.

What I saw at the stadium easily could have duplicated what I saw while covering the Little Rock school desegregation case, or the bus station mob during the Freedom Rides to Birmingham, or the Emmett Till case in Mississippi.

The difference, ironically, was that the predominant number of offenders were Negro. The explosion of hate stemmed mostly from my own people.

I saw the stadium, filled to a great extent by Negroes, suddenly terrified by roving herds of hoodlums who set upon whites—men, women and children—with the most profane language and physical mistreatment. While leaving the stadium, I saw a young Negro woman thrash a white man with an umbrella; I saw groups of toughs battering a white boy on a ramp; I saw conflicts dotting the landscape as far as I could see.

It was apparent to me early in the game that tensions were high. When the Eastern team ran onto the field, the cheers were thunderous. When St. John's team was introduced, there was an avalanche of boos. At the time of Eastern's touchdown, the response was such that I thought the concrete stadium was shaking.

From then on, the outpouring dwindled and a strange sort of revenge moved in. As St. John's amassed their winning margin, a moody dejection set in among certain elements, clearly a small but uninhibited minority. Behind me, I could hear shouts of "Kill him" on tackle plays. Then, I heard comments such as "Let's get out before the fighting starts." My little boys told me about people drinking behind us.

When the fight started on the field, I thought this was a signal for somebody with supervision to realize the seriousness of the situation. I couldn't explain why Eastern coaches allowed bench members to dart onto the field but again, team members tried to restrain the ousted player.

Thank God, the St. John's coach held his reserves on the bench. Minutes seemed to elapse before police rushed onto the field. Too long, I thought, but again the vast majority kept cool, calm. Yet danger was imminent. The existence of troublemakers was noticeable to many persons in the stands. I told my young son to quit waving his St. John's sign.

By the time the game ended, several score more police ringed the field but not enough to make an impact. Hoodlums swung at members of the St. John's team as they made their way to locker rooms, and a wave of youngsters swept across the field in the direction of the St. John's stands, enough to completely fill the playing surface.

Police held some off, but the hoodlums then headed toward the nearest exit, spelling out one thing—an outside fight. Fist battles erupted everywhere, in the stands and out. Youngsters tried to snatch St. John's pennants. Others were slapped, beaten by roughnecks who dashed away.

Like myself, hundreds of parents at the end of the fray tried to herd children through a raging sea of humanity. Attacks, beatings, outbreaks erupted everywhere. My older son was pushed down and trampled as a group of Negroes chased a white boy. I could feel the hopelessness, the tragedy of the situation. I could see the terror and fright on faces of many parents who expected the game to be the highlight of a perfect Thanksgiving Day.

Should the games be canceled? I would hope that we as Americans, white and Negro, turn down such a proposal, which would be based upon the belief that we cannot cope with rowdyism. But I definitely would oppose a game held under the same circumstances. In these particular areas, I see shortcomings:

1. Any such championship game between public and Catholic schools in the near future, at least, will be a game of white vs. Negro. Consider the enrollment. But as Americans, why can't we work together to make the game a success? However, under such

unique conditions, I feel the game program should be geared to goodwill, rather than racial competition.

Why can't the game sponsors establish such an atmosphere, even if it takes the presence of Bobby Mitchell of the Redskins, or Chuck Hinton of the Senators? Why can't the schools which feature the athletic teams stress sportsmanship and make every student who buys a ticket aware of the responsibilities of the theme?

But even in its ugliness, this uprising wasn't entirely racial. A majority of Negroes opposed the misconduct, many were hurt trying to defend whites.

2. Somehow, the school authorities and the police department completely misjudged the ingredients for potential violence. There was little protection for the sports fan and his kids. There was little police manpower as a deterrent against violence; and the little there was was ineffective.

In the school system, some authority should have had a better idea of how to handle mass psychology. In the promotion, there could have been projects for racial goodwill and during the game, the use of the microphone could have been used advantageously to cool off impassioned elements.

The police department showed a lack of awareness of the danger, which is hard to understand, since the game—the biggest in local history—was sold out in advance. Would not an effective race relations detail been aware of such a violent possibility?

3. Negro leadership in Washington has a responsibility to tackle this problem of rowdyism and juvenile delinquency—not by excuses or statements but planned community-wide programs. We cannot ignore it. We must face it. Being closer to the offenders, we can do much more than the institutions or the agencies.

We must begin to develop citizenship programs among our youngsters. Segregation or discrimination may be an excuse but it is not enough. Integration demands responsible citizens, and we must take the first step.

Eating Thanksgiving dinner with my kids, I had to answer the question, "Dad, why did they beat up those St. John's people?"

It was a probing question and I answered, "Son, this game should always be a reminder to you. Play hard, but if you lose, congratulate the winner. A sportsman doesn't use his fists to show a superiority." That was the majority viewpoint on Thanksgiving

Day, but unfortunately there were enough of those who didn't subscribe to this rule of sportsmanship to make the day a bleak holiday.

After the three Washington newspapers published the letter on their editorial pages, an overwhelming reaction occurred. Calls jammed the Johnson Publishing Company telephones, where I am bureau chief for its several magazines. Then came an avalanche of letters from the Washington area and, later, from across the country. A survey showed that the majority of letters and telephone calls were from whites, most of whom praised me for pointing out the responsibility Negro leadership should assume, a factor which the press seemed to emphasize in a digest of the letter. Many whites felt that, if Negro leadership could concentrate on reducing crime, metropolitan problems could be erased overnight. A conclusion could easily be drawn that more whites need to know intimately the problem of the Negro. It is many-faceted and contains an array of sticky conflicts and situations, not easily worked out. The heartening element of the drama is that so many white people are sympathetic to the Negro and anxious to help. Even though most do not understand the deeper aspects, their friendship and their interest are powerful stimuli.

The Negro response, I thought, was at first disturbing and discouraging. Although I had worked closely with Negro leaders across the country, they sent few messages. In the Washington area, I received few phone calls from Negroes. To make matters worse, a few hate missives arrived. One writer referred to me as a "white Negro bastard" and wished that everything evil would happen to members of my family. I was compared to a "house servant" who during slavery times carried every detail of the slave revolt to the master. A man who telephoned was surprised that I would write a letter to a paper without getting NAACP permission. A vandal even slashed one of my car tires—the only act of violence. The editor of the Washington *Afro-American* labeled me an "Uncle Tom" and characterized my actions as typical of a Negro seeking political leadership—a rather facetious way of smearing me. I regarded this printed attack as being of lowest rank and most uncalled for, especially from a fellow journalist. It showed the deterioration of a standard of ethics in the highly charged atmosphere of race relations.

— Many Negroes refused to accept the idea that the outbreak of violence had any racial characteristics or showed hostility toward whites. "Just a boys-will-be-boys disturbance," one leader commented. Another pointed out that of riots that followed games in several cities on the same day, none received as much newspaper coverage as the Washington fiasco. Individual Negroes asked, "Is it because school integration is being used as the issue in this case?" Several indicated that Negroes have been the victims of such encounters for years throughout the United States, so why is it important when whites are attacked?

The commendable aspect of the Thanksgiving Day riot was that the city's Negro leadership acted immediately. A group of Negro leaders issued a statement condemning the "unsportsmanlike conduct and rowdyism," contending that it can "neither be excused or tolerated." This statement, however, was not well received by the Negro community, showing that a gulf existed between the leaders and the mass. Despite this feeling and the handicap of possible further estrangement from their own people, two of the leaders, NAACP President Dr. E. Franklin Jackson and Urban League Secretary Sterling Tucker, agreed to serve on a committee to investigate the stadium riot. Named by School Superintendent Carl F. Hansen, the committee was headed by Dr. Shane MacCarthy, a former White House aide under President Eisenhower, and included Mrs. Alice Hunter, Gen. Lewis B. Hershey of the Selective Service System, Arnold Fine, John V. Hinkel, Philip Larner Gore, Mrs. Henry Gratton Doyle, Alphonse (Tuffy) Leemans, a former professional football star, and myself.

Amid charges that the panel would either whitewash the violence or vilify Negroes, the interracial body began its work behind closed doors. Early in the hearings, it was apparent that the Thanksgiving Day disorders resulted in a greater toll in bodily and property damages than many Washingtonians imagined. The police reported 554 cases, but actual casualties probably reached a thousand because of the large number of unreported incidents. That the majority of the offenders were Negro and the victims white was a disquieting factor which plagued several of our committee members. However, discovery of laxities in many areas of school administration, including the athletic program, the selection of game sponsors and promoters and the sale of tickets, altered the feelings of some who had believed the disgraceful conduct could be traced to Negroes and that Negroes were entirely responsible for it. Several committee members were surprised that no Negro had anything to do with the sponsorship of the game, the planning, the preparation, or the handling of the crowds from a supervisory level, though the crowd was more than 80 percent Negro and Washington's public schools were over 80 percent Negro.

It was apparent also that the school system could also be lax in other areas. In seeking to determine the causes for the game violence, the committee discovered serious disciplinary problems in some of the public schools. A witness testified that "violence was not a stranger to school athletic games," and a probe was begun in a new direction—discipline in the schools.

Following one of our biweekly hearings several days before Christmas, Chairman MacCarthy called to tell me I was to be appointed chairman of the report-writing committee. He said, "This means you'll probably write the report. We need it in two weeks."

"I can't do it," I said, "You're putting too much responsibility on my shoulders."

"You can," he said. A devout Catholic, he added, "And the Lord bless you."

I figured even the Lord and I would have trouble writing the report. As soon as the appointment was announced, its significance for me became both apparent and awesome. In reporting, I had concentrated mostly in Negro news; this report would circulate from the White House to Congress. A white woman called our home and asked if I was a Negro. Getting the answer, she hung up, disillusioned. A Negro called and ranted, "Lousy fool."

For two days I brooded—then I became determined to do it, to show that a Negro can be objective, analytical and understanding. I would try to forget Mississippi and Little Rock, the NAACP and CORE. I would detach myself from everybody, sit down with the testimony, the data, the figures, and come up with a report the committee would be proud of.

Working at home throughout the Christmas holidays, with the co-operation of Mrs. Henry Gratton Doyle and Sterling Tucker, I wrote the report. At the meeting held to discuss it, a committee member said to me, "Booker, this is an inspirational close to an inspirational project. I never would have thought a Negro could objectively handle such a sensitive subject."

Grinning, I said: "Give us more opportunities. We'd fool you."

By means of the report, the committee aroused Washington with a challenging call for action, highlighting the deplorable conditions in homes and the schools. The report touched on lawlessness, on the need for more study of the basic track system that allows a boy or girl to spend 12 years in school and still not be able to read or write or know a trade upon graduation, the need for new authority for teachers in the classrooms, and the desire for fresh, imaginative programs to inspire every youngster, no matter what his skill or brainpower.

In the report was this challenge: "Problems are staggering for citizens of Washington, Negro and white, to work shoulder to shoulder to eliminate. Our city is the most important city in America to demonstrate that Negro and white can work together, live together and play together as a symbol of democracy to nations throughout the world. We can do this even though there are some in Congress who believe the highlighting of our weaknesses is an admission that integration of public schools cannot work. School integration can work, but it requires the help of responsible leaders, parents, citizens and children."

Two holidays, Mother's Day, 1961 and Thanksgiving Day, 1962, have become symbols to me, of a New America, a country in which Negroes have contributed a share of skill, of heartache, of despair. As a reporter, one can easily visualize the path of least resistance and a path that offers the most accolades in the immediate years ahead. For accompanying the Freedom Riders, there was praise from my people, for this represented the determination of many Negroes in America—to achieve first-class citizenship *now*. For analyzing the stadium riot and later serving on an interracial committee to probe the disturbance, there was the moody condemnation that goes with an unpopular cause. Too few Americans today face up to civic responsibility in race relations, the unraveling of the knots of despair and the untangling of the mass of conflicts which contribute to a growing division among the races. For an individual, involvement in such enterprises is like delivering a time bomb.

If the United States is to remain the world's greatest democracy, as we like to picture our nation, we must face up to this challenge. The mass of the Negro population is almost as enslaved today as it was before the Emancipation Proclamation, but today the Negroes know it and a growing number are becoming desperate. If the two holidays with their blend of violence and racial outbreaks mean anything, they point up the critical area of concern for tomorrow.

The average white man in America has no conception, no information, no idea and no concern about the plight of the Negro. Too many think of race in terms of help. That is, they think about the difficulty of hiring a cook or a maid. Even after a hundred years, during which the Negro has struggled to lift himself into the company of friendly whites, whites look at the group with a feeling of disdain and even scorn. Like the American Indian, the Negro was left to fend for himself. But unlike the Indian, the Negro has refused to be quartered in a reservation (even though the Black Muslims want that) and is fighting for his place. Think of the billions we have spent all over the world to teach Asians to read, to train Africans in vocational pursuits, to equip South Americans with business knowledge. How much has been spent at home to lift our own Americans?

While discrimination severely limits the rise of the Negro in every area of life, the fight for improvement goes on. Too many Negroes are impoverished, culturally deprived and disillusioned.

But whites, far removed from the ghettos or the bias, say, "The races are unequal," and the gap widens.

The emphasis on the civil-rights aspect of Negro leadership has brought many breakthroughs, from spotty integration in public schools to more voting rights to occasional instances of integrated housing. Since the 1954 Supreme Court school decision, the Negro community has perhaps experienced its biggest and most dramatic transition. The intellectual Negro class, profiting from integration, has virtually moved from the so-called Negro communities. Many of the community leaders who once fought for better educational and work opportunities are now a part of the new, integrated society. Left behind is a vast group of untrained, unskilled and unequipped Negroes, strong only in size and number. With integration sapping the leadership echelon, this group has become leaderless, unmotivated and victimized by an array of cultists, political operators and hucksters. Too many of the families have long records of welfare and government help, many are uneducated and untrained, and many are existing on the frontier of near-poverty. There is a real need for leadership and service in these areas, but as is often the case, municipalities handle these problems last. Many Negroes who formerly lived in these sections and moved on contend that their plight is a community responsibility—not a racial responsibility. They look down on these people as do much of the remainder of the community—except on the day of an election or civil-rights demonstration.

The growing frustration and despair of this abandoned group ultimately will touch off violent upheavals. Already, crime rates, juvenile delinquency, school dropouts, prison tenancy, and youth unemployment have shot up alarmingly. Racial tensions abound in the Negro ghettos of the big cities, so prevalent that comic Dick Gregory jokes about his child saying there isn't a Santa Claus because "a white man wouldn't enter the neighborhood after dark." As the United States faces the bright future of the automation age, thousands of young Negroes, ill-prepared, ill-trained and ill-equipped, find no other pastime than hanging around street corners, gathering in pool halls or forming gangs.

In a desperation move, demonstrations roared across the continent during 1963, the Centennial of the Emancipation Proclamation, the birthday of Negro freedom. Negroes angrily threw themselves in front of police stretched out in the street, marched and sang in protest of bias in cities ranging from Birmingham to New York City, Los Angeles to Chicago. At one time, the Department of Justice reported more than six hundred demonstrations in 169 cities in 32 states. The surge frightened many Americans, panicked officials, caused the President to deliver a television fireside chat that recommended a new civil-rights legislative program to Congress. Thousands streamed into the Nation's capital in the biggest demonstration of all time. "Dig this," a Harlem demonstrator told a white reporter, "Give us our daily bread—or we gonna take it."

★ ★ ★ 2 The Civil-Rights
Decade

In the 1930's, the 40's and the 50's one of the best
ways for American Negro leaders seeking an audience with a President of the United States or wishing to bring a racial matter to his
attention was through a White House maid or valet. The trick was
simple. Negro organizations wooed the valet or maid, honored him
or her for some outstanding civic work and won a lasting friend.
When the group needed some favor or help, the honoree usually
was in a position to win the ear of the President or the First Lady
during a breathing spell at the White House. This supplementary
channel of communication was very valuable.

The back-door technique was discarded during the administration of President Eisenhower when he named a Negro, E. Frederic
Morrow, to his staff. During the Kennedy administration, the
Negro won recognition he never dreamed of: delegations of leaders
sitting for hours in the Presidential office and then being escorted
for a tour of the White House; invitations by the hundreds to all
types of White House functions; appointment of the first Negro
Associate Press Secretary (Andrew T. Hatcher), and hiring of
the first nondomestic White House personnel, from Negro secretaries to guards, plus countless unprecedented appointments.

This merely was one of a procession of changes in race relations.

From the vantage of reporting from the nation's capital, recent
progress has been swift. In the last ten years in the United States
the Negro has advanced more than in any comparable period of
the 345 years of our American heritage. We came in chains in the
galleys of slave ships. We picked cotton 12 hours a day and

hummed spirituals. When cabins got too small, families were broken up and members sold at auction. We were forbidden to learn to read or write, and masters were fined when they violated the law to teach us. We were described as a hopeless group —smelly, childlike and incapable of learning. A war finally was fought, and when we were freed, thousands trudged up Freedom Road with little more than the shirts and lash marks on our backs. One hundred years ago, we were illiterate, and untrained. For the first ninety years of our freedom, we fought for the right to be educated and trained and qualified to take our place in this democracy. And then suddenly—as if by magic, as if by the combined prayers of 20 million Negroes, the thunderstorm stopped, the skies cleared and there was sunshine. Freedom became more than a word for many of my people.

Few Americans realize the significance of the decade since the Supreme Court's school desegregation decision in 1954. More from fear of change than anything else whites most affected by the decision utilized lung power, pen and paper and, in some cases, fists and sticks, to voice their objections. But for American Negroes, the decision promised an era in which segregation was doomed as a way of life. Historians eventually will interpret the events of the decade and come forth with books on the "ten years which counted."

Here is how one city, Washington, D.C., the nation's capital, and first metropolis to boast a predominant number of Negro residents (54 percent), was affected in this social revolution:

In the 1940's and 50's, the capital was described as the most segregated city in America. Now, it is probably the most integrated.

White House protocol previously restricted Negroes to the roles of cook, maid or valet. Now, we show up at the Executive Mansion in formal dress and sit next to the President.

Earlier, the President's foreign guests were dignitaries from white countries. In the 1960's President Kennedy had as personal guests many black African leaders. At official functions, the President escorted the wives of these black men to the places of honor at

a table. Negroes sat side by side with white at the affairs. On visits
to foreign countries, American dignitaries have danced with black
women at public functions.

Negroes were once hopelessly trapped at the bottom of the civil-
service scale. Now, a White House subcabinet group meets
monthly to discuss programs to upgrade and promote them, and
the Administration's Equal Opportunity Committee makes strides
in finding jobs for us.

Once a President was considered courageous when he answered
a letter from a Negro. However, President Kennedy led a move to
organize a new cabinet department (Urban Affairs) and to ap-
point a Negro as its head.

Time was when a white woman and a Negro who walked the
street together faced arrest. Now, African diplomats with white
wives travel freely and are entertained in the homes of cabinet
members.

The progress in a single decade has been unbelievable, but the
next ten years may bring more. Multiply this by minor revolutions
taking place in the cities and towns throughout America, and you
become convinced America is heading in the right direction.

As a White House correspondent, I have watched this transformation and seen the Negro world of my youth crack and begin
to crumble. Integration is moving swiftly and has caught my operation in the web of change. I have noticed a shift in our magazine's coverage. A few years ago, circulation boomed on the killing
of a Negro in the South or as a result of a violent civil-rights event.
We always received scores of complaints of discrimination and the
weekly output was a culling of the most extreme cases.

Now the pattern has switched to appointment of Negroes to
unique posts, or new plans of the Administration to alleviate some
condition. Many of my friends are working on daily newspapers
or magazines, or holding government press jobs previously closed
to Negroes. Many are living in integrated neighborhoods, their
children attending unsegregated schools and the families attending
unsegregated churches.

A Negro reporter naturally has a heritage of protest, of suspicion, of doubt. We have been schooled for years to find the defects in the system and to rail that democracy discriminates, segregates, subjugates our people. Our crusade has kept alive the hopes and the dreams of many people and probably discouraged an equal number. To an uneducated Mississippi sharecropper I may be a black Walter Lippmann. To hundreds of unemployed laborers in Harlem or on Chicago's South Side, or Los Angeles' western areas I may be a job expert, clamoring for more openings. For a growing intellectual circle, I may be a reporter who manages to twist every national event into a racial advance or defeat—sometimes far out of context, sometimes only a little bit, sometimes not at all. But as a writer, controversial and aggressive in my own way, I have influence in my special Negro world, whose inhabitants have suddenly been recognized as a part of the U.S.A.

Perhaps the 1960 Presidential campaign will always be described by Negroes as their finest hour in politics, because their backing of John F. Kennedy enabled him to edge out Richard M. Nixon. The heavy support given Kennedy was regarded in some quarters as the difference between victory and defeat, and this margin was credited to a phone call to the wife of the Reverend Martin Luther King, Jr. It happened that JFK called King's wife in Atlanta after learning of the minister's arrest on violation of a traffic charge. This incident was publicized throughout Negro communities, along with the word that Nixon had refused to take any action in the case. The result, as far as thousands of Negro voters were concerned: images of a hostile, insensitive Nixon and a friendly, sympathetic JFK.

After his election, JFK named Californian Andrew T. Hatcher as Associate Press Secretary. To many whites, this appointment represented a political payoff, but to Negroes, the elevation of one of their members represented a major breakthrough. Hatcher became a symbol of success—comparable to Jackie Robinson when he broke into baseball's big league. When Hatcher appeared on television announcing one of JFK's news releases, his brown face was easily recognized, and thousands gained new hope. The appointment represented a trend. Later, JFK named

Harvard Ph.D. Robert Weaver as his housing administrator. Events of Kennedy's inauguration were attended by more Negroes than were those of any other President.

The job-status approach wasn't a revolutionary idea. Both Presidents Roosevelt and Truman named some Negroes to positions, but most were in race relations advisory posts. In other words, those individuals served as special assistants and handled functions dealing with a department or agency's relations with Negroes. During his tenure of office, President Eisenhower developed a more desirable method of bringing Negroes to positions on a broader base. His appointment of Chicago lawyer J. Ernest Wilkins as Assistant Secretary of Labor was hailed by Negroes, and the Republicans managed to gain a volume of exposure by his sitting in on cabinet meetings—a first for a Negro. Wilkins' career, however, was cut short several years later when Secretary of Labor James Mitchell succeeded in having him transferred to another post, a shift which Negroes condemned and which later cost the GOP their support.

Eisenhower, who never received more than 30 percent of the national Negro vote in elections, gave Negroes a few jobs. Kennedy, who received an estimated 80 percent in his first national try, seemed to make hiring of qualified Negroes for top-level government posts a major project, rather than carrying out pledges of urging civil-rights legislation to Congress. The plan seemed to work. The nation's capital bulged with the largest contingent of Negroes in VIP slots in history. These capable Negroes shattered old stereotypes.

At an embassy cocktail party, a prominent Southern office holder chatted with a Negro government official just as a photographer raised his camera. "No pictures, please," the Southerner said, lifting his glass, "The folks back home won't understand."

Another Negro showed up at a white VIP's home where everyone wanted to do the "Twist." They figured he was the best dancing teacher. His evening was spent demonstrating the dance to wives of some high-level men in government.

While they waited for a bus, in front of one of Washington's downtown hotels, a group of white school children from Dixie noticed a limousine pull up to the main door. A white chauffeur got out and opened the rear door for a black man and a white woman. The man took the woman by the arm and strode into the hotel. The children gasped, hardly aware that the couple was an African ambassador and his wife.

With lightning-like strokes, integration swept across the nation's capital. What caused this social revolution, not only in Washington, but in cities throughout the country? Sociologists hinted that the emergence of independent African nations pricked the conscience of American leaders and set off the ambitions of freedom for new generations of Negroes. A Central Intelligence Agency man credits the Soviet propaganda machine, which blared forth the details of racial incidents, forcing America to clean house or to lose in a world-wide struggle. Some clergymen reasoned that Americans were ashamed of their racial practices and wanted to do better as part of a moral awakening. The politicians credited the power of the Negro vote for quickly bringing about the reforms. Whatever the reason, singular or collective, a new world is looming before American Negroes, and American whites, too —a life few have envisioned.

For a small band with striking force and maneuverability, the Negro civil-rights movement was one of the most effective in the United States. It was militant, its leaders were outspoken and the following was loyal enough to give the impression of widespread support. After the Supreme Court school desegregation decision, NAACP counsel Thurgood Marshall was Mr. Civil Rights— loved, adored and respected in every community.

When Marshall was named a Federal appellate court judge by President Kennedy, his absence created a void in civil-rights ranks, already affected by the departure of NAACP board chairman Dr. Robert Weaver to the post of the housing administrator, West Coast NAACP director Franklin Williams to the Peace Corps, and a dozen others. It was rumored by some that the Administration was draining off the Negro's top talent to slow down the civil-rights offensive. Most of the persons offered jobs accepted readily, for the opportunities were the most suitable they had ever had. From cities across the country came the recruits: ex-Urban League officials to staff personnel and juvenile delinquency slots, civil-rights lawyers to join departmental units, and specialists in various professional categories to integrate most of the major departments at policy-making levels. After a few months, the assemblage represented the largest stockpile of Negro experts anywhere in the country—including the staffs of the civil-rights organizations.

Coupled with the deployment of large numbers of these Negro experts to government departments and agencies was another shift: whites were named to the major race-relations advisory posts that in the past had been assigned to Negroes. Thus, the New Frontier boasted a crack combine which could easily outduel the weakened ranks of Negro leadership. The result was a public-relations image that painted pretty pictures of gains and shelved the ugly canvas of reality, although it was conceded that the government agencies now dominated the civil-rights arena. The Government, with its resources and facilities, stockpiled more information on Negroes in America than Negro organizations ever had been able to gather, and the Department of Justice, along with other governmental units, attacked on more fronts than could Negro civil-rights operations.

For a while it seemed that the New Frontier had defanged the Negro militancy. The friendship of Negro leadership and the New Frontier warmed until reporters snickered that there was more of a rush to run up to the White House steps than to run down to Mississippi. Professional at handling the Negro power structure, Administration Democrats made maximum use of negotiations, even to briefing the President in advance on the accomplishments of many of the Negro guests so that he would appear intimately concerned and affected. At a reception, for example, Kennedy stopped a prominent Negro guest and asked him about a situation in which the man was involved. As soon as he left the line, the guest confided to friends, "He's sensitive. He even asked about what I'm working on." At a White House session with NAACP officials, the organization's spokesman began to rattle off a long list of proposals. Interrupting, JFK said, "I have read your requests and most of them I don't agree with—not at this time." Next, the Chief Executive pointed out impractical and unworkable aspects of the proposals. Then, while his guests sat confused, bewildered by his frankness, Kennedy noticed that several women were standing and asked that more chairs be brought in. The subtle point, however, was that the men were seated, a factor which, embarrassing to many, further divided the visitors. Later, the President conducted the group to his private quarters, pointing out the Lincoln room and other areas of historic interest. When they left the White House, the delegates were backers of JFK.

Another device was used on a group representing Negro colleges. The spokesman, after the opening niceties, began to read a statement to JFK. Listening carefully, the President then asked about the number of white students enrolled in the Negro schools, obviously asking whether the educators were facing up to the problems of integration in the field. They were surprised at his inside knowledge and found themselves groping for words.

An even worse fate awaited a delegation of Negro publishers. Slated for a 15-minute interview, they rehearsed a statement which would cover the time period. As the spokesman began to read the paper, the Chief Executive reached over and took it, saying he could read the statement a lot faster. With a wave of his hand the President said, "Go on, talk," and chagrin appeared on the faces of the publishers who had spent hours drafting the statement. One said later, "My mind froze. I kept saying to myself, 'This is what we fought for—recognition.' I just couldn't think."

While the intellectual March on Washington gained greater impetus because of the increased mixing of Negroes and whites at the highest levels of government, a new throbbing among the middle and lower classes gathered momentum and exploded a peaceful state of race relations. Uninvited to the VIP functions and hardly able to finance a trip if they were, young Negroes began to flex their muscles. A wave of sit-in demonstrations, in which college and high school students participated, erupted from coast to coast in a national attack on discrimination in public places.

Freedom Rides followed, to test the enforcement of interstate antisegregation laws in transportation. Then came the voting campaigns in the South's Black Belt, a collection of some two hundred
counties in seven states where most Negroes still live in a poverty-
stricken state.

At this point, the traditional Negro leadership was in trouble—
and so was the institution of segregation as it affected many areas
of Negro life. The surge of youth in civil-rights demonstrations
stiffened the back of the leadership, but it also broadened the scope
of the middle class so that it recognized that it had a voice in its
own destiny. Long the kingpin in the civil-rights field, the
NAACP met opposition in the ranks, as accusations of "conservative" and "slow" were hurled at it. The vigor and drive of the demonstrators, most of whom were from CORE, for the first time in
years reduced the influence of the NAACP.

The eruption of sit-ins worried the sponsors of the segregated
institutions. The integration drive caught up with Negro colleges,
Negro businesses, the Negro press and even Negro churches. So
much emphasis had been placed upon integration that merely the
mention of anything all-Negro brought cries of "second-class" from
students. All these institutions felt rising pressures for changes,
and many suffered actual reprisals. Sit-in demonstrators marched
on college campuses. The world of segregation was beginning to
totter—at least in the minds of its sponsors and of many of the
leaders caught up in the integration thrust. They began to see the
handwriting on the wall. Perhaps there would be no drastic change
for a year or so, but change was coming. It was inevitable.

Even more important, Negro leadership realized that the concerted drive for legal integration, which had spanned a half-century, costing millions of dollars and scores of lives, was almost won.
However, the challenge now facing them was even grimmer and
more frustrating than the day slaves were freed one hundred years
ago.

Now that the doors of employment were opening, now that universities, colleges and schools gradually were admitting Negroes,
now that housing developments were considering them as tenants,

time was running out for a Negro leadership that had gained its superiority by emphasizing the defects in American life, by headlining the ugly aspects of discrimination and segregation. The pace of reform was so accelerated that in the years to come there would be the mopping-up battles, the sectional frays and the occasional bias cases, but few more Little Rocks or James Meredith affairs. The new challenge for leadership is to grope for direction in solving basic problems—the low educational and employment qualifications of a great mass of the Negro people, the poor morale, the lack of incentive, the buildup of racial tension, the tragic health and welfare crisis, and the frightful aspects of crime and juvenile delinquency—all indirectly traced to the pitiable status the Negro has held in America for so long.

"You feel like an ant before a mountain," a social worker told me, describing the situation. "You get tired really before you start." This attitude prevails in the Negro community. Even if every Negro leader put his shoulder to the wheel, the problems couldn't be wiped away. Negro leadership doesn't have the power or the resources to erase the mounting backwash of a century of deprivation, but by making the initial effort, it could arouse communities and people to slow down the rate of decay and degradation. Such a campaign could mobilize support from other citizens for more governmental machinery designed to get at the basic causes, instead of continuing to concentrate on the more dramatic civil-rights battles.

An enlightened attitude and a well-designed approach, stressed by officials of the National Urban League, could build a climate of understanding and would help bridge the gap between classes of even our race. It has been easier for us to cope with the problem in ostrich-like fashion—see the deterioration, watch it grow, then run away. As one civil-rights leader explained to me. "Hell, if we ever got tied down with stuff like this, we'd be mired in misery for life. You duck this like soft shoulders on a road."

Others argue that the economic squalor and the impoverished state of many Negroes in America is not the responsibility of leadership but is the responsibility of the Federal Government, the state and the community. They claim that action programs should come from government—better schools, welfare programs with constructive goals, modern low-cost housing, and equal opportunity in employment. "Unless we get relief in these areas," said a leader, "it's useless to try to do anything." Their point seems to be, "Save a few, not all."

# ★ ★ ★ 3  The Power House

Nineteen hundred and sixty-three loomed as the most important year in American Negro history. For almost a decade, the slogan of the National Association for the Advancement of Colored People had been "Free by '63," the historic significance being that this was the year which marked the Centennial celebration of the signing of the Emancipation Proclamation. Bold, aggressive and adventurous, the NAACP proposal shot new life into tired and weary campaigners and inspired them for the final assault on segregation.

As the year came closer, freedom was not in sight. In many areas of the South, a Negro couldn't even walk through the front door of a hotel or restaurant, let alone sleep or eat. He was barred from enrollment at many of the topflight educational institutions. In the North, the Negro was jailed within the tight confines of a ghetto to die early. But there was abundant unrest, triggered by the initial NAACP effort. There were Freedom Rides, the vote registration drives, the demonstrations and the college patrols riding herd in Deep South states.

In December of 1962 on the eve of the Emancipation Proclamation Centennial, the Negro "Big Six"* (the traditional leaders of the race in America) trooped into the White House for a serious conference with President Kennedy. It was not the racial problem in America that they wanted to discuss. The subject concerned greater U.S. aid for newly independent African countries. By all

---

* Roy Wilkins, James Farmer, A. Philip Randolph, Whitney Young, the Reverend Martin Luther King, Jr. and Dorothy Height.

standards of the civil-rights pattern, this meeting was a stroke of misfortune. No single meeting so undercut the influence of Negro leadership. "Negroes want their freedom now in America," one of the participants afterward said angrily, "Here we have met longer with the President of the United States than any other Negro group and we're asking help for Africans, who've fought and won their freedom."

That White House conference, more than any other session, turned the tide in the Negro's fight for equality in America. The NAACP's executive secretary, Roy Wilkins, was the chief spokesman; he was the man the President respected for his vision in the civil-rights field, although for political purposes, the Reverend Martin Luther King, Jr. was perhaps the most important Big Sixer. Wilkins was the skilled negotiator, the diplomat and the firm arbiter, but this meeting and its poor timing almost eliminated Wilkins from the power bloc.

The poor results from the confab dimmed the possibilities of a future Big Six session with the President. A terrible undertow developed.

I spent several hours with aides of the Big Six that evening. They were downcast and gloomy. One said: "We're not going about this right. We shouldn't have been here. We've got to quit begging the Kennedys for this and that. We've got to start demanding our rights."

I heard another say, "How the hell can we tell these sit-demonstrators we came to Washington, met the President and didn't demand help?"

From logistics to timing to techniques went the discussion. Who was responsible for the summit meeting timed on the eve of the Centennial year? Why had foreign affairs become so important when civil rights had long been swished under the rug? Why were some of the chieftains so adamant in scheduling a meeting on African aid? Were the Kennedys behind this move? Were the Kennedys aware of the Negro's mood in relation to gadabout leadership?

Then the conversation took a different turn: "We're headed for a revolution. We're losing our mass support. Unless we go back to them and lead them forward, we're sunk. And to do this will mean some active demonstrations which could touch off coast-to-coast violence. But it must be done."

"To hell with the Kennedys. They can't direct our campaign. We must break all contact. We must give up this protocol life," said another.

This was the dilemma which unfolded. Negro leadership, the Big Six, was losing control of the masses. They knew it. They realized it. They could explain and evaluate their errors point by point. They saw the ominous clouds on the horizon. They began to see their troops deserting their banners. Panic was beginning to break out. So transient is stable Negro leadership and so necessary is a wide audience because of the need for finances, that to sit tight would bring only destruction of their respective organizations. A struggle to regain power quietly started.

What had happened? The Kennedys were not entirely to blame for this confusion. Several of the Big Six toyed with the idea of harnessing the African spirit among Negroes for use in the domestic struggle. There was a growing kinship between the new ambassadors and Negro leaders, and some of the envoys had already volunteered for duties to help ease discrimination and housing in certain areas. The plan was to develop a more co-operative program by swinging Negro support toward financial aid to Africa. But the timing was poor, and the negative reaction which followed from forces trapped in Dixie civil-rights struggles made the Big Six look foolish. They eventually abandoned the emergency aspects of the project.

This was one angle of the meeting.

Another involved the Kennedys. Quite frankly, Administration leaders hoped to gain support for projects in Africa by steering Negro leaders to back them wholeheartedly—even before Congressional committees. (Most other American interests push for projects in Europe, Asia or South America, following a strictly racial line.) The Kennedy charm course in race relations had begun, however, to sour. Far from desiring to press aggressively for civil rights, the Kennedys apparently wanted to pace each step of progress, then news-manage its existence on a political timetable. As a reward for such services to enhance a political image, there were invitations to the White House intimate functions or trips to Africa or Europe, if the Negro was sensitive about his heritage. The Kennedys also had developed an effective G-2 service that nosed into Negro communities, and figured out future plans. They would then either discourage the project before the leaders had time to formalize a program or bulldoze its effectiveness with a counterplan. Many of the Negro New Frontiersmen—most from civil-rights ranks—constantly telephoned to find out what their old friends were up to, and disclosed dates of contemplated activities in confidential messages to a main nerve cell. Negro leaders knew this and also suspected that the Kennedys once had tried to level off the impact of Negro civil-rights organizations by offering their heroes better-paying posts in government. The NAACP lost its most glamorous figure, Thurgood Marshall, in such a deal, it was often gossiped.

With these developments, the Big Six departed from Washington, a thoroughly discouraged lot. The more they thought about it, the more they began to feel the Kennedys had bamboozled them, not in respect to attempts to lift the status of the Negro, but in wheeling and dealing with various Negro leaders to disturb the harmony of leadership. "Really," a leader told me, "we've gotten the best snow job in history. We've lost two years because we admired him for what should have been done years ago."

Then came the invariable split into two camps.

Aging, but still hard-to-please AFL-CIO Vice-President A. Philip Randolph drifted off with the "go for broke" movement exemplified best by two ministers, CORE's James Farmer and the Reverend Martin Luther King, Jr. These men believed in the policy of "striking now and striking hard." They wanted no Kennedy favors.

The other camp could be called the "moderates," but they would object strenuously to the label. The difference in technique probably results from fears that an over-all demonstration, unending and persistent, could erupt into a national blood bath. Yet the NAACP's Roy Wilkins has the strongest organization and a flotilla of experts in mass protest. A series of telegrams from Wilkins could unleash demonstrations nationally, but Wilkins, a New Yorker who in recent years plays the race-relations game like an idealistic businessman, decided to wait—to play for the breaks. If the first wave of attacks failed or erupted into chaos, he could come to the rescue and take over the generalship. His strong point was the NAACP's constant lobbying for a massive civil-rights program to be submitted to Congress. His was the only organization able to lobby effectively for such legislation. The National Urban League's Whitney Young had no such national organization; the League was not geared to put on a direct-action program, therefore his role would have been that of a mediator, in any event, and for either party. Negroes at that time weren't ready to launch a massive self-improvement program, and the League had been caught in an inertia. The last of the Big Six, Dorothy Height, president of the National Council of Negro Women, was a figurehead, largely limited to putting on benefit fashion shows to raise money.

So the schism boiled down to a revolt against the Kennedys in protest to the planned, systematic desegregation program in which Negro leaders would be merely paper tigers in the over-all setting. The Negro "independents" refused to put their salvation in the Kennedys' care, despite the notable progress. They wanted always to be able to wage their own campaign for first-class citizenship.

The NAACP, the traditional standard-bearer for Negroes since World War I, unfortunately bore the brunt of the criticism, even from Negroes. Its critics maintained that the site of the new civil-rights battle should be shifted from the courtroom to the street. For years, the NAACP used the courtroom and gained tremendous victories. Now it was in trouble, not because its program wasn't paying off, but because its leaders advocated an orderly desegregation program in co-operation with the Administration and the country's leading white citizenry. Legal victories were costly, prolonged and demanding, argued the NAACP's opponents, who also felt that the offensive should not be orderly, controlled,

planned or at times—even led. "Storm the cities, any and all," was
the new battle cry. "Give 'em hell!"

The effect of the leadership disunity on President Kennedy
graphically came to light when in February, 1963, the Chief Executive invited more than one thousand Negro guests to celebrate
at a gala White House function. Missing were Dr. King and A.
Philip Randolph.

Some eight hundred Negro VIPs (along with three hundred
whites) tasted shrimp creole, curried chicken, hickory ham, roast
turkey, tongue, assorted cheeses and celery and carrot sticks. These
delicacies were washed down with an assortment of nonalcoholic
fruit punches. In between munching food and sipping punch, the
guests—Negroes prominent in many professions—chatted with
President and Mrs. Kennedy as they slipped in and out of five
historic rooms. The event marked the one hundredth anniversary
of President Abraham Lincoln's signing of the Emancipation
Proclamation, an annual celebration of the Republican Party, which
for years has used the achievement as its sole magnet for Negro
votes. The occasion, described as nonsocial so as to be least offensive to the more militant in civil rights, marked a historical breakthrough for the guests. More Negroes were present at this affair
than at all the combined functions of Presidents at the White
House from the time of President George Washington. Many of
the guests were appreciative that the Chief Executive was bold
enough to schedule what some jokingly called "Cullud Folks Night
at the White House."

But amidst the joviality of the reception, there was pessimism.
"It's taken us a century to get here as guests," whispered one VIP,
"and we're still not equal." As most of the visitors from an estimated
42 states huddled and exchanged words on a variety of subjects
with many of Washington's celebrities, gossip seemed to focus on
one couple—entertainer Sammy Davis, Jr. and his white wife,
actress May Britt. It was whispered that there would be no pictures
of this mixed couple at the affair, because of fears that such pictures could hurt JFK in Dixie vote-getting two years hence. White
reporters chatted about the "close-knit Negro grouping" and how

"well behaved the Negroes were." Much of their feeling—surprising to these prominent Negroes when they read the daily newspapers later—was reflected in their accounts. No mention was made in any column of the presence of the interracial couple, therefore, the first visit of a mixed couple to the White House was not recorded for public view. A small matter, perhaps, but it was one topic that flashed brighter during those hours of the reception than the subject of Cuba. Some believe that many Negroes feel mixed marriage is the solution to the racial problem, and it well may be. What amused the Negro VIPs was the fact that aides to the President of the world's greatest democracy could be annoyed by such a triviality at a time of international crisis.

Striding down the walk toward the White House gate, a prominent lawyer observed: "It's hard to believe that the Negro opinion-makers in this country could be gathered almost completely in four rooms of the White House. But it's true."

Getting into a taxicab, a socialite turned for a last look at the White House and said, "Thanks, Abe. Good night, JFK."

Across town, a cab driver wearily parked his vehicle and ducked into a tavern in the heart of a solid Negro district.

"Through for the night," he told the bartender, sliding onto a stool. "Gimme a beer."

He sucked on the bottle, then opened up. "You'd never believe it, man, but a flock of brothers (the internal code name for Negroes) just left the White House."

"What's going on?" the bartender asked.

"Dunno," came the retort. "But they's high muckydemucks."

The bartender sighed, not too interested in hearing this.

"Must be," the cabby said, "but they were really inside, a whole slew of them."

"Probably a benefit," the bartender tried to reason.

"I dunno," said the cabby. "But them cats were there all right."

Into every community from coast to coast, from the tin-roofed slum dwellings to the penthouse apartments, news of the Negro reception at the White House spread. A special photograph, showing selected Negroes with the President, the Vice President and their aides, was published in many daily newspapers and practically all Negro papers and magazines. Several publicity-conscious guests called their hometown papers on their return and were subjects of social page articles containing accounts of shaking JFK's hand. For sheer momentum, the event was a political milestone despite the fact that some leading Negro Republicans referred to the event as "a cocktail sip" and some of the more militant Negro leaders had flatly rejected invitations. They declared they would have preferred JFK to introduce civil-rights legislation in Congress (which he did two weeks later) than invite them as social equals to the White House.

To arrange for such a monster affair—the largest given by the President at the White House—aides compiled a bipartisan list (mostly Democratic in view of the 80 percent to 20 percent voting ratio) of Negro leaders, opinion-makers, professionals, elected public officials, appointees, judges and entertainers. At no time did the list reach fifteen hundred individuals nor did it include white cabinet members, senators, governors, corporate executives, school superintendents, Wall Street lawyers or department store owners. Preparation of the list highlighted one obscured fact.

A century after the Emancipation Proclamation, the number of success stories is so minimal in relation to the estimated 20 million Negro population, that the social secretaries may have wondered what had happened during the intervening years. The plight of the Negro is tragic, disillusioning, almost pathetic. In no field in America has he reached his potential, despite the volume of governmental propaganda scattered across the world—including accounts of "the huge stockpile of trained and educated Negro specialists who comprise a pool larger than in all of the African countries."

Take any of the professions, the careers, the skills, and you find a few Negroes at the top—only a small fraction over-all. In some trades, vocations and occupations, you find no Negroes. In some industries, you find no Negroes employable in other than semi-skilled or maintenance jobs. In business, the complexion of workmen is virtually lily-white, despite the existence of a few large

Negro insurance companies, publishing firms, banks and the usual service outlets—undertaking, grocery stores and dry cleaning establishments. Several years ago when the Negro Bankers Association met in the nation's capital, a reporter on one of the nation's large business publications urged his editor to assign him to the conference so he could do a piece on the plans of the group. He was turned down. Since the Negro banks handled less than a third of one percent of the nation's banking dollars, the editor didn't feel it mattered what they discussed or did as far as the impact on the total market.

While the Negro VIPs spent thousands on travel to attend the White House reception, President Kennedy, in his first civil-rights message to Congress, best summed up the status of the Negro in America, when he frankly admitted that:

"The Negro baby born in America today—regardless of the section or state in which he is born—has about one-half as much chance of completing high school as a white baby born in the same place on the same day, one-third as much chance of completing college, one-third as much chance of becoming a professional man, twice as much chance of becoming unemployed, about one seventh as much chance of earning $10,000 per year, a life expectancy which is seven years less and the prospects of earning only half as much."

This was the President of the United States vividly painting the picture—with boldness and imagination. This is historic, because too often in the past government officials have hopped on an individual achievement to give the impression that the Negro was climbing Freedom's mountain. The communications industry too frequently concentrated on the exploits and achievements of "the chosen few" and left undisturbed the ocean of humanity which best represents the Negro in America—his world of poverty, frustration and despair. So often our own Negro leaders have entered environments of luxurious living and high society, assuming the dignity of VIPs. Civil rights has become big business, and the thousands of Negro peasants have become merely the pawns of a never-ending drive for finances. Politicians, always sensitive to the popular trends, swept civil rights away from the Negro communities and made it a vote-getting issue, as popular and controversial as foreign affairs. But there is a gap between the fervor of the civil-rights promises during campaign years and the interest in the subject when legislation reaches Capitol Hill. Several years ago, a prominent lawmaker was quoted at a national party convention as telling Southern members, "Why should you object to a strong civil-rights plank? You have the power to stop enactment of law on the Hill?"

Against this backdrop of intrigue, lack of concern and the lethargy among their people, Negro leadership forged its strength during turbulent years of struggle. For this historic reception, who were the Negro leaders JFK could afford to offend by not inviting?

Among Negroes, the Big Six exercise the dominating influence in public affairs. These six leaders more or less are and represent individuals who belong to the highest class of intellectuals and who have recruited among the masses for support. For years this tiny band has inspired a fraction of the Negro population and dominated, led, borne the expense and educated a wide scope of the people to stiffen their backs against second-class citizenship. Most of the Big Six are permanent leaders who, having risen to the top rung and developed a personal power structure, will hold onto their power until death. There can be no replacement except by some element of misconduct or an overthrow of their vote organizations (which is virtually impossible). Negro leadership is a career for them, and unfortunately, some are dictatorial, at times selfishly motivated and resistant to change. They are masters in organization, in projection of their ideas and proposals and in preserving the image that they are "working for the brothers." These men and women also are the integrationists, their organizations being biracial in membership and officership.

But despite the buildup given them in the daily press, the Big Six have no authoritarian rule over Negroes and may not be able to survive as a wider area of Negro life becomes responsibly active in civic affairs. Many areas of Negro life are missing in the control tower of Negro leadership, including the men and women who guide the destinies of the tenants in the all-black ghettos. The Big Six constitute the last remnant of the days when one or two men could "speak for the Negro." And their projection currently is more for ceremonial attribution in order to show a racial unity.

Here is the rundown on the Big Six:

Roy Wilkins, "the old pro," is executive secretary of the 400,000-plus National Association for the Advancement of Colored People, which operates a vast network of state and local branches in every state except Alabama. A former newspaperman, Wilkins is a cool, efficient executive who is buttressed by an integrated board and staff. (Board Chairman Arthur Spingarn and Labor Secretary Herbert Hill, for instance, are white.) Heading the NAACP, the most important, experienced, best-organized and financed outfit in the civil-rights league, Wilkins is the keenest Negro student of public affairs among the six. He is an expert, a general and a leader, but he is not a man to inspire widespread support, in the manner of the late Walter White. In the past few decades, the NAACP accounted for more gains and progress for the Negro than any other group. It is the pioneer and trailblazer. Its legal arm, once headed by Federal Judge Thurgood Marshall, charted a new course in civil rights, the highlight being the 1954 school desegregation decision of the United States Supreme Court. Its Washington director, Clarence Mitchell, is dubbed the "101st Senator" because of his expertise on legislation.

But 1964 finds the NAACP at the crossroads. It no longer dominates the field of civil rights. It is described by many Negroes as conservative and tyrannical in operation. It offers too little opportunity for participation and leadership by the middle classes, except, perhaps, in the South, where the Negro upper class is not too involved in the civil-rights struggle. Its youth program is not dynamic. The NAACP tradition is in danger of being diffused in the future because of declining interest among Negro families who in the past have had only the NAACP to take their troubles to. Its emphasis on solid, mutual interracial achievement, however, continues to project the NAACP as the one civil-rights organization that ultimately could bridge the gap between whites and blacks in an orderly transition, once the effect of direct action diminishes. But with national, state and local government agencies moving into the civil-rights field and paying better salaries, the NAACP has lost many capable officials. It is truly in need of a gigantic overhauling.

Paradoxically, Wilkins is the only one of the Big Six who is currently close to President Lyndon B. Johnson. What this will mean to the NAACP is difficult to contemplate.

James Farmer is executive director of the Congress of Racial Equality (founded in 1942) and the new wonder boy of civil rights. From obscurity Farmer skyrocketed into the inner circle of Negro leadership, although it is debatable whether he maintains a wide enough audience to match his colleagues. Before the barrage of sit-ins and Freedom Rides were popularized by his small but influential group, Farmer, a trained minister who has never occupied a pulpit as a cleric, had no national reputation, and his pacifist group was alluded to as "a screwball outfit." In two years, CORE moved into the front lines as a most aggressive, uncompromising organization. Farmer showed raw courage by personally participating in the first Freedom Ride, which ended on a violent note. At the White House reception, Farmer was behind President Kennedy in the official picture, thus achieving status through publicity. Of all the organizations, CORE probably has the greatest appeal to young Negroes and to young whites who are civil-rights bent. Its active program of demonstrations insures the participation of many persons and has caught on like wildfire in many sections of the country. But CORE has not yet demonstrated permanence as a mainliner. Alert leadership has steered the group to lively orbits of interest that have earned it a national reputation. Whether it can continue as alert and formidable remains to be seen. CORE leaders, however, say they can. At the 1963 convention, the group turned its attention to the problems of the slums—the credit stores, the high-rent housing, and the lack of recreational facilities and adequate schools. Pursuit of such a program well could project CORE into an even more important position.

The Reverend Martin Luther King, Jr. is the organizer of the Southern Christian Leadership Conference. Here is the one Negro leader who has captured the attention of the Negro mass both in the North and in his native South. As the SCLC head, Dr. King has a strong position, but his organization is, on the whole, a motley collection of ministerial combines in various cities. It has little effective weight until Dr. King comes to town or sends a telegram supporting the clerics in a given project. The group's membership, mostly on paper, is best counted when King sermonizes at a given church.

No organizer, no skilled administrator, no expert on legislation or experienced infighter, King's most effective civil-rights argument lies in the field of moral logic. One of the most dynamic speakers, colorful and spectacular in some of the situations in which he has become involved, King is the first Negro who can, with some basis, claim to have influenced a presidential election. In 1960, when Dr. King was in jail and JFK telephoned Mrs. King to express sympathy, the call was magnified enough in Negro communities to prove that JFK was a liberal compared to Vice President Nixon, who failed to take any action. Dr. King possesses all of the personal magnetism and the showmanship attraction that the NAACP leaders lack. His moral arguments and his personal bravery put him in a class with his Indian idol, Mahatma Gandhi. He is the only member of the Big Six who still maintains offices in the South (Atlanta). He will not commercialize civil rights, back down on political alliances, or salt away for personal use any of the money collected on civil-rights missions. He continues to fire away at the problem 24 hours a day.

Whitney Young, executive director of the National Urban League, is "Mr. Harvard," darling of the intellectual set. His organization, comprising some 62 branches scattered across the country, is committed to social work aimed primarily at developing opportunities in major fields for the mass, from which it gets little active support. The League's national reputation is conservative, although the policy really isn't. Few Negroes at the bottom rung can understand the polysyllabic phraseology or have the cash to attend the downtown luncheons or receptions with industrialists.

New in the post, Young represents a force that is not on the violent frontier of demonstrations, protests and marches; he is, however, the man to give Negro leadership direction in moving into new areas of social problems, a neglected front from the point of view of self-reliance. The deterioration of family life, the mounting crime and juvenile delinquency and the need for crash programs of incentive and inspiration are all areas on which Young can focus his skills. His organization probably will streamline and renovate its pattern, moving more deeply into the Negro community rather than resting comfortably in the protected atmosphere of the "talented tenth," the educated upper class. The League gets less press in the white world than any other Negro organization, yet it has the best integration record, the keen experts and the know-how. The challenge, as one League executive says, is that "the problems are so massive, and our forces so small, it's like a small boy fishing in a lake with a clothespin and no bait." Not a leader of the masses and not a drawing card in the Negro community, Young is the brains of the top level, but with so many government experts compiling statistics and acquiring skills, with much more abundance of finance and support, Young's role must increasingly become that of a crusader, or he will be relegated to the background and fast lose status because of a wave of anti-intellectualism growing among Negroes. (The number of college-educated Negroes in the rank and file of the revolution is disappointingly small.)

A. Philip Randolph, the world-famous president of the slowly vanishing, predominantly Negro Brotherhood of Sleeping Car Porters, is the dean of the Big Six. At one time Randolph was one of the most powerful Negroes in America—outspoken, forceful, courageous and dynamic. In the last few years, Randolph has been accorded the honor but gradually has lost control of his dominating position, not only in his union but in the labor movement. His own men, out of respect for him, have refused to oust him. "He helped us," they say, "Now let him alone." His leadership has blunted what was one of the crusading forces for civil-rights activity —labor, particularly the action of its Negro membership. Randolph's organization, the Negro American Labor Council, has split, and many of the younger laborites fight their own battles. At this crucial period in history, some one and a half million Negro union members need a much stronger representative of the labor movement. As a tribute to a pioneer, however, they refuse to elevate Randolph to an honorary post. Thus, one of the nation's former racial champions no longer is a symbol of power; he is only an aged warrior who has fought a tremendous fight.

Dorothy Height, president of the National Council of Negro Women, which in its press releases boasts a membership exceeding 800,000, is the only Big Six member who has to fight to stay in that category. Using any yardstick, Miss Height's only business in this group is that of representing Negro women. Since the days of the late Dr. Mary McLeod Bethune, the friend of Mrs. Franklin D. Roosevelt, the Council has been dropping in influence, program membership and activity. Its rival, the Association of Colored Women, has as large a dues-paying membership, and both organizations, being tax-exempt, are now allowed to lobby on Capitol Hill. Their programs generally center on social affairs with an overtone of humanitarian purpose and on fund raising. It is paradoxical that Negro women, on the whole far better educated than the men, have developed little topflight national leadership; a tremendous pool of brains, insight and know-how has been distributed among many groups. An inspiring Negro woman, such as Dr. Bethune, could be a real force in the power structure, but at present there is little feminine crusading on a national level.

Five of the six recognized national leaders maintain headquarters in New York City, once described as the capital of Negro leadership and the city with the most favorable climate for location of a home base. Internal pressures from Southerners forced both the NAACP and the Urban League to establish regional offices in Atlanta, but even now the Urban League has no great operation in the South. Dixie militancy has diminished the Harlem leadership tradition, and many a Negro from the South who sees the squalor and poverty in the ghetto finds his dreams of tomorrow crashing in front of him. "Lord, they got the vote," a Dixie

Negro said, "and look at how they live. We ain't got nothing, but we live better down home."

In some quarters it is contended that these six leaders do not represent the bulk of the 20 million Negroes, nor are they the opinion-makers for even a good-sized minority. This is a hypothetical proposition. For the sake of argument, and for the sake of explaining how complicated and confusing is the make-up of the power structure, it is possible to line up an array of Negroes who are not Big Sixers but who control the minds of more individuals than the recognized leaders.

For instance, political strategists and government officials who know the Negro world intimately and who need numerical support for various projects consider a man virtually unknown to the white community to be the most powerful Negro in America. The man is Dr. Joseph H. Jackson, president of the National Baptist Convention, an association that boasts an aggregate membership of more than five million persons. Because the Baptist faith pretty well dominates the race, Dr. Jackson, a silky-voiced Chicago pastor and a skillful organizer, has the inside track to major church congregations in every section of the country. To God-fearing Negro Baptists, Dr. Jackson is as potent as was the late Sweet Daddy Grace to his cult.

But Dr. Jackson is no civil-rights fighter; in fact, he is a conservative. He earned the wrath of the Negro press when he opposed sit-ins and called for emphasis on citizenship. During the NAACP's 1963 convention in his hometown, delegates booed him from the stage and he was unable to present $15,000 to the organization for its civil-rights work. Even with his recognized opposition to active civil rights, Jackson showed his organizing power a few years ago in his convention by routing forces (complete with fisticuffs) that sought to put in office as his replacement a friend of the Reverend Martin Luther King, Jr. Dr. Jackson has done little to encourage Baptist ministers to engage in civil-rights activities; he has not even advocated that they conduct vote registration drives in the South or use their churches as meeting places. He is an exact opposite of Dr. King, emphasizing that religion should not be mixed up in the racial controversy. His ability to maintain popularity and his power to rule almost singlehandedly over the major religious faith of Negroes in America are truly social phenomena in this era of revolution.

Coupled with the exclusion of Dr. Jackson from the power bloc, there is another strong and experienced segment that has not attained a seat at the highest policy-making level of Negro life. This group is composed of the Negro politicians, singularly or collectively. Not one of the five Negro congressmen, including the first black Congressional committee chairmen, Illinois Representative William L. Dawson of Chicago and Harlem's Representative Adam Clayton Powell, Jr., has been extended the hand of fellowship, nor has this honor been accorded leading government officials or deputies of the political parties. There is a tremendous gap between the Big Six and the solons, even with the extended vote registration in all parts of the country and the prevailing feeling that the Negro vote is influenced by civil rights or economic rights.

Why is such a gulf between the official leadership and the politician? The ceremonial Big Six is not in a position to barter with these men, who as active vote-getters are more powerful in their own right. The political leaders have tight control of a given area, although the Big Six have more of an invisible, sentimental following. Further, the Big Six, in mythical roles, cannot afford to criticize the Negro legislators even when they oppose civil-rights bills. During presidential campaigns, potential candidates are more anxious to win the backing of a Negro congressman than the NAACP, because they know that the solons, knowledgeable of the vote-getting business and the ins and outs of maneuvering, can produce the vote. The NAACP, for all ostensible purposes, is nonpartisan and cannot campaign. A glorified statement cannot be counted in the ballot box.

Representing the five major cities and having contacts in other cities with leading party officials, the Congressmen as a bloc are far stronger than the leaders. In many ways, they are the real power structure in using the vote as a lever for increased civil rights, although, ironically, the leading civil-rights spokesmen on Capitol Hill are white lawmakers. In too many cases, the legislators, faithful to the line of command, decline the leadership role and become a part of political machinery. Several years ago, when civil-rights legislation was being considered on the House floor, the NAACP tried to gain additional support and contacted Representative Dawson. He refused to listen to them, called their idea impractical and emphatically told them that with his long experience in Congress, he knew more than they about what could be done. Another example is Representative Powell, who for years cavorted publicly with a nondiscrimination amendment to education legislation. When he became the House Education and Labor Committee chairman, he shelved the proposal and dared the NAACP to oppose him, threatening to crush their effort.

Under the presidency of Lyndon B. Johnson, the influence of Hobart Taylor, Jr. will probably rise. The son of a Texas millionaire, Taylor served as director of the Equal Opportunity Committee on Employment under Johnson. Several years ago he gave up a prosecutor's post in Detroit to come to Washington as a member of the Johnson team. Under his direction the Equal Opportunity Committee has achieved considerable success, so much so that Johnson was invited to speak at the National Urban League's Equal Opportunity banquet in New York. Taylor was occasionally criticized for maintaining his close association with Johnson, but in the early months of the new President's administration, he and USIA Director Carl Rowan were expected to be the most influential Negroes.

Besides the aforementioned, other important areas of Negro life are unrepresented at the highest rank. The fraternal world, which attracts a large middle-class following and has a certain influence on the masses, is one. The Elks' Grand Exalted Ruler, Hobson Reynolds with a 400,000-member group, is ignored—probably because his organization is the most consistent GOP backer in the field. There are several youth groups, including the Student Nonviolent Co-ordinating Committee headed by James Forman (probably the brashest civil-rights outfit in America). Newcomers to the cult field, the Black Muslims, also lack representation among the chosen few. The group has less converts and less of a program than many other organizations but is publicized in the press because of its anti-white feelings.

# ★ ★ ★ 4 The Explosion

The mood of the rank-and-file Negro shifted from mediation and compromise. He wanted his rights immediately, and if necessary, he would fight in the streets to get them. He was no longer afraid of police, guns, bombs, night sticks or harsh words. He was tired of conferences, meetings, negotiations and promises. The urgency, the mounting tensions and the growing despair projected a future of uncertainty in the field of race relations.

The Big Six no longer controlled the minds of Negroes.

Neither President Kennedy nor his brother, Attorney General Robert Kennedy, had the charm and persuasion to halt the rising tide.

Negroes were no longer willing to rely on the courts, the ballot or legislation.

A civil-rights crisis was at hand.

The Negro leadership pattern was confused, despite the fact that the leadership itself was at its peak. There were more leaders and more followers going in more directions than any one organization could keep track of. The scope of activity was greater and far-reaching—in marked contrast to the 1930's, when a few men controlled the destiny of the Negro. NAACP Secretary Walter White's word was law, and he got obedience. Discipline was rigid then, and a Negro who opposed White was branded as "Uncle Tom" and banished from the crusading ranks. Now the peacetime civil-rights army was disbanded, replaced by a strenuous guerrilla effort. Only a few generals were around, and they found themselves taking orders, at times from privates.

The pace of battle widened and expanded, until it involved an array of sharpshooters who constantly pressed and unleashed a final thrust on segregation. Ranks, titles, reputations and even lives were lost in the furious free-for-all. Said a prominent civil-righter: "No man can weather the storm for long. The intensity is too great. You've got to be looking over your shoulder for a replacement. Victory is in sight. We can't quit now."

This was the setting in the spring of 1963—the year of freedom, the year of the Emancipation Proclamation Centennial. The previous year Congress had appropriated $150,000 to finance the celebration of the Civil War Centennial, including a series of mock battles—many of which the Confederates won. This was a bit of Americana for the historian, the student and the tourist to relive the glories of segregation. For the celebration of the Emancipation Proclamation, Congress appropriated not a red cent, and the Government and its people probably would have been satisfied to allow the eventful year in Negro history to pass unnoticed. Last-minute protests by some Negro leaders resulted in a delayed schedule of speeches, services and receptions. But even this caused a flurry of criticism. "We're not free," charged Washington CORE leader Julius Hobson. "Why should we celebrate?"

The Negro revolution was as good a celebration as any Government dollar could subsidize. For the first time, the United States was on the verge of a massive revolt that threatened to extend across the nation. Government officials and state and city authorities were panicky. The series of sit-ins and demonstrations, the violent upheaval at Oxford, Mississippi when Negro James Meredith enrolled at the University of Mississippi and the continued brutality in the Deep South states angered Negroes—even though the assault had the backing of the Federal Government. Negroes now defied the demagogues in the South itself.

In the heart of the hurricane were four men—all leaders, all respected, but now struggling to keep ahead of the pack. In the summer of 1963, when the March on Washington walkers jumped the gun in starting, and some ten thousand Negroes and whites prematurely began the mile trek up Constitution Avenue, the recognized Negro leaders scrambled to get in front of them. A. Philip Randolph grinned, "Don't worry, we've been in this position many times in the past. We've been forced to run to keep ahead." When a march official yelled to the crowd that the leaders weren't in front, one of the marchers countered, "We don't need no leaders. We know the way to go."

Although its course steered recklessly towards open violence, the revolution that shook America in 1963 turned out to be one of the most peaceful in modern times. To understand its foundation, take a long look at the four key men.

Roy Wilkins, the old pro, the master mechanic at repairing civil-rights machinery, pressed for a massive campaign with new legislation in Congress, new executive orders, new court decisions, and a firm, forthright stand from the Federal Government to head off possible violence. He believed that the racial difficulties could not be settled overnight, but that the Government should boldly chart a course to bring order from chaos. Never a strong believer in demonstrations to attract the attention of the public, Wilkins felt that the peaceful method of negotiation and conciliation, buttressed by court orders, would bring lasting gains in employment, education, housing, health and welfare.

As a practicing integrationist, Wilkins believed in teamwork of Negroes and whites. He refused to bow to extremists who argued that the NAACP should be all black, barring whites from participation. One of his critics, Representative Adam Clayton Powell, Jr., irked because he has been snubbed for the organization's Spingarn Medal (awarded to the outstanding Negro of the year), launched a bitter attack on the NAACP as being "white-controlled," but Wilkins weathered the storm.

His was the "egghead doctrine," gained after a long and meritorious career. His words were as Greek to the man in the street; his speech was eloquent. His organization was riddled with attacks because of its so-called "conservatism." It is possible that Wilkins' close relationship with the ruling Kennedys softened his demands for all-or-nothing results. Wilkins may have functioned as "a brake."

A. Philip Randolph, the dean, long visioned a huge pilgrimage of angry Negroes to Washington to demand first-class citizenship. Originator of plans for a March on Washington during the Roosevelt era, Randolph didn't get to see them materialize because on the eve of the scheduled march FDR drafted an executive order requiring fair employment in defense industries. Now, as a fitting climax to his full civil-rights life, Randolph wanted such a huge demonstration. Disenchanted with the Kennedys, and having been one of the few labor leaders to refuse to endorse JFK's candidacy, Randolph began talk of a march geared to unemployment. It would be mammoth enough to paralyze Washington and force Congress to listen to Negro demands.

The civil-rights theme eventually became the goal for the march, but Randolph was not the man to organize or to finance such an effort. For previous events in Washington, other groups were forced to shell out funds to pay the bills. This time, for such a large project, other leaders were reluctant to co-operate, believing the money could be used for a more practical purpose.

Further, Randolph's empire had begun to crumble. His Negro American Labor Council, an organization of Negroes in the labor movement, fell apart after Randolph refused to endorse a vigorous attack on discriminatory labor practices and invited AFL-CIO President George Meany to address the outfit. But his idea of a tremendous march captured the masses; it sounded dramatic and exciting. Randolph was king for a few months.

James Farmer, CORE's major-domo, was the leader who inherited the NAACP's "Free by '63" campaign and, in a whirlwind drive, almost hit the bull's-eye with spectacular results. With its far-flung national projects, Farmer's aggressive CORE made the NAACP seem like a reading circle. He knew that with the NAACP playing footsy with government officials, he could always out-maneuveur it in the civil-rights arena. He gave the order, "Full steam ahead," ignoring warnings of violence and maintaining that the peace of a community was the police's role. Farmer's refusal to compromise solidified the independent leaders who defied the Administration and put him in the position of being the unsung hero of the revolution.

The Reverend Martin Luther King, Jr., the "Messiah," saw the Negro's plight in the South and he, unlike the other leaders, represented this section. He dared to live and work in the South. Despite the growing unrest in the North, King knew that Negroes in the South were farthest from the fruits of democracy. Knowing the Kennedys, he realized that politics would not bring an acceptable solution in his lifetime, or on his terms. He envisioned a massive civil-disobedience drive that, although nationwide, would be based in the South. It would be nonviolent and nonracial.

In Washington Negro leaders tried to convince President Kennedy of the need for far-reaching civil-rights legislation. In office for two years, the President had delayed sending a civil-rights message to Congress. Obviously concerned, Roy Wilkins urged meaningful legislation to implement the program to rid the country of discrimination and segregation. After considering the requests and the political expediency, the President recommended only a portion of the program outlined by Wilkins. Negro leaders, understanding the intricacies of politics, realized that gains in this sphere would be slow and that a better technique was necessary to arouse the country. However, many felt that while President Kennedy was sufficiently sympathetic, he was limited by the presidential role. They figured, as JFK advocated during his inaugural address: "Ask not what your country can do for you. Ask what you can do for your country." Following this theory, they felt that as leaders they could help the President realize the seriousness of the Negro's plight by immediately encouraging citizens to seek all the rights of citizenship, from the right to vote to the right to use public accommodations. Also, the leaders realized that despite the Supreme Court decisions the issue of Jim Crow travel lay dormant until a group of Negro and white Freedom Riders tested the policy.

Birmingham is a city long known for its brutal treatment of Negroes. Its civil-rights anchor man, the Reverend Fred L. Shuttlesworth, knew the inside of the jail as well as he did his own church. Finally, coercion and threats to himself and family members forced him to temporarily take refuge in Cincinnati, Ohio. But he never forgot the people of Birmingham he helped arouse, and he returned to the city for special missions. Turned down by city officials on demands to launch a desegregation of the city, Shuttlesworth invited Martin Luther King to make the city the kickoff point for a new civil-rights offensive. The technique: demonstrations.

Immediately, police officials got court orders barring demonstrations. This was the crux of the 1963 revolution. The issue was: Should Negroes violate the law?

NAACP officials privately warned that to move forward in violation of a court order was folly. They believed in the sanctity of the courtroom, where they had gained their impressive victories. They felt that to defy the law was not conducive to good government. "Negroes need to learn to respect the law," a NAACP official told me, "not to learn how to disrespect the law. Suppose white Americans refused en masse to respect antisegregation laws?"

Another aspect was especially bothersome to the NAACP. Almost a decade ago the organization had been outlawed in the State of Alabama and, despite the best of legal help and several appearances before the United States Supreme Court, had been unable to lift the barrier. Alabama thus was a state that had derailed the NAACP civil-rights drive, and now its officials were getting set to snare King in a legal trap.

Government officials viewed the situation as serious. If King decided to ignore the court order and hold demonstrations in Birmingham, a city already inflamed with tension and racial passion, violence could erupt and spread like wildfire across the country. Even King noted the danger of bloodshed. "I want 5,000 supporters," he told an audience, "not 10,000, because I don't believe that there are that many nonviolent Negroes in this city."

Then he made the monumental decision; he and his leaders would defy the Alabama law. But King took pains to explain that, "In no sense do I advocate evading or defying the law as the rabid segregationists would do. This would lead to anarchy. One who breaks an unjust law must do it openly, lovingly (not hatefully as the white mothers did in New Orleans when they were seen on television screaming, "Nigger, nigger, nigger!") and with a willingness to accept the penalty. I submit that an individual who breaks a law that conscience tells him is unjust, and willingly accepts the penalty by staying in jail to arouse the conscience of the community over its injustice, is in reality expressing the very highest respect for the law."

Eventually arrested along with hundreds of his followers, King from a jail cell wrote a passionate letter of explanation to a group of white ministers who termed the Birmingham antisegregation demonstrations unwise and untimely. One of the sections of the letter dealt with the phase of Negro impatience:

For years now, I have heard the word, "Wait!" It rings in the ear of every Negro with a piercing familiarity. This "Wait" has always meant "Never." It has been a tranquilizing thalidomide, relieving the emotional stress for a moment, only to give birth to an ill-formed infant of frustration. We must come to see with the distinguished jurist of yesterday that "justice" too long delayed is justice denied.

We have waited for more than three hundred and forty years for our Constitutional and God-given rights. The nations of Asia and Africa are moving with jet-like speed toward the goal of political independence, and we still creep at horse and buggy pace toward the gaining of a cup of coffee at a lunch counter. I guess it is easy for those who have never felt the stinging darts of segregation to say "Wait."

But when you have seen vicious mobs lynch your mothers and fathers at will and drown your sisters and brothers at whim; when you have seen hate-filled policemen curse, kick, brutalize and even kill your black brothers and sisters with impunity; when you see the vast majority of your 20 million Negro brothers smothering in an airtight cage of poverty in the midst of an affluent society; when you suddenly find your tongue twisted and your speech stammering as you seek to explain to your 6-year-old daughter why she can't go to the public amusement park that has just been advertised on television, and see tears welling up in her little eyes when she is told that Funtown is closed to colored children, and see the depressing clouds of inferiority begin to form in her little mental sky, and see her begin to distort her little personality by unconsciously developing a bitterness toward white people; when you have to concoct an answer for a 5-year-old son asking in agonizing pathos: "Daddy, why do white people treat colored people so mean?"; when you take a cross-country drive and find it necessary to sleep night after night in the uncomfortable corners of your automobile because no motel will accept you; when you are humiliated day in and day out by nagging signs reading "White" men and "Colored," when your first name becomes "Nigger" and your middle name becomes "Boy" (however old you are) and your last name becomes "John," and when your wife and mother are never given the respected title, "Mrs.," when you are harried by day and haunted by night by the fact that you are a Negro, living constantly at tiptoe stance never quite knowing what to expect next, and plagued with inner fears and outer resentment; when you are forever fighting a degenerating sense of "nobodiness"—then you will understand why we find it difficult to wait.

Wholesale arrests of demonstrators, the brutality of the police as evidenced by two widely distributed photographs of cops allowing a dog to bite a Negro man and kneeing a Negro woman on the street, and cruelty to countless children (turned into the battle as an auxiliary force) swung the tide in the Birmingham fray. Public opinion, despite the lack of legal support, fell heavily with the Negroes. With tensions rising in many sections of the country, government officials moved into the picture for a settlement. Assistant Attorney General Burke Marshall worked out an agreement, but only after Alabama businessmen verified what Negroes had been saying all along. The United States departments and agencies in Alabama had a worse record of hiring Negroes than civilian operations. The Government was forced to take immediate steps to set the pace.

With Birmingham as the symbol, America's Negro community exploded with jubilation. King became the symbol, the leader— outdistancing the NAACP, the Big Six, the politicians, the other churchmen. He was hailed as the "Messiah," a title that even Adam Clayton Powell belatedly used when referring to him. A few weeks later, the NAACP's Roy Wilkins flew down to Jackson, Mississippi and was arrested in a demonstration ordered by his organization (despite the earlier policy of obedience to the law), but this was an anticlimax. Whether the NAACP endorsed demonstrations or not really didn't matter. Negroes had chosen new leadership and were rampaging in cities across the country to touch off a full-scale revolution.

When the racial conflict shifted from the courtroom and the conference quarters, the rank-and-file Negro became his own best envoy. Every Negro could participate in a street demonstration, whatever his education or affluence. His century-plus freedom march resembled more of a hitchhike than a steady, onward march. But thrown onto the line were stragglers, grandmas, rabble-rousers, Harvard Ph.D.'s, racketeers, shoe-shine boys, doctors, widows and kids—all shouting, hollering, picketing, demonstrating and making a racket in so many places in so many cities on so many issues, from Jim Crow at a golf course to no wood on the stool of a toilet in Mississippi, that even the civil-rights generals lost control of the field troops. From meager resources in finance, brainpower and know-how, the Negroes built a powerhouse.

By midsummer, more than six hundred demonstrations disturbed the peace in some 169 cities in 32 states. Reactions ranged from sympathy to derision, from co-operation to resentment. Jails filled around the country, but the marches continued unabated. Bond money came from many quarters. Support for Negroes cut through a wide range of classes. There was sadness when Baltimore postman William Moore, a white man, was murdered while walking through Alabama en route to his native Mississippi to deliver a message to Governor Ross Barnett, urging calm and analytical actions to meet the crisis. There was the touch of grimness when a Negro youth dashed through New York police lines and mounted the framework of a new structure to prove that he was not afraid of heights and was qualified to work as an iron structural worker. A white workman sneered, "So that's all the qualifications he's got to have, huh? A damn fool in my book." There was the element of brutality when police grabbed women and shoved them into vans to make the jailward trek. There was meaning to the concerted revolt, for the Negro was unhappy; he wanted his rights now.

The convergence of more than 225,000 Negroes and whites (two and a half times the participation predicted in the press) for the August 28th March on Washington has gone down as the most unforgettable day in Negro history. Besides being the largest demonstration in the nation's capital, the project garnered more publicity on television, radio and in the press, both national and international, than any single racial event. The March was a turning point—a crossroads in strategy and tactics, not only for the Negro masses, but also for the whites in America. For perhaps the first time, the race problem was focused into a constructive view for every citizen of this Nation.

The March on Washington was a mass summit meeting in which the middle class got one of its rare opportunities to express its determination and support for the task of wiping out discrimination. Although the emphasis appeared to be the gaining of support for the civil-rights legislation program of President Kennedy, and leaders spent the morning conversing with Capitol Hill solons, the impact of the March cut much deeper. It was recognizable that for the leader who was aggressive, courageous and dynamic, his flock was ready-made. For the leader who took advantage of the unrest and the declared aspirations, a far-reaching program would win adherents. Thus, the March served as a barometer of Negro feeling; the Negro was not tired and fatigued after almost eight months of unceasing efforts; he wanted even more action, deeper and broader. Leaders—to keep pace—were forced to chart new programs. Again, the national participation of whites and Negroes forged together a solid army of civil-righters. The March was inspirational, and influenced hundreds of crusaders who came from the South. "I got a new charge," a Mississippi farmer told me. "I never realized all of these people were on my side."

When Martin Luther King, Jr., voiced his unforgettable "I have a dream" message, he brought tears to thousands of faces, particularly the black faces—not because of passion or emotion, but because the words and the descriptions cemented together both memories of struggle and the dream for the future. At few occasions had there been much mention of the sacrifice, the devotion, the dedication and the spirit of the men and women who have kept alive the sense of militancy in Negro America. These are the forgotten heroes of American history—those who believed in the American dream and refused to accept the proposition that it didn't apply to them.

The beauty of the Negro's struggle has been that the race has overcome the handicaps of prejudice, finance, the Establishment, politics, gradualism, religion, big business, sectionalism, illiteracy and poverty to demand justice. The Negro has developed little of the Madison Avenue complex, little of the mechanistic organization of the trade movement, little of the machinery of the vast political organizations. What the Negro boasts is soul, heart and belief—unregulated, uncontrolled and unending. "We got soul on Sunday, heart on Monday and belief on Tuesday," said a sit-in demonstrator, "and we just keep rotating these day after day."

Despite the critics, including Negroes who once opposed such a demonstration, the August 28th event became historic, not because of the size of the audience or the lack of violence, but because it set in the soil of thousands of marcher's minds the seeds for action against a major problem. Coupled with this show of interest was the factor of inspiration and stimulation. The event marked the peak of the Negro's struggle for rights in America. The March touched off a new offensive, broader, far-reaching.

But there was a difference that could shape the course of the future. Teamwork among Negroes and whites was the added characteristic. Despite what any authority might say, achieving first-class citizenship has been and will remain the main goal of most Negro Americans able to fend for themselves. This feeling is deep, not easily swept away by recognition or a position. It is a heartening experience to see Negroes, one by one, make sacrifices to bring greater opportunity to the oncoming generations. Families suffer indignities or the passing of loved ones, but even this is taken in stride.

For a long time, Negroes have carried their prejudices quietly.

Many hate the white man as much as he hates them. Several years ago Dr. T. R. M. Howard, the Mississippi civil-rights leader, drove his white Cadillac to Harlem and stopped to see a business friend. When he came out, Dr. Howard was shocked to see a gang of youths trying to turn over his car because it carried a Mississippi license plate. "Wait," he cried. "I'm a Negro. That's my car." The hoodlums dropped the car and ran.

Feelings are that high and are more pronounced among the lower classes. In low-class areas a spark suddenly can turn a brawl between a cop and a Negro into a race riot. This racial feeling has passed from generation to generation. Many Negro parents have told their children of brutalities to members of their families—and numerous families have experienced the savagery of racial violence. Although whites feel Negroes are anxious to forgive and forget, there is an element of Negroes who don't want to forget; they want revenge, and they are willing to bide their time. I was on a civil-rights mission in a southern state when police stopped our car and demanded that we get out and put our hands into the air. Later, one of the companions said: "I was almost ready to knock that cop's brains out." It was a thought that I shall never forget, but is indicative of the latent wrath still uncovered in Negro communities.

I have known families who instill a real hatred of whites into their children. "Trust no white man," the parent lectures, "Don't even talk to them. They are our enemies."

The anti-white theme has been a silent hallmark in the civil-rights struggle, because the white man is basically the symbol of the power structure. He is the government official, the policeman, the union organizer, the businessman, the storekeeper, and the White Citizens Council member. When rank-and-file Negroes think of segregation and discrimination, they automatically think of the white man, and the skirmish becomes racial.

Apparently, the white power structure feared the buildup in Washington would become a military offensive, that "a wild horde of Negroes and fanatic whites" would pre-empt the nation's capital. Some fifteen thousand police, National Guardsmen, soldiers, marshals, and auxiliary law-enforcers patrolled the city in unprecedented concentration, even exceeding precautions taken for an Inauguration. Police formed a cordon around Capitol Hill. Units of troops were situated at many nearby vantage points. Police radios blared. "Check your tear-gas equipment." Liquor stores and taverns were shuttered. Earlier, City Commissioner Walter Tobriner warned citizens to stay out of the downtown area unless they were participating in the March. The spirit was that of an occupation zone, the tone being: "Start something, and we'll really crack heads."

As thousands moved into the city, police deliberately kept their estimates almost seventy-five thousand below the actual figure. Radio and television networks provided first-rate coverage of the March. To achieve what was called "balance" programs were interrupted for interviews of demagogic Southern lawmakers. Many government workers remained away from their jobs because of the atmosphere developed by police, city commissioners and the press. Shoppers avoided the downtown area.

What happened shamed the people of the nation's capital and disclosed an ugly guilt complex. Only three arrests by police were made. A "rather unusual, peaceful day" was reported. The wild fears turned out to be nightmares. Neither morning nor evening traffic jams occurred. There was no violence, no explosion of hate. A Negro woman reported that a white man apologized for stepping on her foot during a march. "Forget it," she told him, and he smiled. Jackie Robinson, despite the warning to keep children away, marched with his son and pointed out to him the civil-rights dignitaries. It was the power and grace of the Negro civil-rights movement at its best, but it also was the new formation of the civil-rights movement—with integrated ranks. This, perhaps, was one of the most important changes introduced by Randolph's pet project. Greater white participation will reduce the intensity of Negro prejudices. The March was the first major step.

In many areas of activity Negroes have quietly excluded whites from their inner circles. A legend originating in Mississippi concerned a Negro grocery-store operator who frequently posted signs bearing misspelled words. Whites traveling in the area laughed at the weird phonetics. In the long run, Negroes laughed at them—the store was owned by the local NAACP president.

Several years ago, I covered a convention of Negro teachers in a southern city. Glancing at the conference program, I noted a speech titled "Controlling Environmental Factors in Nonurban Areas" and thought it too technical for a group of farm teachers. The speaker's name was unfamiliar to me, but I stopped in the auditorium and was surprised. Reporters filled the front row; the room was packed. The speech sounded mature and informational. The speaker was a member of the NAACP national staff, the announced subject merely a subterfuge to enable him to meet teachers later in a private room and explain how they could organize campaigns against school desegregation. The reporters never figured out this one.

Civil rights is a theme, a topic, a religion which engulfs nearly every educated Negro in America. It is a subject which pops up at barbecues, dinners, socials, churches and receptions. We drink late into the night arguing about discrimination. To serve in the civil-rights ranks is to carry out a personal mandate for your people, even if it means the loss of a job. Once outstanding in civil rights, a Negro leader becomes infallible. He can do no wrong—even if he actually does. Negroes are color-conscious, though we urge whites not to be that way, when it comes to our heroes. We excuse, alibi, protect. The March added a new dimension. The infusion of new leadership into a concerted drive certainly will weaken the hysterical, the irresponsible elements that have captured factions of the Negro population for their own benefit. The new thrusts for improvement, unlike in the past, have turned out to be half-and-half, salt-and-pepper, Negro and white, with no tokenism on either side. Thus, with the American race relations picture muddled, a power struggle brewing among Negro leadership ranks, a last-ditch fight from Southern extremists, and passionate threats from the Negro masses, a co-ordinated and integrated assembly of leaders has moved in to bring direction and strength to a project which some had predicted would disintegrate into violence and despair. It is an amazing American saga.

For most of the year the NAACP's Roy Wilkins had been hooted down, attacked by racists such as Adam Clayton Powell, Jr., and forced temporarily to give up his mythical leadership role in the wake of the Birmingham crisis. Yet, of all the Negro leaders, Wilkins showed the greatest courage, restraint and ability. Of the Negro leaders, Wilkins, in the final analysis, was the man on whom the future hinged. Calmly analytical, resourceful as a general and experienced from years of civil-rights fighting, Wilkins had the necessary ability to lead his people to freedom. He had the people, too, with a national network of branches in every major city. He held these people together during a turbulent year, even when he was under direct attack. For Wilkins was the leader who advocated an integrated front, a program and an intelligent technique. He stood by his program when the multitude swept by him. But after the tumult was over, after the headlines faded, after the applause was long forgotten, Wilkins emerged as the key man to head the program of the future.

Wilkins had never allowed racial passion to cloud his mind. He saw the eventual death of demonstrations for demonstration's sake. He saw the need of tangible, clearly planned programs. He realized that Negroes were only a tenth of the population and that how far they progressed, how much they gained depended not only upon their initiative but on selling the program to the American white man. This was his major contribution to 1963. In a year of intense emotional upheaval, Roy Wilkins turned out to be the sober, alert thinker for his people.

Ironically, while writers like Walter Lippmann wrote of "the Negro struggle taking a sharp turn" and others stated that "a Negro revolt was taking place in democracy," the architects and planners of the original dream (the members and leaders of the NAACP) sidestepped and postponed the conclusion of their historic "Free by '63" campaign. Why did the NAACP wage such a forthright campaign and then postpone it on the eve of the great year? What impact will this decision have on the Negro's future in America?

NAACP leaders publicly deny they canceled the "Free by '63"

drive. They insist the NAACP bore the brunt of the advances—even the expenses for lawyers and bonds of the Dixie demonstrators. They insist they sat in on negotiations, on planning, and spearheaded the year's program. Privately, however, some NAACP leaders frankly explain what happened.

1. The "Free by '63" drive was more of a financial campaign than anything else, a device to raise money. There was no solid program to eradicate the discrimination and segregation alluded to in literature—only previously established plans. There had been no co-ordination of an action program to augment the "Free by '63" project.

2. The three major areas for NAACP action were deadlocked. In the executive arena, JFK moved cautiously on major issues, and the organization could do little to press him to expand his program. In the legislative area, Congress pigeon-holed civil-rights legislation. Except for serving as agitators, NAACP leaders were blocked. In the judicial sphere, the NAACP was stalled. Costs were prohibitive, time was consumed and enforcement was based more on individual communities demanding their rights than the issuance of a court decree.

3. Direct action was a risky tactic for the NAACP. In many instances, it involved violation of law, a practice which NAACP leaders condemned—at first. Caught up in the frightening revolution, NAACP leaders finally decided to push in this direction. But this came after the Reverend Martin Luther King, Jr., won his Birmingham fight, and the NAACP was relegated to second billing.

4. The NAACP leaders, representatives of the upper classes, misjudged the temper and will of the Negro middle classes. Because their weapons were designed for an orderly campaign within the confines of a democracy, NAACP leaders considered public demonstrations meaningless and unproductive because they expressed only a protest without reward. They failed to realize the advantage of a super-demonstration, the jailing of thousands as against the jailing of a single person for a court test, the massing of thousands in a given place downtown, in contrast to a meeting in a Negro church.

5. Veterans of nearly a half-century of crusading and well entrenched in the civil-rights movement, NAACP leaders felt that without their support, no other movement could succeed. They believed they had the national organization and the numbers and could easily outflank any single individual who rose to leadership in a given section. NAACP leaders spent as much time trying to control the influence of rival leaders as they did in devising and mapping plans for a concerted effort. As it turned out, the NAACP lost control of the revolution.

Had the NAACP forthrightly moved ahead on a well-established Centennial program, it would have been in a position to chart a course that Negroes would have respected. As it was, the NAACP's colors came in second in a reversed turtle-and-hare race. In an *Ebony* article, "The Mood of the Negro," senior editor Lerone Bennett wrote about the failure of the NAACP to attract the masses. He said:

"The dilemma of the NAACP was spotlighted recently by a young schoolteacher who asked a speaker what she could do about Birmingham. The speaker urged the teacher to join the NAACP or the National Urban League. She replied: 'You don't understand. I want to do something.' The speaker said she could do something in the NAACP and the League. The teacher said: 'No, you don't understand. I don't want to pass resolutions or debate. I want to go out in the streets and do something.' "

Caught up in such fervor, NAACP leaders found little support from Negroes. They were harshly criticized for having conditioned Negroes into believing 1963 would be the year of change. The attacks on the organization reached a new high, punctuated by Adam Clayton Powell's charge that the NAACP was "white-dominated." Wilkins was accused of being "a moderate" and "lacking in color." There was open speculation that the organization had lost its usefulness, and having served its purpose, was deteriorating into a social organization. It was tragic that NAACP officials received such a rough going-over after their forthright campaign of previous years.

But there was little reason, little sanity in the uprising.

Wilkins did not panic, even at the NAACP's annual convention when Baptist leader Joseph H. Jackson was booed so loudly that he was unable to speak. Tempers flared when James Meredith, the Negro who braved mobs to enter the University of Mississippi, cautioned a student audience to "build constructively." Criticized by the meeting chairman for his moderate views, Meredith later admitted that he cried in his hotel room afterwards.

Wilkins took the brickbats but continued his steady program. At year's end, he was again the leader to whom Negroes turned for advice. His organization had regained its pre-eminent position. Although sporadic outbreaks had demonstrated indignation, the Negro wanted dignity. The crusade was in a new stage. As one civil-righter said, "The more freedom we get, the more we want. When we get it all, we're going to be so mad because we didn't get it when we should have, that we're going to start fighting all over again. Then we will realize that the freedom we thought we won by smashing accommodation barriers isn't the freedom that gains adequate education, housing, employment and health. But to get this, we can't fight in the streets."

When the civil-rights revolution left the streets, Roy Wilkins was again the general—for the infighting on Capitol Hill, the strategy in the courts and the executive sessions with the nation's leaders.

## ★ ★ ★ 5 Money Bags and Carpet Bags

Reports from the field showed that the Republicans were losing a heavy percentage of the Negro vote in the closing weeks of the 1960 Presidential election. GOP strategists hurriedly scouted the scene, talked with advisors and agreed on a last minute plan of counterattack. Two days before the election, Secretary of Labor James P. Mitchell presented to President Eisenhower a document which received wide publicity in the Nation's press. The title of the special report: *The Economic Situation of Negroes in the United States.*

In the foreword of the study, the Secretary, campaigning hard for the Republican Party's slate of Vice President Richard M. Nixon and Henry Cabot Lodge, carried this hard-to-believe message: "A notable development in the United States in recent years has been the steady improvement in the social and economic status of Negroes. In education, type of work, income, housing and other areas for which measures are available, the historic differentials between whites and Negroes have narrowed." Included in the report were the latest statistics on population, employment status, occupation and wage and salary income, all subtly interpreted to influence the reader to believe that differences between white and Negro standards were slight after 8 years of GOP prosperity.

The last-minute GOP effort had little impact on the Negro vote in the fourteen states where it is important, possibly because up to that time the party had shown little interest in winning the racial vote. But this technique of utilizing economic and social data marked a new political turn. Had it been a conscientious, sincere

66

effort to project honestly the plight of the Negro, the gesture would have been hailed as a sign of progress. In its race-relations aspect the project backfired, provoking many social scientists to challenge the conclusions and insist upon undoctored interpretations, especially on the eve of a major political event. The furor created in the Negro intellectual set precipitated new demands for pure research and objective analysis.

For years the National Urban League had served as the official record-keeper for Negroes, its experts able to assess a condition, report objectively on data and present a detailed history. However, few giants of industry, government, business or civic affairs were interested in such data. They wanted to hear the brighter side of Negro progress. More emphasis was placed on developing a wholesome climate of race relations by pointing up the positive side of Negro life—the appointments, the job gains, etc. Even during the Eisenhower years and the early Kennedy Administration, the Government stressed the appointment of a few Negroes to key posts more than the discrimination in Government agencies. More attention was focused on the few instances where antibias committees had prodded industrialists with Government contracts to hire a token number of Negroes than on the industry-wide barring of Negroes in skilled posts. Far more notice was taken of one or two unions that accepted a few Negro members than of discriminatory apprenticeship training programs. Even this stress on the positive side, although giving whites a false sense of Negro economics, had some benefits. It kept alive the widespread issue of discrimination in employment—for Negroes, at least. It also opened the door for the Civil Rights Commission to launch new probes of conditions in America and virtually take over the function of record-keeping in race relations in the new era.

Government exploitation of data on the Negro in an effort to show progress and consequently win Negro support is not unusual or unique. Starting with Franklin D. Roosevelt during the New Deal days, politicians learned how to use this information skillfully to attract votes in the North and possibly encourage Negro leadership to realize that the racial problem was being solved—by degrees.

New Deal speakers roamed the country, addressing crowds with glowing accounts of progress. Even Eisenhower aides at one time estimated the annual Negro income at about 20 billion dollars—more than the entire income of Canada—a figure which touched off a boom along advertising row and caused agencies to cast their nets at this lucrative market.

The trick of using Negro statistics is to compare figures of to-day with those of yesterday and note the percent of gain or improvement. It is not unusual for politicians to make a statement to the effect that "Negroes have gained more in four years of one Administration than in all of the previous eighty years of free-dom." Certainly, some Negroes have gained comforts; life is moving that fast. But the statistics are never compared with the figures for whites. Several years ago an Eisenhower appointee, speaking in New Orleans of federal gains in employment, made the challeng-ing announcement that under the Republicans the rate of increase of Negroes in government employ there was 300 percent. News-papers carried the story of the amazing development, although few reporters checked to find that employment of Negroes in New Orleans had gained from a total of two people to six in the case to which the speaker referred.

There appears to be a conspiracy to lull Negroes with glowing accounts of progress. Not since 1921 has the Labor Department staffed a Division of Negro Economics. During World War I the Division was established to examine the first migration waves from the South to the North and to develop some program "to keep Negroes on the farm." Efforts were made to improve living condi-tions and wages in rural areas of the United States. Gradually, the Division began to move into the complex field of employment and Congress, dominated by Southerners, abolished it by denying an appropriation. The government "snow job" technique has been a pattern since civil rights began to move its way into the headlines as a major domestic issue. But while the politicians and the press developed the general climate of complacency, conditions among Negroes deteriorated.

Before the 1963 Negro revolution, government officials rarely would speak on the plight of Negroes. Few admitted that the economic condition of the Negro was, on the whole, miserable. This is the critical problem today. A million Negroes are unemployed, some without skills or education—hopeless job rejects in the era of automation. Yearly wages for some Negro families in Southern states fail to reach $400 a year. Thousands of Negroes annually receive compensation from relief, welfare and jobless insurance—wards of the world's richest country. A majority of Negroes are doomed to ghettos, poverty, malnutrition and existence by dole.

Several years ago, *Ebony* editors searched the country for Negro millionaires. They queried correspondents in the major cities. They couldn't find 100, 50 or even 25 who could qualify by a financial examination.

One of the first government officials to speak out honestly on the Negro situation was Assistant Secretary of Health, Education and Welfare James Quigley, who in a 1961 speech in Washington declared:

Many people involved in the area of employment, whether in government or private business, will admit that the Negro has been discriminated against in the past, both as a job seeker and job holder. Many of these same people with a sanguineness I don't share, profess to see little discrimination in employment today. In my view, some real progress has been made. It is much less, however, than many believe.

Let us look at a few facts. According to the last census, although there has been an increase in the average income of non-white families, there has been an actual decrease in that average income in relation to the average income of white families since 1952. In that year non-white family income averaged 57 percent of white family income: in 1960, it averaged 55 percent. The disparity is even greater when we look at the incomes of single men and women. In 1952, the non-white individual's income was, on the average, 69 percent of the white individual's: in 1960, it was 57 percent. It is plain, that, in a sense, instead of progress there has been deterioration in the Negro's relative standing. He may be taking home more cash than ever before but he is not keeping pace with the growth of individual income in this country, much less closing the gap.

Take another example. The percent of Negro workers has doubled in the last twenty years in professional, clerical, sales and skilled jobs; but only about 23 percent of Negroes workers in such jobs as compared to about 58 percent of white workers.

Now I don't say for a moment that these figures can all be attributed to present-day discrimination. On the contrary, I am aware that there are other considerations, disparity in educational background for one, that contribute to the gap between non-white workers and white workers. Having said that, I would point out that differences in education background can't account for a situation where 22 percent of white college graduates are employed in jobs as managers, proprietors and officials of comparable standing and only 5 percent of Negro college graduates are so employed (or where, in almost complete reversal, five times as many Negro college graduates are in service and laborer jobs as white college graduates).

Equally as frank on the unemployment question, Quigley said:

Are we serious about attacking the hard-core unemployment? The rate of unemployment has run twice as high among non-whites as among white. A recent survey of twenty major cities indicates that although the Negro work force is 15 percent of the total, Negro unemployed are 34 percent of the total unemployed as compared with a general rate of 7 percent. (Recent surveys in major industrial centers estimate that the rate of unemployment among non-whites is a good deal higher.) I think if we mean business on these programs all of us—government (Federal, State and local), private business and labor, volunteer groups, have to do much more in assuring equal opportunity.

A summation of the Negro's economic might was unveiled in the first Manpower Report to Congress in 1962. The report, among other things, stated:

In 1962 non-whites made up 11 percent of the civilian labor force but 22 percent of the unemployed. On the average there were 900,000 non-white workers without jobs during 1962, with an unemployment rate of 11 percent, more than twice that for white workers. (Among adult men) the non-white workers' unemployment rate was two and one half times higher than that of the white. In part, this is due to the heavy concentration of Negroes in occupations particularly susceptible to unemployment. . . . Nevertheless, within each broad occupational group, unemployment is disproportionately high among non-white workers, partly because these workers tend to be near the bottom of the skill ladder for their occupational group.

An appraisal of this report came in a speech on "Urbanization of the Negro" by Housing Administrator Robert C. Weaver. The Harvard scholar declared:

Persisting discrimination in employment, in training and in upgrading harasses Negro Americans. We often hear that the situation is improving, and it is for the well-prepared colored American. The reverse is true for the untrained. And because of their magnitude, each ten years the Census records the fact that the gap in median earnings between whites and non-whites is wide and sometimes wider than before. The economic situation of the Negro in the United States, taken on the average, is not improving as rapidly as the situation of the white.

Averages, however, are misleading. They can be meaningless if there is high frequency at either extreme or at both. The latter is the case in this instance. Thus the median income actually represents remarkable economic progress of Negroes at higher income levels at the same time that there has been retrogression among low-income groups. In 1959, for example, there were some 1,160,000 non-white families earning $5,000 or more in the United States; 145,000 had incomes from $10,000 to $15,000; 28,000 had incomes from $15,000 to $25,000, and 6,000 earned $25,000 and over. It has been said that Negroes in the United States have a total annual income of 20 billion dollars. These, too, are consequences of urbanization.

At the other extreme, in 1959, some 1,200,000 non-white families earned under $2,000 a year and another 1,400,000 earned between $2,000 and $4,000. The majority of these faced poverty, and almost all had too little resources to sustain a decent standard of living.

This latter status was almost universal among those families earning less than $4,000 and residing in urban areas, unless they were single-person families.

What does this graphic analysis mean? A reporter figures that almost two-thirds of the Negro families in the United States earn wages inadequate to provide even the normal comforts of life. More Negroes earn under $2,000 a year than earn over $5,000. The trickle of Negroes into the higher pay scales isn't enough to compensate for the broad base of low-income families who now dominate the metropolitan pattern of our country, following the migrations of the war years.

But if this data is not alarming enough, consider more of Dr. Weaver's appraisal:

> If we judge family stability by the presence of both husband and wife, we find that it declines with migration and increases with rising income. Among southern rural non-whites, there is considerably more stability than in northern cities, at every income level. And in both South and North, the stable families become more numerous as income rises.
>
> In the northeastern and midwestern cities, we find very high percentages of households with female heads among the poor non-whites. Thus, if we take households with incomes under $3,000 and limit ourselves to families whose heads are in the 35- to 44-year age bracket, we find over 50 percent have female heads; for families with incomes between $3,000 and $4,000, the percentage drops, but is still over 20 percent; for families with incomes between $4,000 and $5,000, the percentage drops further, to between 10 and 15 percent.
>
> Among southern rural non-whites, in the poorest families with incomes under $3,000, the percentage of families with female heads is only 20 percent; and it falls in higher brackets to about 5 percent. Thus we may say that in northern cities there is by one measure, approximately two and one half times as much instability among non-white families as in southern rural areas; and among the poorest families there is about four or five times as much instability as there is among those better off.

Hampered by an insecure parental, financial and cultural background, dwelling in the dingy atmosphere of the ghetto with its accompanying frustration and despair, the Negro faces an uphill battle to become part of the American main stream. His resources of leadership, finances and strategies are limited. His inspirational symbols are few. The near-poverty status of the Negro virtually presses his nose in the rubble of humanity.

Only a few Negroes find opportunity in the face of discrimination, segregation and prejudice. Improved conditions for the few have set them apart from the majority of their underprivileged brothers and sisters, establishing two extreme classes—the Money Bags ($10,000 or more a year) and the Carpet Bags (the poor in mind, spirit and income). To fill the vacuum between the groups a new middle class is emerging, from whose ranks will come the new leadership, still hungry enough not to be satisfied, and still close enough to poverty to realize that conditions are not satisfactory. Meanwhile, a new class struggle is ripping the Negro community. The once-united front is now wracked by disagreement. The Money Bags, who supplied the leaders in the integration movement, are pulling away from the Carpet Bags in views, outlook and neighborhood. The so-called "Negro rich" are taking advantage of the widening opportunities for integration in employment, education and housing. Integration is more than a word for them.

Typical of adjustments required by this trend is the experience of one of the first New Frontier appointees in Washington. An outstanding civil-rights specialist from a southern area, this lawyer saw his life virtually reverse. His practice had consisted mainly of civil-rights cases, his wife had taught in a Negro school and his two children had attended segregated schools. When he came to Washington, he specialized in labor cases, his wife was one of the few Negro teachers at a white school, and his children attended predominantly white schools. It took this family months to adjust to the new surroundings. "I had no idea such a life existed," the lawyer told me, "Before, I responded as a Negro with Negro views.

Put into the white world, I found myself fighting to be objective because of my prior experience."

In my Maryland community, school segregation barriers came tumbling down, and for almost three years, not a Negro family would send their children to a public school two blocks away from the settlement. Instead, they boarded a Jim Crow bus mornings and traveled some two miles to a Jim Crow school. Parents argued that their kids would become emotionally disturbed by the treatment they received. It was a revelation to talk to the first Negro student pioneers and see how they reacted to integration after an early start in segregated schools. Their first months were far from perfect. They were unhappy and wanted to transfer back to the Negro school. These were problems our community leaders never anticipated when we argued for school integration.

A brilliant Negro qualified for a top slot in a northern city but flunked the physical examinations given by a white doctor. Aroused by what he considered discrimination, the man went to a Negro doctor and passed the tests. Finally, after leaders took up the case, the two doctors, white and Negro, met to give him the test. The conclusion was the same. He flunked the white doctor's tests and passed the Negro's. It was finally determined that he was so emotionally upset around whites that his reactions showed on the tests.

Such glimmers of integration touch the lives of thousands of Negro families in America and have a profound effect on the course of race relations. Once exposed to the big white world, many Negroes will not retreat back to the world of Jim Crow. The brave move on and upward as do the highly trained, the skilled, the talented, the qualified, but the unskilled and the illiterate fall back, neglected, ignored. Integration has helped only a few Negroes.

The rise of the Negro Money Bag class is an American success story, but like every other gain affecting the race, it is a mark of tokenism. Only a few Negroes are wealthy. Few Negroes hold upgraded employment in government, industry, labor or business. A good yardstick is the fact that throughout all of government there are less than one half of one percent Negro employees in the higher job categories. Yet this penetration is higher than any in other spheres of American life; the low-grade status of Negro employment can be readily understood. In the art of money-making or the world of business, the Negro also has done little.

With the exception of those in professions (mainly, the ministry, law, teaching and the medical fields), Negroes have acquired funds, for the most part, from insurance firms, funeral homes and small service industries such as grocery stores, shoe-shine parlors, barber shops, beauty parlors, restaurants or tailoring shops. But the total financial stake in business is still insignificant. A recent report showed that the "major Negro-owned financial institutions, which include 51 life insurance companies, 21 savings and loan companies and 11 banks, had total assets of a little more than a half million dollars. According to Leroy Jeffries, vice president of Johnson Publishing Company, the assets of the top 83 Negro-owned financial institutions fade into almost total insignificance when compared to the 478 billion dollars of the white-owned institutions in the same category.

But this progress is commendable, considering the financial state of Negroes and their lack of confidence in their business specialists. There is more money passing through Negro hands, but the bulk is not funneled through a Negro economic world. Perhaps the most amazing accomplishment of the Negro is his financing of the civil-rights crusade for more than a half-century. Millions have been poured into legal campaigns, funds and drives to contest discrimination and segregation. Our national organizations are primarily supported by Negro dollars. The best example of the co-operative economic might is shown in the development of the cults, from Father Divine to the Black Muslims. Thousands of little people pool their resources to form a treasury for leadership to plot a course for their self-improvement—sometimes not in their best interest. But the economic idea is sound and could be widely extended throughout the Negro community.

Suffering from the effects of the integration crusade, the Negro businessman had to use racial nationalism more than efficiency of service to attract customers in the past. Now that the masses again are becoming nationalistic and shouting "Buy Black," the Negro businessman finds himself out of touch again. He is too wealthy for his customers, and they consider him a member of another class. Few Negro business organizations are nationally recognized, and not too many leaders have status or prestige—even as a symbol of success for young Negroes. The reason, perhaps, is that the black community hasn't particularly honored them for forging an unusual record against tremendous odds or given them the acclaim bestowed upon articulate civil-rights leaders.

Nor have business leaders been particularly close to the civil-rights struggle. Forty years ago the North Carolina Mutual Life Insurance Company in Durham was founded by a man who trudged all over the state to interest Negroes in investing their money. Today, the company is one of the largest Negro financial institutions, with assets of 800 million dollars. Furthermore, North Carolina Mutual is constructing a 5-million-dollar building in the downtown area and is considered one of the state's most substantial businesses, operating in ten other states and the District of Columbia. With such financial leadership many other areas could have developed the structure for teamwork and co-operation. This is a dynamic example of a downtrodden people using the tools of capitalism to help themselves. Business is a pathway that few Negroes in the United States have used, yet it offers unlimited opportunities.

Several years ago, I visited Winston-Salem, North Carolina, on an *Ebony* assignment to do a story on a Negro bus company. Figuring that the firm boasted a collection of old school buses and transported Negroes to and from church, I made plans to stay in the city only a day. But I found that the Safe Bus Company had a fleet of more than fifty buses, had regular city routes, transported whites and was a respected business. The president told me that Negroes a half-century ago proposed the company after merging several "jitney bus companies" to form the enlarged firm. "We quit fighting one another," he said, "and started working together."

Another example is Chicago businessman L. B. Fuller, a cosmetics manufacturer. He successfully produces several lines of products, one geared for white trade and another for the Negro market. Scores of other Negroes have moved onto the business front and made contributions, but this side of life has been over-looked in the haste of the press to cover dramatic news. When the 1963 demonstrations erupted in Birmingham, many reporters covered the story, but few came away with any account of business-man A. G. Gaston, a Negro who became a millionaire in one of the south's most segregated cities.

With such distinguished business heroes dotting the horizon and thousands of Negroes forging ahead in unique positions, the gap in Negro ranks one hundred years after slavery is as great as that between white and Negro, not only financially, but socially and culturally. This is not particularly revolutionary. American Negroes have been divided by coloration of skin and religious de-nominations. Today, however, the differences of activity and con-tribution have expanded the orbit until the average white person cannot figure out what the Negro wants or needs, nor does he understand the community. The use of the term *freedom* as a catch-all answer is even more confusing, because the lowering of discrimination barriers alone is not going to help many of the Negroes in the Carpet Bag category. Such a transformation may cause the problems of crime, juvenile delinquency and welfare to become more acute, unless all spheres of government launch spe-cial rehabilitation programs to salvage the victims of racial oppres-sion.

Social workers tell disheartening accounts of Negro families sunk deep in human wreckage: "Several of these families have been on relief for three generations. None of the women have wed legitimately. All of the children are illegitimate. Talk to them is like rain water. It dries quickly without a trace. The situation is grim enough to be hopeless."

"Why should I work," said a Chicago Negro, "I don't have to. Live with women and pimp. Life's too easy. I got five women to shack up with any time I get ready."

The ghetto is a place where a man can live by his wits. A card

shark can gamble, run some numbers, play it up in night clubs
and be a community playboy. A confidence man can fool laborers
out of their money and live handsomely. In every block or so lives
a mystic, an oracle, who advertises in the Negro press. The ignorant and superstitious troop to his place, unload their cash and
leave without considering that the man is a phony, a fraud. The
quickest way to make a fast buck is to hit the numbers, a police-
protected enterprise in most Negro sections. Police generally are
used to keep an eye on whites (the businessmen, that is) in the
neighborhood, or to dissuade visitors from entering. A spiraling
record of arrests is the result of the poverty and the lack of incentive
or moral value. The Negro tenancy in jails and prisons is far out of
hand. This smacks of reverse subsidization. The government
would rather pay to feed prisoners than to help Negro students
and rehabilitate wayward families.

On the eve of the 1961 Inauguration, Lester Granger, former
Urban League national secretary, submitted a report to President
Kennedy, titled "The Time is Now." It outlined the public wel-
fare crisis. In the report, Granger noted:

> The very humanity of federal-state public assistance programs
> assisting over 6 million people—dependent children (38 percent
> Negro), the aged (17 percent Negro), the blind (30 percent
> Negro), the sick and the disabled (38 percent Negro)—empha-
> sizes the inhumanity of denying such aid when the family's bread-
> winner is employed, no matter how inadequately, or when he is
> "employable," no matter how theoretically.
>
> These legal categories pose problems for the non-white and the
> non-black. The Negro suffers out of proportion to his share—as
> 11 percent of the population, but this is in part because of other
> sides of the quadrangle.
>
> The problem then is "theoretical employability" in the face of
> joblessness and the "technical ineligibility" of a submarginal job,
> as much as a cross to the white West Virginian, the coal-less miner,
> as to the urban Negro.
>
> The nation can no longer tolerate these pigeon-hole categories

which have allowed us to ignore destitute and near destitute Americans.

We propose: that such categories as "employed" and "employable" be eliminated or greatly liberalized in the federal grant-in-aid programs to the states.

The wide disparity in income, aspirations, living standards and education is an index of the encompassing system of discrimination that has blocked Negro progress in almost every area. Whites have used the Money Bag as the symbol of accomplishment by toil and sacrifice. Few whites stop to consider the overwhelming number of Carpet Bags who are victims of such a cruel system.

While serving as a member of the committee investigating the race riot at D.C. Stadium, I was shocked to hear school personnel casually speak of Negro children regularly coming to school without breakfast and of their skipping school because they didn't have shoes. Why has this predicament been covered up so long? Why didn't school officials make the facts known to community leaders, lawmakers or District Commissioners? Poverty in the Nation's capital, within sight of Capitol Hill, should be of greater concern to legislators than poverty in foreign countries. Negro children in other cities are also victims of the same conditions and lack of concern. One has only to check welfare figures or to notice the condition of school buildings. A social worker recently told me:

"At the present rate, there is no answer to the Negro problem, except death by malnutrition over generations. The weak are so weak now—educationally and culturally—that they can never compete. There is no rehabilitation. The system is as vicious as the Nazi horror in Germany, but the American style is subtle and modern. You are not killed mercifully. You are allowed to suffer for years."

# ★ ★ ★ 6 The Middle Class

A Negro taxi driver pulled up to a stop light in downtown Washington, momentarily slumped over the wheel, then lifted his head as if to shake sleep from his eyes. "Tired," he told the passenger, "One more trip tonight and I will have made my quota. Then, I'm heading home to get some shut-eye."

"You better go now," said the passenger.

"Can't do it," replied the Negro, shaking his head, "but I'll let you in on a secret. I need the money. Me and my wife got a plan. We both work at the Government Printing Office, and I moonlight at night. We got to do it to feed and clothe our kids and put some away for their college."

An elderly Negro woman had worked for 35 years as a maid in a downtown department store. Management felt that because of her age, 68, she might want to retire and qualify for social security benefits. "No, sir," she told them, "I ain't worked for myself all of these years. I'm working for my little grandchildren. My daughter's got three kids, and her husband's gone and I'm gonna see they don't wind up on relief."

Neighbors were horrified when, soon after a family with seven children moved into a Washington residential area, the home became a mecca for travelers. Always the visitors carried patched-up, weather-beaten suitcases and wore the flashy clothing of the rural South. Utterly disgusted at the turn of events, a civic association committee called on the head of the household, a wiry man of 45 years, who explained: "Yes, ma'am, I know what you are talking

80

about. I agrees with you. We had too many folks here. But I told my kin down home in Mississippi the day I bought a house up North, I was going to give them the chance to improve themselves. In a few months, all the kin that wants to leave will have come and be out of here. And then I'm gonna be a good neighbor."

Multiply these cases thousands of times by a combination of dedication and devotion, add the stimulation of religious faith and inspiration, subtract the toll of casualties caused by horrors and broken dreams: the result is the pride of Negro heritage—the emerging middle class. The new middle class is the buffer group between the Money Bags and the Carpet Bags. In five decades, these people have breached the wall of discrimination and segregation.

It is an accomplishment for a middle-class Negro family to buy a home or save money to train its youngsters. It is also a badge of honor. Even with the handicap of a meager income and the insecurity of employment, thousands of Negroes struggle to accomplish this goal in an economic jungle alive with credit racketeers, real estate sharks and enterprising lawyers on one side and vice, police corruption and slum indifference on the other.

The Negro community is replete with stories of grandfathers attending night school to learn to read and write, of mothers taking shorthand and typing on week ends to qualify for better jobs and of clubs and organizations raising money to feed and clothe needy families. Despite the Negro class system and its organizational rivalries, there is a kinship in time of distress or trouble.

To be a Negro in America and to work to lift yourself is a trying, bitter, exhausting struggle. It is an existence which at an early age brings maturity, not that acquired through a first-class education, but the kind gained from firsthand knowledge and experience of a rough-and-tumble life. Despite what whites think among themselves, or what is written in textbooks, Negroes in America learn the facts of survival early, not in the orderly world of classrooms but in the chaos of ghetto city streets. For a century, a young Negro child could hope only to become a school teacher or a preacher and eke out enough money to live, while a white child could aspire to become President, or an advertising executive or a Wall Street

banker. Negro youngsters knew of color barriers, prejudice, hate
—even violence. With such terrible odds and handicaps, many
talented youngsters wound up among the uneducated, the unskilled, the untrained. They literally gave up the pursuit of dignity. To stay alive was all many could do.

Year after year, generation after generation, Negro families
pressed to keep a thin stream of qualified sons and daughters ham-
mering on industry's doors. But most were sloughed off into the
tenement world of poverty and frustration.

The middle class is the pride and the hope of the Negro race.
Every time I think of these plodding people I am reminded of a
headwaiter in a hotel of a major city. He was a big, tall man, and
he looked like a general in his uniform. Given the opportunity,
he was smart and intelligent enough to have become a lawyer or
doctor. His family was poor, and he had to be content with his
headwaiter job. But this man wanted much more for his sons and
sons of other families. He made a special effort to hire college
Negroes during the summer. Today his legacy is a new group of
Negro professional people, but his contribution is unrecorded in
history books and his name has long been forgotten. So it is with
many of the middle class.

While economists utilize certain descriptions for the term *middle class,* ranging from income levels to white-collar occupations,
a Negro reporter must disregard these statistical labels. The term
is not so much used as an economic trademark as it is a symbol of
people who are pressing forward to succeed in America. Of course,
this group is struggling, the average family income being well
below its white counterpart. In too many cases, because of the discrimination in employment, security comes from moonlighting
and even, in some cases, from lucky "hits" in the numbers.
Mothers, fathers and some sons work to keep the bills paid. Unlike the typical white middle-class family, which is staid and
conservative, the Negro middle-class is driving and pushing. It is
neither satisfied nor discouraged.

Statistically, the Negro is a flop in America. Using charts,
graphs, records and tests, Negro accomplishments are meager ex-

cept in areas of crime, juvenile delinquency, welfare and educational dropouts. This cloud hangs over the entire race. Critics often overemphasize these figures when contending that the Negro is inferior; at the same time they ignore the horrors of discrimination and segregation used to keep the Negro in a lowly state. The development of the middle class, with its storehouse of well-knit and resourceful families, is the answer to any bigot in Congress, government or business, many of whom have banded together in past years to keep the Negro "in his place." The vitality and the determination of the Negro middle class have destined the Negro for eventual integration on the American scene instead of the settlement preference afforded the American Indian or the fifty-first separate state advanced by the Muslims. These Negroes have survived the most hostile years of their civilization and have weathered the storms boldly, bravely and courageously. Certainly, they have not been "the most favored sons and daughters" on the American scene.

Several years ago, a Negro was honored for faithfully serving thirty years as a messenger in a government department. The Secretary and top aides attended the ceremony and presented him with a gold watch, all of which was publicized in the daily newspapers. On the way home, the old man turned to his son and said, "You keep this watch long after I am dead. Remember you are a college-educated man because your dad didn't want you to follow in his footsteps. And I worked as a messenger to make my dream come true."

Such perseverance and patience were commonplace in the past, and are commonplace now despite the flurry of civil-rights endeavors. However, in the past, this quality was often misinterpreted by whites as a sign of the Negro's complete loyalty to a *status quo* arrangement in race relations. The task of earning a living was such a difficult proposition that many middle-class Negroes refused to commit themselves openly to campaigns or proposals for equality to which they were secretly pledged. Thus, in the South, the politico's favorite slogan was "We know the nigger." The image long perpetuated was that of the old faithful "boy" who really wasn't concerned about his son or daughter getting an adequate education, job, home and health protection. All the benefits the Negro was supposed to get were the leftovers from the white man, a sort of hangover from the slavery tradition. Negroes suffered a long time before they were able to help themselves.

The northern migrations, politics, the world wars, religion, unionism and the integration campaigns left an imprint on the swelling Negro middle class, shaping its size, income, beliefs and development. Where would we have been if our forefathers hadn't trudged northward during the wars to the metropolitan areas and slowly developed a political foothold? Not as far along the road as we are today, with resistance in the South still based on violence and fear. A million and a half Negroes belong to labor unions, and this influence has developed a new crop of semiskilled and skilled workers adjusting to the rigorous livelihood of industrialism. Politics became a method of advancement with shrewd use of the vote. The civil rights issues, never actually consummated, were always interspersed into platforms and kept alive. The role of the Negro organizations, varied and often in disagreement, broadened the scope of campaigning and gave the middle class a variety of programs in which to participate.

The coming of age of the Negro middle class is a marvelous accomplishment. Although diverse in make-up, from porters to salesmen, from Baptists to Catholics, from segregationists to integrationists, from the few plumbers to auto mechanics, from preachers to cultists, this group is the most vibrant, the most adventurous, the most seething with excitement and activity. This is the group which balances the ship of state and provides the foundation for the progress of the future. From its ranks comes the restless, the aggressive, the ambitious youth who touched off the national siege of sit-ins, walk-ins, step-ins, dwell-ins and study-ins. The Negro middle-class parents of today, compared with their parents, are less patient and cautious, and more educated. Their children are even less patient. And their grandchildren will be still less patient, and considerably more educated. As the middle class grows, so will the expansion and intensity of the desire to become first-class Americans.

While the civil-rights revolution is more publicized and has, perhaps, been the main catalyst, activity among the middle class has spread into many channels. A remarkable increase in home ownership among Negroes throughout the country has been noted by government officials. Savings and investments have grown. Negro businesses are expanding. A tremendous spurt has been made in education, as P.T.A. and civic groups move to improve the quality of the ghetto schools. Negro publications have begun to advocate self-improvement in conduct, manner and qualifications for employment. More discussion and comment, more exchange of views, more clashes of opinion prevail in Negro communities than at any time in history.

What is freedom to the middle class? Most whites conclude that Negroes want the privileges of living in predominantly white communities, seeing their children attend integrated schools, and eating in downtown restaurants. Unlike the more advanced Money Bag set, the middle class as a group doesn't see integration as the answer. A majority would prefer better housing, jobs, education and security with integration only an issue as it affects the opportunity. It could be argued that the middle class has been forced into segregated patterns so long that the desire for integration is remote from their aspirations at this time. This is not altogether true. There is more of a sense of racial pride and dignity among the middle class than the upper class, more of a responsibility to "help the brother."

Consider this example: In selecting a home in the North, a Negro professional generally would be concerned with (1) integration of the neighborhood as a prestige symbol, (2) integration of the schools and (3) quality of the house. For a middle-class Negro, the requirements would be different. The economy of the real estate purchase and the neighborhood atmosphere would be the chief considerations. Without thought to integration, many of the Negro middle class are not white-conscious, have no desire to imitate whites or even, in many cases, to associate with whites. (Segregationists, probably, will be gratified to hear this.) But they resent the fact that discrimination exists because of their race and color.

With so many divergent views, theories and approaches, the Negro middle class is the melting pot, steaming and boiling with a passion and intensity never before witnessed. The multifaceted uplift crusade is a testimony of the broad-based interest among the middle class. For those who argue that the Negro is becoming revolutionary, there is the fact that in recent years Negroes have invested millions in new church structures and community buildings. For those who contend the Negro is slovenly, lazy and a ne'er-do-well, an upsurge in education has boosted hundreds of Negro youngsters into topflight interracial institutions. For those who stress that the Negro is united and operates in a machine-precision manner, freedom of speech has become a new item in his community, which is flooded with leaders of every type, method and manner. But progress is not enough; the Negro is still far off the pace. He knows it and is angrily trying to catch up.

When Kennedy Administration publicists announced that 38-year-old Luke C. Moore, a former assistant district attorney, was to be the first Negro marshal in the Nation's capital since Frederick Douglass held the post in the late 1800's, there were few hoorays from the community. Most Negroes felt that Moore was over-qualified to hold the spot, which in the past required not even a high school degree. At first Administration officials were taken aback. Said one: "Hell, these people are getting choosy." Not choosy so much, it's that the middle class no longer is swayed by hubbub over individual success; it is more concerned with the over-all situation. And politicians belatedly are finding this out, since it is the Negro middle class that is the main source of the vote.

"I'm poor. I'm old. I'm tired," the Negro chauffeur told the owner of a television shop in a Dixie city. "But I just want to see what color television looks like." The white man was kind and directed him to a corner of the store where a color TV set was turned on. The old man looked a while, shook his head, and turned away. "Thanks," he said. "Ain't nobody telling me I haven't watched color TV."

That Negro chauffeur had gained fresh pride and a status symbol, since few Negroes in the city could afford color television. Many symbols Negroes have used appear trivial, but to the individual they were priceless in inspirational value. Big cars, quality clothes, medals and jewelry are some of the symbols Negroes have used, even as they have adored leaders, ministers and sports heroes. I remember a maid in Youngstown, Ohio, who prized a diamond ring more than any other possession. She rubbed it constantly, keeping it sparkling and attractive. When friends joked about her overfondness for materialism, she'd retort, "I got this from scrubbing floors and every time I see this jewel shine while I'm on my knees, I get happy, and do a good job." Southern Negroes of the middle class had a penchant for big cars, and I often wondered why. A friend told me: "You can't use a jalopy down here. You got to pick up and go. If your car breaks down en route, you can't get service, you can't use the rest rooms, and you can't call from a phone booth in some places." A new car thus was insurance against the humiliation of discrimination, as much as a new TV set was a substitute for a ticket to the downtown theater.

Like the symbols, Negro idols have inspired our middle class. Few, of course, are in government, industry and business, therefore the sports heroes and the entertainers have shouldered a big burden. The immortals range from Bill Robinson to Sammy Davis, from Lena Horne to Harry Belafonte, from Joe Louis to Sugar Ray Robinson, from Jesse Owens to Jackie Robinson. Entertainment and sports have become the lucrative fields. Children of the middle class aspire for success in these fields because those celebrities are best known. This may be unfortunate because the discrimination in other fields has narrowed the career horizon almost to a occupational monopoly of teaching and preaching. Only in recent years have our leaders concentrated to steer youngsters into wider fields of endeavor—as discouraging as the outlook appeared.

"It was impossible," a Negro high school principal told me recently, "Our students wanted to train for jobs they can get, not ones they couldn't get. Too many had become defeatists because they knew the chances were they could never become a scientist or chemist, so they settled for being a soda jerk or a car wash and quit school. The sit-ins have done more than anything else to catch the imagination of these youngsters and inspire them to stay in school. Demonstrations have proven to these kids they can use their energies to make a better world and in that world there will be better jobs. And they need education to get the jobs."

This is the type of spirit which has inspired the middle class and proved to its younger members that they will become the chief recipients of any real advances in the employment field. Because they have more education and training, this group will be in position to claim positions and promotions in government, industry and business, and also some of the scholarships to universities to train for the scientific posts. The Negro father who for years worked as a custodian in a factory yet had the skills to become a steam engineer, the Negro worker who held a semiskilled job in a plant but could have qualified for the production line, the Negro carpenter, denied membership in the union and unable to obtain work, and the Negro mother, saint of our people, who has toiled to keep her clan alive and in school—all will live to see the day when the barriers break before their eyes. But their struggle, their protest, their sacrifice to face the torture of bias and the keen disappointment of rejection based on race will be forgotten. Their role in holding the faith and providing the pool of Negroes eligible to qualify for the white- and blue-collar jobs will be overlooked in the fast pace of current events. These members of the middle class are the true heroes of the Negro advancement. And for the most part, neither their leaders nor the country has seen fit to honor them.

A testimonial to their greatness was their stamina to forge ahead against overwhelming odds in employment. National Urban League Associate Director Mahlon T. Puryear recently declared:

> Discrimination in employment has been more pronounced than in many other areas of American life. Throughout the years of

our economic history, references to "Negro jobs," "white jobs," "Negroes need not apply," "for whites only," "our union contract will not permit us to employ Negro workers in categories other than maintenance and janitorial occupations" and "management does the hiring, so we don't have anything to do with discriminatory hiring practices" have been and unfortunately, to a regrettable extent, still are the standard cries.

Even the United States Department of Labor, in a pamphlet titled *America Is for Everybody* stated that the Negro is largely restricted to unskilled, semiskilled and menial jobs. A paragraph says:

> Figures reveal that only 20 percent of the Negro work force is engaged in clerical, professional, technical and managerial fields, compared to 60 percent of the white labor force. This disproportion is too great to be blamed on the increasingly smaller gap between the educational evils of the two races. A similar disproportion exists in unskilled and semiskilled occupations. Seventy-five percent of all male Negro nonfarm workers are engaged in jobs in those categories, while only 33 percent of all white male nonfarm workers are employed in those occupations.

Appearing in 1963 before a House subcommittee on labor, Mrs. Cernoria Johnson, the Washington representative of the National Urban League, testified:

> Figures on unemployment also give a very clear indication of the job disadvantages faced by Negroes. Unemployment rates are generally higher for them than for whites. One factor contributing to these high unemployment rates is the disproportionate number engaged in unskilled work, where unemployment is regularly heavier. Another factor is the frequently lower seniority of Negro workers because of their more recent entry into the work forces of a particular factory or office.
>
> In the 1958 recession, unemployment rose in all groups, but it continued to be roughly twice as high among Negroes as among whites. Nearly 14 percent of non-white male workers . . . a large proportion of them from unskilled and semiskilled occupations . . .

were unemployed and seeking work in 1958, compared with an average of about 6 percent of white male workers. By 1961, both rates were lower, but nearly 13 percent of non-white men were still unemployed, compared with 5.7 percent of white men. This percentage comparison remains today.

Crossing the job wasteland at the dawn of the automation age, the Negro middle class faces its most difficult challenge. The cutback in unskilled and menial jobs, coupled with the heavier volume of Negroes competing for these jobs as against the availability of semiskilled and skilled positions, certainly can hamper the future development of the ranks. A National Urban League survey of the employment situation among Negroes in 1963 revealed four crucial areas:

1. The present plight of the Negro workers in America is becoming worse and will become permanent unless constructive measures are immediately undertaken.

2. Critical areas exist in every census region.

3. Current and projected unemployment trends are such that little hope of better times ahead can be held out for Negro workers who look to us for improvement of their lot.

4. Repeatedly from our local affiliates comes the phrase "little is being done." This phrase represents a reporting of fact, not a desire to defame character or to disparage the positive accomplishments of government, industry, labor and education thus far. We cannot state too strongly, however, our conviction that all good work to date, however lofty in motives, however progressive in intentions, however effective in accomplishments, is not yet enough.

What does this mean to the future of the Negro middle class? Race-relations specialists are beginning to suspect that unless the Government moves firmly into the picture, the Negro middle class may be sharply curtailed and even wiped out. It could be that in years to come there will be but two Negro classes: the "rich" and the "poor" (the description "rich" will apply to Negroes able to clothe, feed and house their dependents). Unless more Carpet Bag families are lifted, unless more unskilled are processed for trades, unless more illiterates are taught to read and write, unless more jobs are made available through apprenticeship and retraining programs, the marginal Negro middle-class families, now far below the white middle-class economic status, might well be dragged to the bottom rung of society—to join the underprivileged, under-educated, underemployed, underpaid and underutilized Americans. Meanwhile, the more successful Negro middle-class families could, by becoming increasingly self-supporting, easily be assimilated into the Money Bag set, with its accompanying sophistication and snobbery.

This is not an optimistic outlook for the pride of my people. It is an extreme prediction, but it is still a possibility unless changes —far more than the Government experts have ever engineered— are put into effect. At the core of the Negro's problem in America is economics. In the first century, he has harnessed his low income and some energy into civil rights projects so that all Americans realize that the Negro is dissatisfied, angry and ready to demonstrate for his advancement. If he is ignored, if his demands and requests are rejected, the growing impact of Negro middle class, the hope for the future, could be diminished. Said a Negro worker: "I ain't got the faith of my father. He died early after working in a steel mill beside a blazing furnace. If I'm gonna die early, I ain't gonna do that. I want to work in the front office."

Many of the Negro middle class want to work in the front offices. What happens if they don't?

# ★ ★ ★ 7 Negro Politicians and the Vote

At a private meeting in the Nation's capital, the fifth Negro congressman since Reconstruction and the first from the West Coast, Representative Augustus Hawkins of Los Angeles, revealed a significant diagnosis when he said:

"Only in politics can the Negro wield influence in America. He can never hope to make an impact in the world of business, finance, labor and Government—all vital cogs in the operation of a democracy."

From personal experience, Representative Hawkins knew his subject matter. For 28 years he had served in the California legislature and participated in the authoring and passage of many bills, ranging from fair employment practice to workmen's compensation for domestics. When a new Congressional district in Los Angeles was carved in 1962 from a predominantly Negro area, Hawkins got the opportunity to fulfill a lifetime dream of serving in the nation's second highest legislative body. At no time was there any doubt as to whether the Democrat could win in the populous low-class district.

When the new Negro legislator arrived on Capitol Hill, no welcoming committee appeared. No knot of reporters came to interview the man who represented a step forward for America's largest minority. But here was a politician who had the earmarks of political greatness; he was tough, articulate, broad-minded, balanced and a statesman. Disclaiming political showmanship, Representative Hawkins once commented: "You don't need noise to get something done. All you need is organization, an organization of people, groups, creeds and races. A street-corner crowd can't do much to get the job done." The 55-year-old lawmaker spent his early months in the nation's capital, quietly learning the ways of the House, the committees, the procedures and the lawmaking way of life.

Ironically, Representative Hawkins cannot be recognized by the hundreds who troop into the House galleries. He is light-skinned enough for even Southerners to claim that his skill is due more to an overinfusion of white blood than to the fact of his Negro blood. The Congressman likes to tell of his early days in the California legislature when a colleague turned to him and said, "There's a new nigger in here." Representative Hawkins smiled, then retorted, "Yeah, I know. I am he." Washington correspondents recently had a guessing game to pick him from a group at the National Press Club. All flunked the attempt.

Give or take a few anecdotes about his color, Representative Hawkins could well be the man to set the example on Capitol Hill for statesmanship. He is an individual who has lifted himself, taught himself, battled the opposition and still maintained the outward character of a balanced lawmaker. He does not carry the Negro vote in his pocket nor the race problem on his shoulder, but he is aware and alert. At present Negro politics is a conglomeration of both the best and the worst, the professional and the dedicated, the slick and the uncouth. In some instances, Negro politics is as second class as is the status of citizenship in various parts of the country; in other cases, it is impressive and responsible. The usual yardstick for measuring the value of American politicians is their service and devotion to the populace, and it is by this concept that Negro politicians must be judged. Civil rights is an issue dragged across the Negro community in order to get votes, much as a trainer holds a bone over a dog to teach him tricks. The mythical Negro vote bloc often labeled in election years as a decisive factor is a reportorial conception used to give election coverage a varied flavor. An example of the failure of the American Negro to take full advantage of an opportunity is in the area of voting—one of the few channels in which he has had unlimited possibilities.

I don't refer to the southern areas where the Negroes' right of franchise has been denied, but rather to the metropolitan areas of the North where he can vote and doesn't, or where he can vote and is misled by the tactics of the professional politicians, including many Negroes whose sole interest is self-aggrandizement. The wise, intelligent use of the franchise is an important weapon for the Negro, but we haven't learned to utilize effectively the rifles for short-range duty, let alone the cannons.

Only in the last twenty years has the Negro vote been sizeable enough for recognition as a possible factor in an outcome of a national or state election. Only in the event of a close race in which candidates cannot afford to alienate the smallest number of voters has this become important. Politics previously was as lily-white in its organizational structure as some of the industries. Usually a Negro preacher or undertaker was the contact man for "getting out the vote," and when he did accomplish this, the reward was usually money or continued status as a consultant on what the Negro wanted. Earlier, little unity or co-operation existed among Negroes, although dedicated militants were active prior to the civil-rights years. Now Negroes are learning the tricks of big-time politics; for some, Negro politics is becoming a profitable career.

The Negro vote is a "poor vote," traditionally the vote of underprivileged, underemployed and discontented masses. Slick politicians don't use the strategy of statesmanship with a planned program of housing or employment to woo this level of voters. Political machines with the lure of relief, welfare and city hall favors can have more impact than the dynamic speaker who orates about foreign affairs. What Negroes can work in such an atmosphere? Only the politically oriented with an eye on eventual power and income via a career. Few Negroes who start political careers from the precinct level are ever able to qualify for Federal posts.

The Negro vote, like other minority votes in America, remains clannish and nationalistic. No white man is considered strong enough to win the vote on his own merit, even with a tremendous civil-rights platform. A determination of his liberalism is generally made by which Negroes support him and whether he has the backing of the bosses. There must be Negro advance men in the neighborhoods and communities. He must be briefed thoroughly on the petty dislikes of Negroes in particular sections. Because of this peculiar feature, reports, rumors and gossip bearing on anti-Negro qualities of a candidate can achieve wide circulation in Negro neighborhoods, and dishonest politicians deliberately set off such campaigns to undermine the opposition. A common tactic is the accusation that a candidate lives in a house with a restrictive covenant, or he lived at one time in such a home or his parents did. Housing segregation guarantees the presence of Negro political leaders for a while to come, and some of the leaders are quite content to have the restriction to remain.

How effective are Negro politicians? Do they get out the vote? Do they transform power into progress? Is civil rights their major issue? Who are the Negroes who run the power structure? Have the Negro politicians been the forerunners in Government moves in the civil-rights area?

These are the questions asked most by those who assess the state of affairs in Negro politics. In a general sense, the Negro politician is effective in that he knows the secret of transforming support into votes under the most harassing conditions. The politician is closer to the man in the street than the Negro leadership, which caters to the higher classes. The national politicians have developed such confidence and independence that few are concerned about the goals of civil-rights leadership groups to align with them. Their strategy is to line up with political leadership and work within the framework of the party or administration. Civil rights, to the Negro politician, resembles more of a campaign issue that can be shelved once an election is past. There is no "do or die" spirit if platform promises are broken. Negro politicians have learned to make excuses quickly, even to blaming the other party. Leadership in this sensitive area, especially for enactment of law, seldom comes from Negroes; ironically, civil-rights progress is captained by white lawmakers on Capitol Hill in co-operation with leaders of the major Negro civil-rights organizations. In too many state legislatures and municipal bodies, the elected Negro representative is not the spearhead for major civil-rights reforms; often, he is not the best-qualified.

The most powerful Negro politician ever developed in America is 77-year-old Representative William Levi Dawson, a veteran of 21 years on Capitol Hill and the boss of Chicago's teeming South Side. In his dual capacity, Dawson runs the Negro area in Chicago with an iron hand and, because of his seniority, is chairman of the House Government Operations Committee, which yearly oversees billions in United States expenditures. In the sunset of a stormy political life, Dawson manages to hold onto his fief in Chicago but has lost his national power.

In the Truman era, Dawson was powerful enough to be considered as the ex officio Negro member of the cabinet, a sort of race-relations advisor who handpicked Negroes for high posts and helped set policy affecting Negroes. As vice-chairman of the Democratic Party he ran the national political show for minorities. Of all of the lawmakers in Washington, Negroes feared Dawson most. A conservative in civil rights, he was firm and heartless on occasion if it appeared a person or group was attempting to embarrass his party, even on civil rights. At one point, he told civil-rights leaders to "go to hell" when they urged him to support a particular move. Never one to support militancy publicly, he even had Negro representatives appear before the convention platform committee and denounce the tentative proposals as "weak." He was considered "safe" in respect to civil rights, and had become a favorite of the ruling elite.

This peculiar characteristic—his neutrality in civil and civic rights—for a while dissuaded Negroes from banking on the use of the franchise as a means of winning first-class citizenship. Dawson's contribution was his perfecting of the total organization of a Negro community for voting purposes, but he lacked the vision to make this arrangement productive in terms of a social program. In Chicago, with such an organizational voting strength, Negroes are no better off than in any other city. Dawson's organization fought urban renewal because such projects would dislocate the voters. It discouraged school integration. It has provided little civic leadership. And to make the picture still more bleak, the Dawson organization fought Negro groups that tried to change the *status quo*. When the NAACP branch attacked Dawson for failing to speak out against local conditions, Dawson's men ran a slate of candidates at the next election and took over leadership of the branch. When Edward Berry, crusading head of the Chicago Urban League, launched a fight against slum housing conditions, he ran into numerous obstacles. In the nation's second largest Negro community many leaders realize the danger in giving such vast power to one man. Once in the driver's seat and backed by a machine controlling the masses, a Negro politician becomes like any other politician—color-blind. Evidence of unrest came in 1962 when Dawson's machine tried to unseat a white man, Alderman Leon Despres, from representing the heavily Negro Hyde Park District. The Dawson-backed candidate, Attorney Chauncey Eskridge, claimed support of the Reverend Martin Luther King, Jr. and White House aides, but Negroes backed the white man, who campaigned for human rights more than did the entire Dawson machine, with a seven to one vote.

Well-known both in and out of Negro politics are Harlem's celebrated "Mr. Inside-Mr. Outside" pair—Representative Adam Clayton Powell, Jr. and J. Raymond (The Fox) Jones. Unlike Dawson, these men boast no precise, smoothly oiled machinery. Also, unlike the Chicago leader, the pair hasn't submerged civil-rights issues when they could be used to voting advantage. As pastor of the country's largest Negro Baptist church, Powell is a polished orator and brimstone pulpiteer who uses the agility of a hungry evangelist to electrify an audience. A long-time civil-rights advocate (dating back to the 1930's when he instituted breadlines at his church, spearheaded "Buy Where You Can Work" campaigns to get jobs for Negroes in Harlem and edited a fighting newspaper called *Peoples Voice*), Representative Powell earned the title Mr. Civil Rights when it was unpopular even to whisper about integration. Powell yelled it. Barging into politics, the son of a pioneer Negro clergyman found no great difficulty lining up support. His church membership was enough to guarantee

his election as councilman and, later, as the first Negro congressman from the East Coast.

For a long time Powell was the voice of the American Negro,
echoing what Negroes thought but couldn't afford to say. Negroes
overlooked his personal life; that was his reward. Powell's criticism
burned many a government official. President Truman angrily
barred him from the White House after Powell remarked that Mrs.
Truman was the "last lady of the land" because she attended a
meeting of the lily-white Daughters of the American Revolution.
But Powell never held his tongue; an attack on bias was imminent
anytime he spoke at carefully planned press conferences. Never
a paragon of virtue (which he himself admits) Powell wears many
mantles—as a solon, civil-rights fighter, Negro nationalist,
preacher and family man with a series of wives. The role he probably plays best is that of the civil-rights crusader, because his words
lift the aspirations of those who lack the education to evaluate his
actions. He captivates his parishioners and constituents with his
charm.

In America's largest Negro community criticism of Powell is
generally outlawed—even by the Negro press, civic leaders and the
little people themselves. His popularity remains a substitute for
any examination of a long list of attainments for "my beloved Harlem," which still is a tenement slum that might be described as the
most blighted neighborhood in America. Its percentage of voters
is one of the lowest among northern Congressional districts.

"What has Adam done for Harlem?" you ask a native. He twists
his head at a peculiar angle, raises an eyebrow, figures you are a
square and not worth telling. "What the hell have you done?" he
retorts and struts away, leaving you to wonder what makes you so
smart to criticize Powell when the cards are stacked against you in
Harlem. In recent years, except for a flurry of comment about his
use of funds to allow staffers to enjoy foreign travel, Powell has
managed to hold his own as the first Negro chairman of the House
Education and Labor committee. He has started numerous bills on
the road to passage and has been an effective, hard-driving wheel.
His concentration on committee activities has sidetracked his nor-

mal civil-rights actions, and his recent statements on the latter subject have seemed confused. When Powell attacked the NAACP for being "white-controlled" and said that Negroes should control their own destiny, most civil-righters sighed, saying, "Where has Adam been in the last few years? We've integrated." But in Harlem and in other all-Negro communities, the last bastions of nationalism, the Powell attack was well received. "Adam's on the warpath again" was the repeated comment. Nobody in such a setting questions Powell's philosophy.

The other half of the Harlem political team is virtually an opposite. J. Raymond Jones is a close-lipped, secretive, straight-living, crusty politician. His nickname "The Fox" implies he is far shrewder than Powell at political tactics—which is true. Jones has a reputation for a clean political life. A few years ago, he was questioned by a New York State Crime Commission concerning accusations that judgeships were being sold, but Jones denied the charges. Probably the top Negro mastermind in politics, Jones has a solid record to back up his reputation. When Tammany Boss Carmine De Sapio decided to punish Powell by trying to oust him from Congress for supporting President Eisenhower in 1956, Jones served as general for Powell's forces and handed De Sapio a stinging defeat. Five years later, Jones masterminded the election of Mayor Robert Wagner, against a De Sapio threat and a Powell rebellion. Studiously political—enough to know that his poker face and gravel-toned voice are not vote-getting assets—Jones plays the role of "Mr. Inside" with an imagination that surprises most Democrats. Offers of a post or job failed to move him until 1963 when he agreed to run for City Council to offset disruption of the political team by other candidates. He shies from publicity. But he has become adept at prediction and marshals election forces with such skill that many VIPs seek his counsel. "I'm a politician," Jones tells reporters when they ask about Harlem's woes, "not a doctor." "Let no one go hungry in Harlem," Powell once said, then flew off to Europe. Both men got rich; Harlem is still poor, but it is a better place because this team held down the fort for a decade or so.

A wealthy businessman in his own right (head of Michigan's largest undertaking firm), Representative Charles C. Diggs, Jr. is the Detroit representative in Congress. Unlike Negro political leaders in Chicago or New York, Diggs is not a boss, but he is recognized as the one man who has been successful in aligning all factions for teamwork. Except for labor influence, Detroit has no single boss, but the city boasts a high caliber of Negro political leadership and representation on elected bodies. Labor's effective vote registration and indoctrination programs probably account for the advances of Negroes in the Motor City. In a co-ordinate drive, Negroes in Detroit have elected representatives to the city council, the school board and the state house. They also helped elect the first Negro on a state-wide ticket (when Otis Smith became state treasurer). Detroit is the model city for Negroes in politics, even though the race vote is lopsidedly Democratic (Nixon got only 17 percent of the vote in 1960, the lowest Negro rate in the United States). Politics is in a healthy state; it is integrated, and Negroes refuse to follow Dawson and Powell in building personal machines that exploit the racial theme. Administration officials regard the Negroes who come to Washington from Detroit as best equipped to deal in integrated settings, primarily because of the political make-up of that city.

Diggs is a product of this system. Representing a high percentage of whites in his district, he has developed a fairly competent operation in service to his city and state. His civil-rights activity has included personal trips to Mississippi to probe inequalities. On one such mission, a home in which he was staying was bombed. Diggs, however, is not a veteran in legislative affairs and so far has not distinguished himself, even to fulfillment of the aspirations of his people back home.

The fifth Negro congressman, Representative Robert N. C. Nix, represents the Fourth District of Pennsylvania, a predominantly Negro section of Philadelphia (the third largest non-white community in the country). A painstaking lawyer but a lackluster lawmaker, Nix quietly attends to his political chores, rarely speaking on the House floor or leading any civil-rights move. Of the

Negro legislators he is least known and probably has least to show for his tenure of office. However, this is part of the Philadelphia story: Negro politics in Quakertown resembles a plantation system, with white overlords dominating the vote, the leaders and the organization. No independent Negro is in politics in the city. Politics is second class with most of the faults of the old political rule still prevalent. Negro leadership has failed to develop in this populous area, and the downtown bosses have exploited the large Negro vote for their own purposes. Whether a Negro political leader can forge a united front and do a better job is a moot question. A Powell-type leadership would represent a threat in this situation, because the city's masses would be an easy touch. But all of Philadelphia's story is not bleak: Negroes have the highest percentage of vote registration in their areas than in any other section of the country. This is an example of the plantation system producing good results.

Six men with vote kingdoms, all Democrats representing majorities in five cities, are the accomplishment of a minority just beginning to come into its own. The Borough of Brooklyn in New York City and four cities (Baltimore, Cleveland, St. Louis, Missouri and Kansas City, Missouri) soon may send Negroes to Congress. And 25 other Congressional districts boast a heavy Negro constituency. The cities probably will become the laboratories for Negro public servants new to their responsibilities. Already, two Negroes serve in high municipal roles. Edward Dudley is president of the Borough of Manhattan, New York City and John B. Duncan is a District of Columbia commissioner. There are also approximately one hundred fifty Negro councilmen, more than sixty judges, some seventy state legislators and countless numbers on school and welfare boards.

A forecast for Gary, Indiana by Mayor George Chacharis shook up a 1962 Democratic dinner. In a city whose population is one-third Negro, the Mayor predicted that Negroes would run as candidates for justice of the peace, constable and state representative despite the opposition from some party leaders who "preach civil rights and citizenship but only think of Negroes as bootblacks and household servants." He concluded, "Look for a Negro in my position in twenty years."

The election of Negroes on state-wide tickets, such as the victory of Edward Brooke as Attorney General of Massachusetts, marks a new era in politics. Integration, too, has begun to catch up with the Negro politicians, precipitating a division of thought as to the Negro's approach in the next decade. Some still cling to the theory that Negroes should segregate, operate their own vote machines and become an auxiliary to the regular party organization; others call for total integration of Negroes in the regular organization, signalling the death of the Negro boss system.

While the migrations to the North have given the Negro his vital striking force, a more dramatic development is occurring in the South. Black Rip Van Winkle has awakened from years of apathy and is finding his way to registration places and the polls. Defying threats of intimidation and harm, Negroes are registering to vote for the first time in many Deep South counties that had closed polling books to them since Reconstruction. In Mississippi, two Negroes campaigned for Congress. In Georgia, the white Mayor of Atlanta, Ivan Allen, was elected by a combination of Negro and white votes, while Negro Leroy Johnson went to the state senate. A Negro woman was elected to the school board in Houston, Texas. Eight cities in North Carolina have Negro aldermen.

Reinforcing this trend, Attorney General Robert Kennedy inaugurated a tough government drive to knock down the remaining vote barriers in the South. Two foundations financed a registration drive with a $325,000 grant, enough money to increase Dixie voting by a half million in two years.

By latest surveys, less than half of the Negroes eligible to vote are registered. In the North, where there are no restrictions, registration doesn't reach 60 percent of those eligible. The picture is blacker in the South, where less than 30 percent are registered. In about two hundred counties of the Black Belt, the figure is very low. During the next decade, many Negroes for the first time will experience not only the thrill of casting a ballot but also will gain the maturity of judging campaigns and candidates on subjects far broader than civil rights. Out of this experience a new crop of sensible, balanced voters will graduate.

The learning process could be greatly accelerated if Negro leadership, nationally and locally, made an effort to use its influence to harness what could be the Negro's real power weapon. At present none of the major Negro organizations make any effort toward political action. There is no national citizens committee to examine the records of parties and candidates and give direction at a grass-roots level to thousands of Negroes who have followed the advice of leadership to register to vote or to participate in marches and demonstrations. After an appearance before the platform committees of the major parties to urge inclusion of civil-rights measures, Negro leadership officially takes a vacation until after Election Day.

What happens in the interim is a disgrace. Both parties establish special Jim Crow divisions to influence the Negro vote. Both parties print leaflets, pamphlets, fliers, booklets and news releases all designed to woo the Negro voter in his own neighborhood. Facts are twisted and distorted, yet no civil-rights leader complains. Scores of Negroes are hired in Washington to augment the public relations staffs, their jobs to propagandize. Much can be written about the slush, the phoney issues, the whispering campaigns and the tactics pursued by politicians. Coverage of the campaign in some of the Negro press generally depends upon the amount of advertising given to individual newspapers and not to the significance of the news. As one Negro politician told me, "Every four years, I make enough to take a vacation."

Big names, particularly in the fields of sports and entertainment, are used to barnstorm across the country as attractions for appearances of candidates. In recent years, a growing number of upper-class Negroes (most with civil-rights reputations) have participated in the campaign as the first requirement for qualifying for Federal employment in the event the candidate wins. The situation in 1960 resulted in the biggest job hunt in the nation's capital since the Depression. After Kennedy's inauguration, there was more excitement among Negro campaigners over who would get the topnotch jobs in government than about the enactment of civil rights and economic legislation, the major inducement among the Negro masses. At a time when the Negro unemployment rate was almost twice the white rate, it was ironic that the speakers who campaigned about New Frontier benefits now were more concerned about their own welfare.

A word about the future of the Republican Party among Negroes. In plain truth, the GOP has negligible support among the middle and lower classes, which, in essence, make up the Negro vote. Some experts consider the Democratic Party's emphasis on economic programs, from welfare to unemployment insurance, to be the key to winning Negro communities. The GOP big city report attributed the poor showing to a lack of organizational strength at the precinct level. However, as a reporter who has covered many campaigns, I believe the basic problem is that the GOP leadership is unwilling to make a strenuous effort to win the Negro vote, because such a move would be extremely expensive and probably wouldn't net the results the use of such moneys in other areas would bring. As a substitute and an answer to any charge that the party is ignoring the vote, the Republicans at election time employ public relations techniques in the campaign. Generally, the effect is an increase of noise but not of votes. It's a common GOP practice to give Negro ministers money and expect them to preach on Lincoln freeing the slaves.

There is little substantiation to the contention that the GOP cannot win votes among the Negro mass. In Cleveland's Eighteenth Councilmanic Ward, virtually a solid Negro area, Attorney John Kellogg has been elected for years, and before him, his uncle. This is probably the most Republican Negro area, but Kellogg, a pro at methods of holding the vote, has never received any recognition from the national committee. The same is true of Chicago Representative William Robinson, named the most impressive freshman in the Illinois legislature a decade ago. Regularly, Robinson wins his legislative seat in a Democratic section, but he has been given little recognition by the GOP powers. While many

GOP candidates are unattractive to Negro communities, there are many others who get support, proving that there is no vote bias against the party. Unless remarkable advances occur in the next few years (which seem impossible at this writing), the Republican party may become, except for a sprinkling of Negro bluebloods and professional people, a predominantly lily-white party.

An opportunity to observe the conduct and direction of the Negro vote will be presented when Congress gets around to granting home rule powers in Washington, the only big city in the country with a racial majority. Because of the racial ratio, Southern factions on Capitol Hill have succeeded in bottling up any legislation, but sooner or later, the metropolis, with about 54 percent Negro population, will become self-governing. In the nation's capital live the Negroes with the highest standard of income and education in the country. Will Negro leadership seek a racial autonomy? Will it insist on an integrated front? What type of campaigning will best lure the Negro voter? What issues will be the dominating ones? Can the Republicans make a strong showing in this city? These are questions that haunt the politicians. Under the watchful eyes of Congress, Negro politics in Washington could become a model for the country or could increase the fears of citizens in southern localities that racial solidarity is the ultimate goal of Negro voters. Certainly, the granting of the franchise in Washington will produce an acid test for leadership.

As Richard Nixon goes down in history as the man who turned his back on the Negro and lost the Presidency, so John F. Kennedy became the best-loved Chief Executive in history. Applauded for appointing Negroes to high offices and urging passage of new civil-rights legislation (a usual procedure), JFK went farther; he broke down many a racial barrier in an informal way.

Watching the Inauguration Day parade, he noticed that Negroes were not marching with cadets from the United States Coast Guard Academy. Calling for a probe, he discovered that none were enrolled and immediately took corrective steps. The first Negro in the Academy is now a senior. On a West Coast visit, JFK showed up at a debutante ball at which the daughter of en-

tertainer Nat (King) Cole was presented. Many a colored parent
became flustered at the sight of the President of the United States
at this social function.

These incidents enhanced JFK's reputation and established a
new code of race relations in office. The oft-repeated slogan in
Negro sections is, "Lincoln freed us, FDR gave us jobs and JFK
gave us pride in ourselves."

Why were the President, his brother, the Attorney General and
the Democratic National Committee so concerned with the
Negro? And why has the Republican National Committee concluded its big city report with a warning that the party must move
into the metropolitan areas? They have discovered the potential
Negro vote. In another decade, this vote can change American history.

In his book, *Population Perspectives*,* Dr. Philip Hauser, chairman of the University of Chicago's Sociology Department, pin-
points the reason:

> Streams of Negro migrants not only moved from the South to
> the North and West, but also from predominantly rural to pre-
> dominantly urban areas. In 1910, only 27 percent of the Negroes
> in this nation lived in urban places, as defined by the Census
> Bureau, that is, places having 2,500 or more persons. By 1950, about
> 60 percent of the population was urban and by 1960, the propor-
> tion of Negroes living in cities approximated two-thirds. This trend
> could easily make about three-fourths by 1970.
>
> In 1950, over 90 percent of the Negroes in the North and in the
> West, about 48 percent in the South, lived in urban places. By 1950,
> non-white population in metropolitan areas numbered 8.3 million.
> This number reflected a fourfold increase since the beginning of
> the century and an increase of over two-fifths (44.3 percent) be-
> tween 1940 and 1950.

While whites say, "Lord help me," sell city homes and move to
the suburbs, Negroes with Dixie sharecropping and farming back-
grounds continue to unload from the Twentieth Century Over-

* Philip Hauser, *Population Perspectives* (New Brunswick, the Rutgers University Press, 1961).

ground Railroad with little more than a satchel of clothes and hope. They've been arriving for the past twenty years and only neighborhood politicians and relief workers have been concerned —until recently.

By the year 2000 many U.S. cities, the final stops for urban-bound migrations, may be predominantly Negro—in both the North and the South. In 1960, the Census Bureau reported more than 15 cities with "exploding Negro populations," and experts pinpointed areas such as Atlanta, Detroit and Philadelphia as places to watch, that is, to watch Negroes take over.

# ★ ★ ★ 8 Pray, Man, Pray

A century ago, the Negro had only a shed or a weather-beaten cabin to pray for deliverance from the white man's cruel world. Church, to him, was a place to rest from a week of toil and pray to the white man's God that he some day could go to heaven and "put on a pair of silvery wings."

In America today, the Negro has a choice of worshipping. He can go to towering modern churches in some cities and sit with whites praying to enter their heaven. Or he can enter a luxuriously furnished church, bought and paid for by Negroes, and pray for a better life hereabouts, hoping to enter the white man's heaven by a side door. Or he can join one of the numerous cults and bang cymbals, blow horns, dance a jig and rejoice at the good life. Or he can join the Black Muslims and hate white people instead of loving God.

The multiplicity of ways of "climbing the King's highway" is symptomatic of the unrest in the Negro's religious life; it frustrates many Negroes while at the same time it disturbs many whites. Continued integration has widened the doors to many religions but has thrown a bombshell into almost every aspect of God's world. For generations whites have believed Christianity was their exclusive faith. Now they have to worry about Negroes sitting beside them in their churches, and in accordance with the enforcement of the ethics of the faith, must remain mum while Negroes compete with them for jobs, housing, an education and the right to marry their daughters. More and more, Americans are being forced to face the moral challenge of religious teaching. This is difficult for whites to accept; it is similarly difficult for Negroes.

When leaders of the major faiths met last year in Chicago for the first National Conference on Religion and Race, a project designed to co-ordinate the efforts of major denominations in America in an all-out effort against discrimination and segregation, New York City lawyer William Stringfellow told some six hundred delegates that the conference was "too little, too late and too lily-white." A Jewish delegate arose to condemn the prospect of "4 days of breast-beating and self-flagellation." The Reverend Martin Luther King, Jr., the lone Negro speaker, delivered one of eleven major addresses, but his speech was given on the final day—after the business was concluded—implying that his presence was an afterthought. Missing completely from the sessions were delegates representing the National Baptist Convention, the largest religious body (5 million members) in America, whose leaders rejected the invitation. Perhaps they fear integration would decimate the rank of their churches.

The religious picture in America is confusing, jumbled and loaded with racial suspicion. The problem will not be solved overnight. In the name of religion, many unkind and harsh words will be said. In the name of religion, many cruel actions will transpire. Integration of religion threatens to immobilize and weaken the influence of one of the Negro's major professions in America, its biggest business and one of its main sources of leadership. Resistance will come more from Negro clerics than from leaders of white churches.

Religion has been a stand-by of the American Negro; it has strengthened him and inspired him to continue along a rugged course. As he becomes aware of its hypocrisy and superficiality, he will become bitter and angry; many will repudiate religion. Few can argue that religion in America has not been hypocritical in the area of race relations. Negro religion is merely a Jim Crow wing of Christianity. It sprang from deep roots in slavery and separated from the main stream during Reconstruction into a gaudy network of denominational auxiliaries, faiths, cults and a few all-Negro sects. During slavery, some plantation owners allowed Negroes to sit quietly in the lofts of their churches, but most built sheds in which the Negroes could sing and shout, under prescribed conditions of not learning to read or write about freedom. In later years, the expanded Negro Church performed more of an accommodative role, serving as a center of activity because of discriminatory policies in public places and as a beacon of hope for the future—peace and goodwill in heaven.

Many educated Negroes early questioned the morality of Christianity, not in its precepts, but in the programming of its policy-makers. Unfortunately, because prejudiced men controlled the church structures, their weaknesses and failings affected the destiny of the religious institutions more than did the application of the Ten Commandments. This is true today in America of the so-called White Church and the so-called Negro Church. The gap between the two institutions is wide enough to make one wonder whether there is the same reward for lifetime loyalty. At a Southern mass meeting, a civil-rights leader said: "We are born in Negro hospitals, go to Negro schools, attend Negro churches, enroll in Negro colleges, work at Negro jobs, die in Negro hospitals, have wakes at Negro funeral homes and are buried in Negro cemeteries. How can your minister preach to you that you are going to a white heaven?"

This is a difficult question to answer, and Negro ministers are no longer able to answer it with embroidered Biblical phrases. Memberships are demanding a vast improvement in life around them. Sadly, because of the slowness in the fulfillment of the desired goal, congregations have experienced decimation in the ranks of Negro churchgoers, especially among the low-income groups and the young. There is growing despair among the Negroes whom the Church once was able to comfort and counsel. The deterioration of morale among Negro churches poses the biggest danger in American race relations. If leadership acts to plot a peaceful transition, progress can be orderly. If not, a wide segment of Negro life may be responsive to demagogues who use religion as bait.

The Church remains the largest, the richest and the most influential power in Negro America. Its total membership dwarfs the combined forces of civil-rights groups and labor's one and a half million Negro members. Its leaders maintain power in cities across the country, not singularly but collectively. The Church's program touches more individuals than any other institution in Negro life. It produces the backbone for every movement launched in this country.

Consider these figures from the 1963 *World Almanac:*

| | |
|---|---:|
| National Baptist Convention, U.S.A. | 5,000,000 |
| National Baptist Convention of America | 2,668,799 |
| National Primitive Baptist Convention of the U.S.A. | 80,983 |
| African Methodist Episcopal Church | 1,166,301 |
| African Methodist Episcopal Zion Church | 780,000 |
| Apostolic Overcoming Holy Church of God | 75,000 |
| Church of God in Christ | 392,635 |

Several months ago in Washington, a ranking government official who is responsible for some aspects of vote-campaigning mentioned the Negro Church as "my secret weapon" in politics.

"Names and addresses of ministers are more valuable to us than those of schoolteachers or doctors," he declared, "A directory of church leaders is worth its weight in gold." Leaders of both political parties, sensitive to the whims of the populace, generally agree that the key to the Negro community is through the churches. Undoubtedly, many whites think of Negro power in terms of civil-rights groups, because of the considerable publicity centering on the militant units. But they are wrong. The churches are the silent power.

In many ways, the Negro Church has been a sleeping giant. In civil-rights participation its feet are hardly wet. The reason, perhaps, is because the Church is a victim of its own heritage—segregation. Its strength came from segregation, and its leaders hardly shared any desire to shift the foundation. It has procuced few great names, few distinguished scholars or theologians. Most of its leaders are

mediocre clergymen who have developed skill in politicking, shouting or mass psychology.

The Negro Church is big business, the largest investment the
Negro has in property and finances. Next to teaching, preaching
is the most popular profession and because of fluctuating requirements, most any individual who has been "called" can find a
bloc or congregation to listen to his message. Negro Baptists claim
to own almost a billion in real estate; the Methodists count their
assets in millions. Cultists include apartment houses among their
resources. When Sweet Daddy Grace died a few years ago, his
estate grossed more than 15 million dollars. If a Negro minister has
no Cadillac, or if his congregation doesn't send him to Europe an-
nually, he is not considered first class.

The improvement in the economic condition of the Negro set
off an extensive church-building program but also caused a class
policy to infiltrate religion. In almost every city, upper-class Negroes
attend churches where the ministers use an intellectual approach
in sermons. Other upper-class Negroes switched from the Baptist
and Methodist to the Congregational, Episcopal and Unitarian
churches. A small percentage accepted the Catholic faith. But the
great mass remained with the Baptists, Methodists and the cults,
where the average fare was geared to the superstitious, the ignorant
and the deprived.

As a boy, I once attended an evangelistic campaign at a church.
The visiting evangelist was a handsome, brown-skinned man who
with a few well-chosen words could induce women to jump up,
shouting and leaping into the aisle. The old folks described him
as "a preaching man," and they accorded him the honor due a visiting monarch. At one service, he said he wanted to raise five hundred dollars for God. That was a huge sum in a steel mill town like
Youngstown, Ohio, but he nevertheless leaped and pranced on
the pulpit throughout most of the service while his special "heavenly choir" sang most compelling gospel music. The program was
opened with a collection—"blessed dimes," which were placed in
a specially blessed mayonnaise bottle by donors who paraded to the
front of the church. Several songs later the evangelist called for

"spiritual dollars" in memory of dead mothers and fathers. As some
members of the congregation moved up to place the bills on the
table, the evangelist scored those who remained in their seats, asking them whether they appreciated how their fathers and mothers
had struggled to give them food. As his choir sang, one of the women
shrieked and almost fell over a railing (she was caught in time by
a fellow chorister. The incident sent a scare over the congregation,
and you could feel the tension sweep the place. I had a dollar in
my pocket, but it was to pay for a schoolbook. Since my parents
were living, I felt I didn't need to pay such homage. Still later, after
the evangelist had delivered an emotional sermon on getting to
heaven, he took up another collection. This time it was "the holy
offering."

Several people started to leave, but the evangelist ordered the
ushers to close the doors and put Bibles in front of them. "Let no
man or woman be damned tonight because he stepped over the
Lord's Book," railed the preaching man. Trapped, I thought. The
heavenly choir sang, but still not enough people went forward.
"Everybody come," shouted the preacher man, and row by row the
folks again paraded before the table. I dropped my dollar and felt
strangely fooled. Many others dropped bills they couldn't afford.
Three weeks later I saw a newspaper item which said the preacher
man had been shot to death in a midwestern city by the husband
of a woman choir singer he was traveling with.

Years later, as a reporter, I was assigned to cover a national meeting of a religious organization. Trying to find its president, I finally
happened upon him at a party in a hotel room. Liquor, women
and entertainment were on hand—which was all right with me.
My stay at the gathering ended abruptly, however, when the president recognized me. Realizing a reporter was present, he raised such
ructions that I was ejected posthaste. The president was typical
of hypocrites all too frequently found in positions of leadership:
he shunned publicity about his worldly conduct—behavior of
the very type he publicly campaigned against.

An even more disturbing experience occurred during an interview with the late Bishop Sweet Daddy Grace, a former real estate

salesman who used a slick tongue and high-power public relations tactics to become one of the richest, most powerful and most respected cultists in the United States. Magazines and newspapers competed to write articles about this man, who at one time was worth more than 40 million dollars. Sweet Daddy was considered a "good" Negro because to many whites he was a freak and a buffoon who didn't advocate any civil-rights advances.

Entering his castle in the nation's capital, I was steered by two athletic-looking guards to his eating area, where he was propped on a high chair at the head of a table with some forty or fifty followers crowded around him. As he finished eating, he inquired whether any of the crowd wanted the remainder of his food.

"Yes, Sweet Daddy," came the chorus. Sweet Daddy broke up a piece of toast and began dropping crumbs into the mouths of followers, for a dollar apiece. In a short time, 15 bills were piled at his plate. He next broke a piece of bacon and sold it, then what remained of a scrambled egg and, finally, a heap of potatoes. Every so often, he would toss a food particle into the air; the followers fought to grab it, like kids at a penny toss.

"This is holy food," Sweet Daddy explained to me, "Sweet Daddy is eternal, and they all want to get like me." Scooping up about 35 dollar bills, Sweet Daddy told me to follow him through the luxuriously furnished castle. At every door was a servant anxious to please his holiness, the former house salesman who learned the trick of making a fortune among the Negro masses.

Tragic and pathetic, you might say. But it is a part of Negro religion, originating among the illiterate, ignorant lower classes, victims of a power-drunk elite which narcotizes the minds of such people. Several years ago when sessions of a Negro Baptist organization were televised in Louisville, Kentucky, viewers were shocked. Fisticuffs broke out on the stage. An *Ebony* photographer attempting to take pictures was injured when a minister, in an effort to eliminate a permanent record of the fight, pushed an opposing colleague off the stage so that the latter landed on the cameraman. Reporters who covered the AME Bishop elections said that as various ministers campaigned for the high office, money was distributed in a manner that would have embarrassed hardened political precinct workers.

"Clean the slate," cry the young. Some tire and join integrated churches or the upper-class congregations. For years, the job appeared hopeless. One of the earliest Negro clergymen who attempted to develop his church into a social engineering project was the father of Harlem's flamboyant Congressman Adam Clayton Powell, Jr.

Establishing the Abyssinian Baptist Church in Harlem, the senior Powell pioneered in adapting the program of the church to the needs of the community. He set up classes to teach members to read and write and had workers help them find jobs and housing; he became a spokesman for a vast area of underprivileged people. His voice rang out many times in sermons of protest against conditions. In such a setting, the junior Powell got a head start in winning recognition. During the Depression of the 1930's, he led employment drives, set up soup kitchens in the church and expanded the civic program. He became a symbol: the "new Negro preacher."

The armor of the crusader was not donned by Negro clerics across the country. Few of the church leaders were either dynamic or crusading. Here and there, a Negro minister instituted programs to help members improve their lot. The Negro ministry, for the most part, fell far short of conducting self-improvement programs or even civil-rights projects. As a minister told me, "All these people want is to hear me shout on Sundays and so I give them a shouting sermon on Sundays, and the other days of the week I have off."

Failing to organize its forces, the Church expressed little concern for its members except to impart the knowledge that heaven was the answer to earthly woes. Despite the escapist belief, however, the Negro minister had status, prestige and a following in his community. A single church in a city might have more members than even the NAACP branch or civic groups, but its size was no index of its civil-rights attitude and activity. During the Little Rock school crisis, Mrs. Daisy Bates corralled support in Negro communities without the backing of many of the city's leading ministers.

At no time did she have a sizeable number of clergy behind her, and from the pulpit many of the prominent ministers openly opposed her integration effort.

During the Mississippi vote crisis a few years ago, the president of the state Baptist organization urged fellow ministers "to stay out of this vote business" and preach the gospel. "Don't let these radicals get into the church," he stressed. Imagine a religious leader urging followers to give up their citizenship rights!

But then came the Civil-Rights Era and the bus boycott in Montgomery, Alabama.

Of great importance in considering the bus boycott is that perhaps for the first time a group of Negro ministers banded together in a struggle to lift their people in a given situation—one which became world-wide in news interest and seemed to inspire similar ministerial heroism in other sections of the country. A Negro minister engaging in such a controversy brings with him a congregation, a group of dedicated, self-sacrificing Negroes who can use the power of religion to sustain them in the darkest hour. When Negro church people are aroused, they cannot be beaten. The bus strike was the spark that ignited the Negro church, and from the suffering emerged a man who would become the new messiah of civil-rights—the Reverend Martin Luther King, Jr.

With a trend, a leader and a new organization, the Southern Christian Leadership Conference, ecclesiastical forces moved into the civil-rights field. In many cities, ministers joined the call for crusade. In Philadelphia, they led a city-wide boycott against companies that refused to hire Negroes. A lone minister, the Reverend Fred Shuttlesworth, struck hard at conditions in Birmingham, Alabama. Clerics pushed in Albany, backed up the line in New Orleans and struggled with bigots in Atlanta. Ministers began to mention voting, civil rights and sit-ins in pulpit messages and Negroes received a fresh view of the unfinished business of democracy.

While the guerrilla forces of the Negro church were moving into position on the front lines, support came from white churchmen. On July 26, 1962, in a speech at the National Press Club in Washington, Martin Luther King, Jr., the club's first Negro luncheon speaker, said:

> More and more the voice of the church is being heard. It is still true that the church is the most segregated major institute in America. As a minister of the gospel I am ashamed to have to affirm that eleven o'clock on Sunday morning, when we stand to sing "In Christ There Is No East or West," is the most segregated hour of America, and the Sunday School is the most segregated school of the week. But in spite of this appalling fact, we are beginning to shake the lethargy from our souls. Here and there churches are courageously making attacks on segregation, and actually integrating their congregations. Several parochial and church-related schools of the South are throwing off the traditional yoke of segregation. As the church continues to take a forthright stand on this issue, the transition from a segregated to an integrated society will be infinitely smoother.

Striking evidence of this new approach of religious leaders came in the adoption early in 1963, of an action program at the National Conference on Religion and Race in Chicago, the first such gathering of representatives of 70 religious groups. The publication, *Christianity and Crisis*, in a special conference report by Stephen C. Rose, listed the following proposals:

> Whites should seek membership in Negro congregations and vice versa; the formation of direct action groups of laymen to meet problems; solicitation of open-occupancy pledges and sponsorship of voter-education drives; unequivocal preaching: rejection of offers of free land for church construction from promoters of segregated developments; elimination of discrimination in hiring qualified Negro employees in schools, hospitals, and so forth operated by religious institutions; use of pension funds and other investments as weapons in the racial struggle by withholding investments from institutions that practice discrimination and consciously investing in Negro banks in order to increase available mortgage funds and integrated housing developments; purchasing only from companies with nondiscriminatory employment policies; encourage members who are teachers to work in ghetto area schools; spark revision of text-

books that give an outmoded picture of the Negro: begin a "justice corps" of young people to augment the direct-action approach of the student nonviolent movement and CORE; encourage similar inter-faith meetings on a local level.

With liberals in religion, both black and white, now dedicated to the task of re-posturing the church to conform to the practice of brotherhood, conservatives continue to oppose such drastic changes. Included in the opposition is the majority of the Negro ministry. Negro ministers, like Negro teachers, Negro college presidents and Negro businessmen, fear integration because they believe their professions will be wiped out.

Controversy in the Negro church centers on integration and the new demands for social engineering from the church pulpit, the offices and the classrooms. The Reverend J. H. Jackson, president of the National Baptist Convention of America, refuses to lead his organization down the civil-rights trail, or to support sit-ins and mass demonstrations led by ministers. For the first time he is being opposed within his church by a significant group. Adherents of the new theory generally are believed to be disciples of Martin Luther King.

In his declarations, Dr. Jackson, pastor of a large Chicago church, argues that religion should not be used to further the "radicalism of the 60's." Contending that "it is not enough to sit at another man's lunch counter and close up his store," Dr. Jackson believes that "You must build you a store."

"We need protest, have to have it. But a Marian Anderson, a Roland Hayes, a Negro who has accomplished some creative excellence can achieve more than one thousand sit-ins," Dr. Jackson maintains. He also disapproves kneel-ins at white churches and does not favor integration of churches. He feels that Negroes involved in kneel-ins are not sincere. "They will kneel in at a white church," he says, "but won't even go to prayer meetings at their Negro churches. This is hollow hypocrisy." His philosophy is best summed up by this statement: "Negroes should not fight just for civil rights. We should struggle to solve the bigger problem of making America better. Yes, we must protest and demand rights guaranteed us by the Constitution. But we must also produce. We must harness our creative energies."

A conservative by any standard, Dr. Jackson nevertheless, controls the majority of the 25,000 clergymen who belong to his organization. Assaults by liberals thus far have failed to dislodge him. "Reverend King may be your hero," he once told a reporter, "He is not mine. There are no wings growing out of his back."

Will integration diminish the power of the Negro church? Will it remain the strongest all-Negro organization? What will be the new role of this historic institution?"

"The fear of losing many members isn't at our doorstep yet," said a prominent Negro minister in Washington, D.C., "But we face a cutback sooner or later. Frankly, most Negroes aren't emotionally ready to accept integrated religion." He pointed out that even upper-class Negro churches are managing to hold onto their members by moving from slum areas to the recently expanded neighborhoods, buying church structures of departing whites. "This will hold us for a while," he said. He felt that the exodus from the Negro church will start more from the top in the Protestant ranks and the middle for the Catholic ranks. His explanation was this:

> Our most educated members, who earn fairly substantial salaries and have many contacts among whites, are already beginning to leave our churches. They are the first recruits. But the economic factor is keeping others who believe in an integrated church from leaving us. They just cannot afford a mixed church and don't want to be embarrassed. The Catholic Church has the best opportunity to recruit among Negroes. Its neighborhood system already is producing, and I wouldn't be surprised if this faith makes the most spectacular gains among Negroes.

The restlessness of the middle class, another minister said, will force the church to change it programming radically to serve more community needs. And if the Negro minister is to remain a leader, he will have to lead his congregation in more than prayer. Whether the Negro church goes in the direction of a community developer or a civil-rights advocate, or both, remains to be seen, but one fact is becoming clearer: the Negro church is abdicating its duties in the low-income areas and moving its churches lock, stock and Bible. As it stands on the threshold of what could be a golden era, the church appears to be concentrating on its middle and upper classes and giving up (probably for financial reasons) its responsibilities in slum neighborhoods.

A good illustration of what can happen in the field of organized religion is the revolution blazing in the cult world. For years, Father Divine, with a 5-cent cup of coffee and a 15-cent meal, got a chain of heavens going throughout the country and did well during the Depression years. While his following grew, another cultist, Sweet Daddy Grace, stepped into the picture with more pageantry and business operations and subsequently acquired a string of hotels, apartments and gaudily dressed patrons. Then, came the Muslims, and in a generation, this cult wiped out the image of the escapist cults and even greatly influenced the tempo of the Negro church. Man for man, the Muslims reaped more publicity and cash and made their way to a bargaining position at the table of religious leaders—a feat no other cult ever accomplished. Masses today want jobs, housing and an education—not prayer and singing, and some members are angry enough to fight for it.

A blood-curdling human sacrifice more than thirty years ago set the stage for the most fanatical and disciplined cult ever organized by Negroes in America. Today, the cult known formally as the "Nation of Islam" and popularly as the Black Muslims has spread into more than eighty cities, controls the minds of an estimated 70,000 to 250,000 Negroes, has millions in real estate and cash and openly advocates a future racial war in which the white man will be toppled from power. Black Muslim leaders preach "We are told by the white man to bury the hatchet. We'll bury the hatchet in his head."

Advocating anti-white philosophies and denouncing the Bible in shocking terms, Black Muslims first tormented, then began to destroy the weakest link with which a great number of Negroes held onto a vestige of democracy-religion. These Negroes were not college-educated, nor were many high-school educated; they were the mass of illiterates and least educated who swarmed to the cities from Dixie's rural areas. They were downcast, hungry and disillusioned. The Muslims gave them a sense of belonging, hope and status, meanwhile making new crowd heroes of ex-convicts, who run the cult in a fear-ridden atmosphere, along a road that can only lead to a violent extinction.

This outfit started in Detroit as a successor to one established by a flimflam artist, Wallace Don Fard, who served a 3-year sentence in San Quentin prison for a narcotics law violation in the early 1930's. Calling himself "the Supreme Ruler of the Universe," Fard changed his name to "F. Muhammad Ali" and worked out a royal lineage which included birth in Mecca, as the son of wealthy parents of a tribe from which Muhammad had come. His bloodline was that of the dynasty of the Hashemite sherifs of Mecca who became kings of the Hejaz. To add more legitimacy to his claim, he said he had been educated at a college in England and had abandoned a diplomatic career to "lead Negroes out of slavery in the wilderness of America."

This cult differed from those of Father Divine and Daddy Grace in that racial hatred was more pronounced. It was apparent that Fard was cementing this factor into the foundation of the organization. The cult grew until private homes could not accommodate its members. A temple, still known as Temple 1 of the Nation of Islam, was purchased. The cult disintegrated, however, when local authorities ordered Fard to leave Detroit after one of his followers, was arrested for an amazing crime—a human sacrifice. On November 21, 1932, a Muslim induced one John J. Smith to present himself as a human sacrifice so that he might become "the Saviour of the world." At the given time, Smith lay across an improvised altar, and the Muslim jabbed a knife into his heart. Arrested, the Muslim claimed that some women social workers were scheduled to be his next victims. The deluded man was committed to an asylum, but Fard completely disappeared.

A friend, Elijah Poole, gathered the straying adherents. Calling himself Elijah Muhammad, the Messenger of Allah, he claimed to be an apostle of Fard, who supposedly had gone to Mecca. He credited Fard with lifting him from the Detroit gutters and teaching him in 3½ years "the knowledge of Islam." Poole had previously used the names "Gulan Bogans," "Gulam Bogans" and "Mohammed Rassouli" in devious efforts toward financial self-improvement.

Born in 1897 on a farm near Sandersville, Georgia, Poole was one of 13 children whose parents had been slaves of a white family of the same name. His schooling extended only through the fourth grade. Leaving home at 16, he went to Detroit and worked as a common laborer in several manufacturing companies. Poole became anxious for a change in occupation and status.

It took the frail, cunning Poole 31 years, but by a bizarre climb he moved into the racial power structure. Even though believers in the orthodox Muslim church openly denounce him as a fraud who uses their religion to deceive and exploit Negroes, he forged ahead in our society as a recognized cultist leader. He has been described by the press as "the bravest and boldest black man in America." With a powerful following, he has virtually silenced the Negro press against publicizing any of his "hate" record or the strong arm discipline of his following. His organization has grown in financial strength; experts estimate its real estate and cash holdings to be worth millions. The cult operates school systems in Detroit and Chicago, an adult-education program and numerous businesses. Because of its policy of patronizing only Negro businesses, Negro Chamber of Commerce groups have turned a deaf ear to the racial hatred line in order to reap the dividends. So accepted are cult leaders that they appear before numerous university audiences in debate against recognized and educated Negroes, and few times do the cultists feel they have lost the battle. Steadily they have taken over the mantle as the "Little Negro's" fighter and, having reversed their policy of discouraging members from voting, the Muslims now are a powerful voice in elections, especially in the swollen slums of the big cities.

When Representative Adam Clayton Powell, Jr., refers to Muslims as "my dear friends" and joins them on platforms in Harlem political meetings, it seems possible that the cult has gained a new image in the eyes of the professional politicians. Few of our political leaders dare attack this group for fear of punitive revenge. Even prominent churchmen hesitate to criticize it and thereby subject themselves to bitter charges of being "Uncle Toms." Newspaper editors who railed against the Ku Klux Klan seldom lift a pen to analyze the Muslims critically.

Why this strange acceptance of an outlaw band of black racists intent on dominating the Negro world with a combination of power, fear, racial pride and theology mixed to produce an explosive formula? The climate in Negro life has deteriorated in recent years to such an extent that no questions are asked of any individual or group fighting on the antidiscrimination front. "How can we be choosy? The Muslims are doing some good," a Negro once explained, "They're making the white man realize Negroes are willing to fight for what they want." Although prominent Negro leaders are aware of the danger embodied in the Muslim movement (and many have spoken out), even these leaders realize that the man in the street certainly will not condemn the Muslims. "Give 'em hell," a Washington cab driver urged the Muslims, "Soften up the white folks so they'll give us food and jobs." Added to the neutrality stand of a great majority of Negroes is the increased publicity given the Muslims (not with any reporting in depth) by the press, radio and television. Elijah Poole has become the most quoted, most publicized and perhaps the most feared Negro in America. As one reporter said, "If white folks can't muzzle this man, why do they think I should do it?" At one point, publicity given the Muslims reached such a peak that other Negro leaders joked about starting similar campaigns in order to get the white press to take interest in their work. Traditionally, however, cults have received ample linage in the daily press. Father Divine and Daddy Grace were lovable characters whose quaint customs made fascinating "Negroes ain't ready" features. The cultists were freaks who were good for racy articles, and reporters besieged them for copy. The same type of coverage was focused on the Muslims, but it became apparent that the Nation of Islam was a little more than idle chatter. Elijah Poole meant business.

Structurally, the Nation of Islam is, like most Negro businesses, a tightly controlled family operation. Elijah Poole has conceived an operation that provides careers for his six sons and a few sons-in-law. While Poole, now better known as Elijah Muhammad, retains absolute authority, his sons and in-laws occupy the most influential slots. The sons are so trustworthy that only they can serve as messengers to the various temples, carrying secret messages and returning with the cash. The financial arrangement of the cult is so secret that only the power elite can discuss it; expulsion is a threat used to discourage curious members.

With a facade of outright demagoguery, a system of personal identification with numerical mumbo jumbo and the pageantry of platoons and uniforms, the Muslims steamrollered in cities such as New York, Chicago, Detroit, Los Angeles, Boston, Philadelphia, Cleveland, Milwaukee and Baltimore. Their aggressiveness astonished even the most militant Negroes. Said Poole to his following:

"I am not trembling. I am the man. I am the messenger. You should be glad to know God has raised up one in your midst who has that kind of nerve." (When arrested for sedition in 1942, he was nabbed hiding under his mother's bed.)

As if the avowed intent of the Muslims is not bitter enough, a power elite is trained to push their attack. Its forceful and domineering leader is Raymond Sharrieff, the Supreme Captain of Islam. A son-in-law of Poole, Sharrieff is the mastermind for the shock troops and develops the program that trains the male members for the coming War of Armageddon. Considered boss of the hard-driving cadre of "fighting men," he brooks no interference. Outside of Muslim circles, Sharrieff is little known and seldom makes public speeches.

Although Poole's son, Wallace, and Raymond Sharrieff, the prophet's son-in-law, are considered heir apparents to the leadership, the best-known Muslim is a smooth ex-convict, Malcolm Little, better known as Malcolm X. From 1946 to 1952 he served time in the Massachusetts state prison on a breaking and entering conviction. Earlier he was a marijuana user. Wallace Poole, for that matter, was convicted on a charge of failing to report for civilian duty at a state institution, as ordered by a draft board. He appealed a 3-year prison term and is awaiting action on the case.

From prison to platform—that is the route Malcolm X, as a militant, free-wheeling Muslim philosopher, has traveled in the last decade. On some of the finest college campuses he has debated, argued and discussed issues of segregation and integration with some of the best minds in the country. He has spoken at Howard University, the City College of New York, Wesleyan College (Connecticut), the University of Chicago, Cornell University and Morgan State College. His radio and television appearances probably outnumber those of any other Negro leader. He has addressed congregations of many Negro churches.

Few intellectuals can match Malcolm X's eloquence on the speaker's platform. Before large crowds, he has humbled James Farmer, director of CORE; Bayard Rustin, a former aide to Martin Luther King, Jr., and Willoughby Abner of the AFL-CIO. His weapon is simple: an array of charges against the white man. With such a frontal assault, Malcolm X puts most opponents on the defensive, then tears into them with biting comment about "the Negro's inferiority." "Can you stand here and contend you're equal in America?" he'll ask a Negro, followed by, "Isn't one hundred years enough time to give the white man?" As a demagogue, pure logic is not his forte; he appeals to passions and prejudices and stirs up assemblages to reject reason.

When an airliner carrying more than 120 Atlanta residents crashed in Paris two years ago, Malcolm X, in addressing a Los Angeles crowd, cried:

> I would like to announce a very beautiful thing that happened. As you know, we have been praying to Allah. We have been praying that He would in some way let us know that He has the power to execute justice upon the heads of those who are responsible for the lynching of Ronald Stokes on April 27 [shot fatally by police].
> And I got a wire from God today.
> Wait! All right. Well, somebody came and told me that he really

had answered our prayers over in France. He dropped an airplane out of the sky with over a hundred and twenty white people on it, because Muslims believe in an eye for an eye and a tooth for a tooth.

He gets rid of one hundred and twenty of them in one whoop. But thanks to God or Jehovah or Allah, we will continue to pray and we hope that every day another plane falls out of the sky.

But when Malcolm X mocked the tragic death of President Kennedy, he was suspended by Elijah Muhammad who said that his subordinate's action was an inaccurate reflection of Muslim attitudes.

While sociologist C. Eric Lincoln explains the phenomenon of the Muslims as "the fruit of oppression—the hate that hate produces," other Negroes, such as Chicago Urban League Director Edwin Berry, blame the rise of the cult on continuing discrimination in America. The plain fact is that the Muslims plant a seed of hatred which can flourish in rich soil.

But encouraging is the crusade of America's leading churchmen to halt discrimination and segregation and to utilize the power of the Church to bring brotherhood on earth as well as in heaven. Nineteen sixty-three was the turning point for religion. Enforcement of a standard of ethics will put into the struggle millions of God-fearing Christians in the United States, and this alone will develop a climate of understanding and compassion to solve the many racial problems still to come. The Negro Church also must rise to the occasion—as it has done so heroically in the past. "Follow me" is no longer a hymn, but a command for Christians to act.

# ★ ★ ★ 9  The Eggheads

Like the plodding turtle in the fabled race with the hare, the American Negro, after a slow, agonizing start, is flexing his muscles for an educational spurt. Already Negro youngsters are trudging to white schools for the first time in the Southland, and many will be following them in growing numbers to high schools, colleges and universities. In the North, angry Negro mothers picket overcrowded schools in ghettos, demanding better training for their children. Federal authorities, with blueprints and appropriations, are on the verge of trying to wipe out America's underdeveloped areas, with crash programs in manpower retraining, education and methods of curbing juvenile delinquency.

A new spirit has gripped the American Negro. Education is a status symbol and the Ph.D. degree is as treasured as the mortgage on a $25,000 home. More Negro students are enrolled in high schools, graduating and going on to college. This is the golden era for the Negro—and in the process a harvest of Negro intellectuals of talent and ability will be realized.

In the past, a few Negroes have won national and international recognition. There are individual success stories in almost every profession and career; one or two Negroes have worked to the top of the heap and gained accompanying prestige. More than one hundred and fifty Negroes are listed in *Who's Who in America*. Many more would be if they were affiliated with large industrial corporations, major universities or colleges. A number of successful Negroes are completely unknown to the majority of Americans. To most whites United Nations Under Secretary Ralph J. Bunche symbolizes the successful and prominent Negro.

Yet when President Kennedy was hunting for government executives after his election, he experienced little difficulty in recruiting Harvard-educated Negroes. He selected two Negro Ph.D's for key posts—Robert C. Weaver, for service as the nation's first Negro housing administrator, and Samuel Z. Westerfield, Deputy Assistant Secretary of State for Economic Affairs.

Brilliant examples of the Negro's victory over environment, these men, nevertheless, are exceptions. They are Negroes who forged ahead despite the barriers and obstacles. While these pioneers reached the top, hundreds faltered along the way and thousands never got started.

"Have you ever seen a foot race between an athlete and a one-legged boy hobbling along on crutches?" Dr. Samuel Proctor, noted educator, once asked an audience, "And the fans expected the one-legged boy to stay in the race?"

He explained the parable in contrasting the inequities between whites and Negroes. Statistically, whites have produced more experts, more award-winning researchers and scientists, more inventors and planners, more everything. But whites also have more income, more education, more job opportunities, better housing, and better health. Despite this disadvantage, the Negro has not become totally disillusioned, as has the American Indian, nor has he been hopelessly outdistanced.

"The Negro cripple has run so long with handicaps," says a distinguished educator, "that when he gets on more equal terms, he might become a whiz."

Negro achievements are legion. In one hundred years, the illiteracy rate has been lowered to less than 8 percent, an enviable record of determination and pride. While educational experts bemoan the disturbing dropout rates of high school students, little is said about the Negro's increased school enrollment (from 81 percent to 87 percent in 5 years, 1956 to 1961). The number of Negroes in college, full and part time, has steadily spiraled.

During one of the school integration crises in a southern city, a Negro leader frequently split verbs in conversation. A reporter drew his attention to this. The leader retorted: "Well, I'm one of them there folks who's got a fourth-grade schooling. These kids deserve a better break."

But in an age of automation, the Negro's victories in education scarcely are enough. Under the glass on the desk of a government official in the nation's capital rests a letter from an ambitious job applicant who starts off, "I is a Negro college graduate."

The official is a Negro, a man dedicated to the thankless and sometimes difficult task of helping recruit Negroes for high-grade positions in government. Why would a Negro VIP retain such a missive with a preposterous grammatical error? Is this an omen of failure? Does this show disillusionment creeping into the picture?

On the contrary, the official keeps the letter to re-emphasize the need for better quality education for the Negro in America. In the nation's capital, where discrimination in government employment became as obnoxious as the Communism issue a few years ago, the inability to place Negroes is often blamed on racism. Under close scrutiny this charge in many cases proves to be unfounded. Realizing this, the official maintains his sense of objectivity by keeping all factors in focus.

Poor education is a real handicap to the Negro. Discrimination and segregation in employment opportunities and inequalities in education have, for more than a century, shortchanged our parents and their parents, back to the days when it was illegal to teach a Negro to read and write. Continued exclusion from major colleges and universities—in the North because of economics or quota barriers and in the South because of outright discrimination—has limited the number of Negroes able to climb the ladder. It also has created a peculiarly constructed society. For example, more Negro women than men go to college,* yet few women take an

* Most Negroes who attend college are from the South where it is felt that a woman needs education to protect her in a segregated society.

active role in civil life, locally or nationally. The Negro intellectual set is far smaller than the comparable white group, and anti-intellectualism is far more prevalent in Negro communities. (Writers like Richard Wright, James Baldwin, Frank Yerby and Ralph Ellison have achieved national popularity, but they and a few others are exceptional.) An educated Negro, usually a preacher or a teacher, often is labeled a snob in many sections where appeals to passion or prejudice over-balance the appeal to reason. "Culturally deprived" and "unteachable" are terms used to describe so many of my people, survivors of poverty-scarred generations who weathered the empty years. In our midst has been built a separate education system, from kindergarten to college. It is inferior, poorly equipped and second class, yet two-thirds of the educated Negro class emanate from this system. Despite widening opportunity, too many Negro youths are still being prepared, in an age of automation, with the tools of the horse-and-buggy era.

The long court fight to integrate schools dealt a cruel blow to the world of Negro education, shabby by academic standards of excellence as it is. A decade or two ago the thrust for litigation on behalf of integration crippled Negro education, because experts realistically had to appraise separate education as inadequate and inferior and paint it as an institution that produced second-class candidates. A spirit of support had to be developed among the masses, because intellectuals, for the most part, opposed such a step for fear of losing teaching jobs. Parents had to be sold on the idea that their children were being shortchanged; some leaders who refused to accept the latter doctrine were verbally horsewhipped as "Uncle Toms" and "sell-outs." In no time, this conclusion influenced many Negro leaders. Negro educators, including some who were not qualified for the profession, found themselves fighting for their very limited existence.

Ten years ago some Negro leaders tested in court the policy of transporting Negroes miles beyond white schools to attend Jim Crow schools. Now the leaders advocate sending Negro children miles out of their community to attend white schools. Tomorrow, the strategy may be to concentrate on improving the schools right in the heart of Negro neighborhoods and teaching children the elementary lessons of pride and confidence.

Many believed the NAACP civil-rights war whoop of "Free by '63" after the United States Supreme Court's 1954 decision against school segregation. It is realized now that the judgment was premature. Negroes still face hurdles and barriers previously concealed by the intensity of our integration drive. There are the conflicts, the educational battle of theories of rehabilitating many Negroes, and the resultant emotional depression that clouds the mind of many youngsters and stunts their growth toward maturity. We have in our midst the growing despair of those who refuse to continue in school and contribute to an alarming national dropout problem. In both North and South, there are community problems of enhancing curricula to capture the imagination of our youngsters and of developing new educational methods to reinforce, via the medium of the public school, our badly mangled family life— a peculiar problem few educators want to touch. The problems of crime, juvenile delinquency, crowded housing, poor health standards and unemployment within the growing slums are spotlighted because the trend toward integration has made the Negro community a part of the whole. Before, no one bothered to know what was going on across the tracks or in the blighted areas where we live— except the researcher, the sociologist or the budding novelist. Before, many of our leaders concentrated in putting most of the eggs in the basket of integration as a catch-all for progress.

The educational situation is depressing and disillusioning, one of the most difficult Negroes face in America, but one that blossoms with hope. The will of the Negro to succeed, the refusal to lose faith after generations of hardship and the fierce determination of many youngsters to overcome the handicaps add up to the conclusion that eventually the national leadership will inspire a massive educational drive. Many leaders admit privately that of all the fronts to wage a campaign for improvement, education should be foremost, and not merely in terms of a continued clamor for integrated education. Improvement of standards is needed in the ghetto schools and in Negro colleges, where for years thousands of youngsters will continue to receive their diplomas. As long as the Negro in America is severly handicapped by educational deficiencies, progress will be spotty, slow and limited in scope.

Several years ago, when the Kennedy Administration launched its Equal Opportunity drive to increase the number of Negroes in high-ranking jobs in government and industry, one factor became increasingly clear: the difficulty of finding candidates who could pass existing civil service examinations. At a Howard University meeting of Negro educators this was brought out by Don Frye of the Housing and Home Finance Administration, who said:

As a result of noncompetition or limited competition with whites and because of primary educational discrimination, academic standards of Negro educational institutions have tended to be low. In Atlanta, one of the most progressive southern cities, the average achievement level of the Negro high school graduate was equivalent to the national average of a sophomore in high school. This lost ground can't all be made up in college, and unfortunately, some colleges have not always tried desperately enough to do so.

You heard the results of the standard Federal Service Entrance examination, on the basis of one or two exams. It's improving, but you heard the results for the last full year.

In one college I personally gave the secretarial test to 15 young ladies who were about to receive a 4-year degree in secretarial science. None passed. This is a test a sizeable majority of all high school graduates who take the test pass. Quite possibly, neither the students nor the professors thought that the maximum effort was worthwhile because, due to discrimination they could obtain only routine jobs. But if Negroes are to take and keep their rightful place in the economic world, and if the current favorable climate, as represented by those who are at the conference, is to continue and grow, the standards must be sufficiently high to enable Negro graduates to compete successfully with all graduates of all races.

Some colleges have not foreseen or do not believe a new day, a new era is here and, as a result, are doing very little to steer students into preparation for fields which might provide additional outlets for their talents. Too many colleges are still preparing too many teachers, preachers and farmers. Only by wide dispersal of the best Negro talent will barriers be broken down and future graduates be accepted without regard for race. Every well-placed Negro is a salesman for another Negro.

To approximately fifty presidents and executives of Negro institutions of higher learning who heard this message, this was a mandate for improvement. It was a sobering warning to educators who developed what Assistant Secretary of Labor George L. P. Weaver described in a Pittsburgh speech as "the first generation of Negro leaders." Said Weaver of the contributions of the so-called Negro college: "They later provided the first teachers for the publicly supported colleges and public schools, the educated Negro ministry and the first opportunities in such professions as medicine and law. These colleges and universities have produced leaders who enriched the main stream of American culture."

At similar parleys and conferences throughout the South, the plight of the Negro colleges has been and will continue to be discussed, not only by education specialists but by the parents and even the students. College presidents are concerned about the collapse of their "academic prowess" at the dawn of the integration era. Howard University President James Nabrit contends, "We must increase the levels of achievement in all our colleges and put more exacting demands upon our students and ourselves. We must let our students know that their opportunities in the world of tomorrow will depend upon their spirits and the tools they possess. The limitations on them will depend upon their own inadequacies." Hampton Institute President Jerome Holland states, "We cannot delay for a moment the preparation of our young people for the fruits of a new day. We must return to our campuses in a mood of urgency and raise the standards of our programs."

Confronted with alarmists who contend that the separate institutions will shortly be swallowed up by integration and the fatalists who argue that Negro colleges should be junked for the cause of better education, Negro college presidents have witnessed a revolution in mind and thought on their campuses, while at the same time they have tried to adopt crash programs to remedy the deficiencies. The sit-in movement which swept over the campuses was more than a revolt against the system of segregation; it was a signal for vast changes in the administration of the separate institutions. Like the Negro church, the Negro college has been an escapist in developing wide-awake, civic-minded and responsible graduates. It, too, has suffered, because for too long a period it has graduated classes equipped only to perform mediocre services within the realms of segregation and discrimination.

A college president tells the story of a student who, having joined the sit-in demonstrators, was visited by a parent who demanded that he quit. "I didn't send you to college to parade before a white folk's store," ranted the parent. "I know you didn't," the student said, "but if I can't be treated like a human being, it doesn't make any difference whether I have a degree."

This is an important discovery for a young man at a Negro college. In my day, many colleagues from the southern states had no such conception of democracy; they had been brainwashed in public schools to accept an inferior status, even in aspiration. Their role in achieving a college education would be to return either to preach about or to teach the same docile philosophy. But these kids are awakening today, demanding more in terms of curricula, programming and the freedom to think.

The tragedy of the sit-in was that its dramatic attraction soon drained off. Eventually, when professional agitators took over the national student groups, the scholastically poorer students took up the cudgels. These same students, a professor told me, could have turned against the college president and picketed his home, demanding better equipment, better instruction and a more intellectual atmosphere on the campus. By doing this, the educator explained, sit-in demonstrators could have performed more good in the long run than was accomplished by the demonstrations directed against a five-and-ten cafeteria.

Negro private colleges, established and endowed in many cases by Northern philanthropy or by religious institutions, carried the torch for years. They kept education alive among Negroes when every other force tried its best to stifle our ambition. The stories of how many of the early educators connived, fought, bowed low and politicked just to keep their institutions provided with funds to operate have never been told. Neither have the accounts of many whites who served as educational missionaries on faculties to bring guidance and knowledge to the few ambitious students. But this pioneering spirit, this determination, this search for unequalled education has bogged down in recent years in a swamp of educational poverty, professional insecurity and misdirected leadership. A foundation official was interested in putting a sum in excess of 30 million dollars into a Negro private school to bring it up to such a standard that whites would be willing to attend. After countless inquiries and trips to schools, he gave up the mission as fruitless. According to a reliable source, he could find neither the educator young enough in ideas or the school with sufficient equipment to make the start.

At my own alma mater, Virginia Union University in Richmond, I remember a white man leaving his hat on when he entered the president's office. This was a sign of supremacy, I suppose. The students in the hallways booed and warned him that if he didn't take off his hat, they would. Redfaced, he obliged. This was the spirit of any student body, defiant and determined.

Union was a poor school. The buildings were in disrepair, the cafeteria menu resembled a relief diet, and few professors earned $5,000 a year (but they were dedicated to their jobs). Yet on our campus in the heartland of Virginia, students could speak on any issue, discuss any problem. We couldn't enjoy freedom of thought in the city, but we experienced it on the campus.

This was not true on the campuses of the state-supported schools, which had larger faculties and more numerous buildings. It still is not true. The integration drive has caused state legislatures to pour millions into these universities; physically, they resemble first-rate institutions but few have ever developed "a soul" or "a backbone." At one of the state universities for Negroes, men and women were not permitted to speak to one another, except for an hour daily. The curricula in many cases were designed not to educate the Negro and prepare him or her for a pioneering future, but merely to placate graduates so they will accept a sterile, noncontroversial existence in a much-disciplined world of teaching. State legislators, by threatening to withdraw funds for buildings or salaries, did more to restrict and hamper effective work than the officials they hand-picked to control any educational progress among Negroes. It was joked in communities that before a Negro became president of a state college, he had to know how to say "yes sir," to bow low and to chauffeur a governor around the campus.

Much is written about professors on American campuses who have stood for unpopular causes and been fired from their jobs. Little has ever been written about the tragic circumstances of faculty members on state-supported campuses. They are forbidden to participate in militant groups such as the NAACP, CORE or the National Urban League. They are barred from encouraging students—after graduation—from registering to vote and becoming active in civic affairs. Freedom of discussion in campus parleys or school newspaper articles is banned. How can responsible men and women be developed in such a juvenile atmosphere? How can students be inspired to think, to ponder, to probe in an atmosphere of fear? Yet such conditions prevail in these institutions. The schools are inferior because state legislators want them to be.

Several years ago, when a Negro educator retired as president of a publicly supported university, he made this confession to a close friend: "The philosophy of operating a Negro college is to prepare our students not to compete with whites." His friends were astonished. "I must be frank," he said, "We are not preparing these students. It's not unintentional. It's the way they've forced me to do."

This confession could come from any of the presidents of the Negro state-supported schools. In only three states in the South, Texas, Arkansas and North Carolina, are Negroes serving on the boards handling the destinies of the separate schools. In one southern state, the university president must check with a law-maker to get his approval for any administrative action he takes. In another university, faculty members have told how the president patrols the campus and permits no visitor to come to the school and speak to classes except with his permission. "This is the most sterile environment I have ever worked in," said a professor, "Nothing controversial can even be whispered, whether it be race relations or birth control."

At an Alabama school, an employee of the governor of the state served for years on the board of trustees. Scarcely qualified for such a post and lacking in knowledge of educational techniques, he was one of its most powerful members because of his link to the governor. But the picture is changing. When a governor of North Carolina visited a state-supported Negro college, he was booed by the students. The president became excited and reprimanded them for their poor manners. That produced a wave of subdued laughter. The students had read in newspapers of a speech in which the visiting governor had discussed race relations. They had voiced their objections to his views in their own way. At another Negro institution, the president met with the student body and described with emphasis plans for modernizing the campus—new buildings, manicured lawns and paved roads. When he finished, a student asked him whether he had also given consideration to a better-paid and more qualified faculty.

This is evidence of the foment building up on both state-supported and private Negro campuses. It is precipitating a revolution in the field of education. For Negro students to develop such confidence is encouraging. The challenge will be to channel the energies into developing better graduates, inspired, well-trained and free of racial prejudice. Better-prepared, better-educated and better-conditioned faculty members are needed to fulfill this goal. Recuitment could well include more white educators. The transition will eliminate the lackluster college presidents who have held onto positions because of political connections rather than capabilities. This is not to say that all Negro institutions are second-rate and their presidents incompetent. A few institutions succeed in accomplishing a worthwhile function—even some state-supported institutions, several of which have integrated their student bodies in recent years.

The greater struggle to survive confronts the presidents of about forty private Negro institutions that in many cases lack the funds to build new buildings, develop the campus family they need and hire the necessary staff. Their curricula will have to be re-examined and their purpose re-evaluated. Some, no doubt, will become junior colleges, since in this era of automation, more than confidence is needed for survival. Whether Negroes will support more fully these private schools, whether foundations and industry will value their services, are questions only time will answer. So far, the response hasn't been encouraging. The United Negro College Fund receives less money in a year for its 32 member institutions than does Harvard.

The lack of enthusiasm among Negroes is due to a general feeling that the schools rate scholastically lower than other institutions, in which sons and daughters will never enroll. Even presidents of the Negro colleges admit that many of the best minds matriculate at integrated universities when such opportunity is available. However, the institutions still educate thousands of Negroes, and most attract more applicants than can be enrolled.

Despite the dire warnings from Southern educators that integration in depth will not occur on white university campuses in the foreseeable future, there will be a continued influx of the more qualified Negro students at both the undergraduate and graduate level, in both the North and the South. Educational specialists feel the present generation will probably be the last to rely on Negro colleges for an education. The migration of students from the North to attend Negro colleges in the South will be lessened as specialized job openings provide more incentive for youth to prepare themselves.

Why send your child to a Negro college? That was a question my parents asked themselves. For my generation, the theory was that Negroes needed to know one another and that the experience was necessary since Negroes live together. One had to develop prestige and status in the Negro community; thus, earning a fraternal membership in many instances was more important than winning a degree. Progress in race relations completely reversed this belief. Today, the acceptable Negro youth is a keen, well-balanced person equally at home among Negroes or whites. He is not supposed to carry a chip on his shoulder. He is supposed to be articulate on current events beyond the scope of civil rights, and well-trained in his specialty.

Likewise, there is an increase in the number of Negroes attending interracial institutions. Fifteen years ago, the percentage was below one percent. Today, it ranges higher in some schools, according to the most reliable sources. Most universities refuse to stockpile such information, contending that there is no racial identification on records. But this certainly is the trend, and because of it, the new generations will produce substantially more qualified graduates in a variety of specialties. Numerous organizations place Negroes in white colleges through guidance programs, scholarships, and financial aid. The most outstanding, perhaps, is the National Scholarship Service and Fund for Negro Students, which has put more than eighty-five hundred students into some three hundred and fifty accredited schools on scholarships totaling an estimated $3,600,000. Governmental programs, including the Peace Corps and the employee recruitment efforts, also have encouraged the scholarship aspirations of many Negroes.

But all this promotion has yet to begin to inspire the mass of Negro youth to lift their sights. Too many Negro youngsters in both North and South dread facing the challenges of integration by attending mixed colleges. At this time, unfortunately, many of the children of the men who guide the limited Negro education attend northern prep schools. A story is told of an educator whose children attend New England schools making a case for the limited educational program of Negroes in the South. "It takes time," he told an audience, "We must be gradualists in switching the course of education." They said to him, "Then you bring your children back here, and suffer with us." In another southern city, a leading Negro businessman pondered whether to send his son to a northern school. "Well, I finally decided to send him to a Negro institution. You know I didn't want him to get all mixed up. He's already behind, being a Negro high school graduate, and just pushing him into stiff competition might ruin him for life."

But to enroll in college, one must graduate from high school.

This is the gray area, the no man's land for the pitched battles in the months to come between educators, lawmakers, community leaders and Negroes. To gain a formal high school education is an impossible goal for too many Negro youngsters in America at this time. This is a problem in both North and South. More and more, Negro leadership is turning its attentions to this subject of education, as are the lawmakers and the community leaders. What they see is a complex and distressing situation that cannot be erased overnight. In the *Journal of Intergroup Relations,* School Superintendent Carl F. Hansen capsuled the problem in his predominantly Negro Washington school system:

> Restricted employment opportunities—especially in the technical, office and executive fields, restrict non-white income, status and training incentive. This, in turn, is reflected in large numbers of nonacademically interested youngsters, school dropouts, delinquency and parents who show little interest in school problems, since education alone does not open doors to jobs and decent homes or dignity in a nonintegrated society.

> The schools that are mainly Negro usually are in the overpopulated portions of the city and are usually overpopulated themselves, with resultant diminution in educational facilities and values.

> Racial desegregation has increased the availability of public schools to Negro pupils, but the poor housing, limited employment and culturally deprived ghettos are strong deterrents to improved quality of educations and upgrading of educational ambitions.

> The foregoing circumstances create other hurdles for integration such as: (1) a dwindling supply of white personnel applying for public schools in totally non-white areas and even in the public school systems as a whole, (2) increased teaching and non-teaching loads because of increased needs among the changed pupil population, (3) an increasing pupil population that demands even greater system-wide efforts and expenditures to provide an instructional program through which every child may develop his abilities to his highest potential level, and (4) nonintegrated experiences for pupils in all white and all colored schools.

In almost every city and state, the problem is similar: the Negro youngster, for the most part, lags in the education race. At a meeting of the Virginia Teachers Association, Otis E. Finley, Jr., National Urban League associate director for education and youth incentives, called for new standards:

> The drive for equality of opportunity in the public schools must be accelerated, but at the same time we must all work and pay for a new standard of excellence in our schools if education is to fulfill its role as a true national resource.
>
> We must not squander the tomorrow of 3,250,000-odd Negro schoolchildren in the South, who need better facilities, better libraries and better incentives.
>
> It is apparent that progress in school desegregation is not really progress unless it is broad and fast enough to meet the need of the times.

An expert in such matters, Finley advocates a broad, bold program to reach youngsters. Says he: "Most textbooks and vocational counseling aids, including films, used in our public schools today were written or produced from the vantage point of an all-white society. The position of Negroes and other minorities in contemporary American living is largely overlooked. Again there is sufficient research to suggest the value of self-identification in the motivation of youth."

# ★★★ 10 The Image Makers

At a formal banquet in May, 1963, at one of the new hotels of the nation's capital, a tall, lanky white man brought a Negro audience to its feet with a stirring address. The speech, one of the most illuminating on the subject of race relations, was given by Vice President Lyndon B. Johnson of Texas before the Capitol Press Club. Timed a few days after the Birmingham demonstrations, which had sent racial feelings soaring in many American cities, the appearance was a high point in the Vice President's political career. Johnson's earlier activities had included alliances with Dixiecrats on Capitol Hill and the casting of negative votes against civil-rights legislation. As a Texan, he possessed an unimposing record in race relations in the eyes of many of the banqueters—even as chairman of the President's Committee on Equal Opportunity in Employment.

Few Americans learned of this speech by the man who was then the Administration's second highest official. Press coverage for the affair was minimal. Neither wire service bothered to report the speech or the occasion at which a Negro press club honored the Vice President and presented North Carolina Governor Terry Sanford as the guest speaker. At a time when national reporters emphasized that Washington was "a city about to explode with racial violence," coverage of such an event certainly would have had some effect in comforting those who felt that all Negroes carry razors, umbrellas (to jab with the metal point) or guns to rampage against whites.

To an industry that can accuse Presidents and cabinet members of "news-managing," Negroes certainly can justly complain about the news treatment of their people. For too long, Negroes have known and grown to accept "news managing" of their affairs, attitudes and selection of leaders by most of the communications industry. And for too long, the industry has not recognized Negroes as even a part of the community, locally or nationally, except as an undesirable part.

I have often wondered why the national conferences of the wire services,* newspaper editors and editorial writers refuse to invite Negroes to discuss civil rights for the black man. Is this not a subject as important to democracy as international affairs?

I have often wondered how a daily reporter could win a major award on a series of stories exposing the second-class citizenship status of Negroes. Is such a project unique? The Negro press crusaded for years, and few won even a mention.

I have often wondered why the major journalism schools refuse to recognize the Negro press and do not attempt to improve its quality, as is done among white newspapers and magazines.

I have often wondered, even in these times of massive protest in which race relations has become a separate but complicated field, why few newspapers, magazines or broadcasting outfits employ reporters or editors skilled in background and interpretation? I know of one so-called Negro radio and television chain that has a one-man news staff for 12 stations, as compared with a full complement of crazily named disc jockeys.

Of all of the creative fields that are characterized as liberal and understanding, journalism ranks in lowest esteem; it has done little for the Negro, not only in the hiring of qualified personnel but in interpreting his plight. This is not a blanket indictment because there are some newspapers, magazines and broadcasting firms that have contributed magnificently. But these few are overwhelmed by industry-wide lethargy, mostly at the local level, that has set the Negro apart and segregated him as an outsider.

As a lifelong journalist, I am critical of my profession, which I

---

* U.P.I. editors and publishers sponsored a session on race relations for the first time at an October, 1963, conference in Chicago.

love and feel is important in the maintenance of a free society. It has done much, along with the movies, to establish an image of the unworthy Negro. Negroes were unacceptable as candidates for space in departments of society, housing, education, women's pages, civic news and business but could rate a mention in crime, entertainment and sports. These policies still are in force in many newspapers, but recently those in metropolitan areas outside the South have begun to change slightly.

When I was a youngster, one of the dailies in Youngstown, Ohio hired a Negro to write a daily column of Negro news notes. This would enable an employer to see whether the maid or chauffeur was attending gospel meetings. Into this column went everything about Negroes—weddings, church notes, obituaries and even a few two-line ads. The comic aspects of such a collection can be imagined, and acquaintance with the man, who in the town was regarded as one of the "bridges" between the white and Negro communities, made it even more humorous. The man drank heavily and often during some of his sprees, he got facts garbled—which frequently made the column enjoyable reading. For years, nevertheless, he was the Negro representative in the daily press.

In intervening years, the Negro image has changed slowly. The first step was to get newspaper editors to capitalize the word *Negro*. Then came the campaign to remove the word Negro from personal descriptions in news stories. That was followed by the struggle for inclusion in general news columns and equal opportunity in hiring. Over the years, meanwhile, the image of the Negro was shaped, blighted and blemished. The Negro is not a citizen, according to many segments of the press; he is merely a piece of property, a casualty, an outsider, an "invisible man" (as writer Ralph Ellison describes him) or a migrant. Tragically, too many white Americans share this view, because many reporters feel this way.

Several years ago, the Negro Big Six visited the White House to confer with President Eisenhower in what was probably the first meeting of its kind. The meeting was well publicized, and each of the Negroes was well known, thanks to the press. At a press conference at the White House, one of the reporters turned to NAACP

Executive Secretary Roy Wilkins and said, "Sir, What did you say your name is?" I don't know of anything which could have been more embarrassing to Mr. Wilkins at that time.

This is not an exception. Every Negro leader can spell out experiences of being misquoted, having a speech misinterpreted or even being ignored by newspapermen at press conferences. The quality and extent of coverage in the field of race relations leaves much to be desired. How can communities, if their newspapers employ education editors, allow schools for Negroes in the ghettos to be second class, with curricula designed in too many cases for ninth-grade students not being able to read or write with skill? Are not the quality of education, the program and the production an education editor's concerns? Newspaper editors who believe in the integrity of their profession (as they often state) could battle in the areas where Negroes are forced to accept menial jobs, but they don't.

Leaders of the communications industry, the authorities on freedom of speech and the critics of "news managing" themselves violate a code of integrity and honesty when it comes to the Negro. They talk and write in glowing terms on democracy and its institutions. I feel the profession, more than any other, represents the hypocrisy in America to Negroes and corrodes, in too many cases, the faith of those of my people who wish only a fair shake.

Let me give some examples of the double standard. In the letter I wrote to the three Washington newspapers following the race riot at D.C. Stadium on Thanksgiving Day, I took pains to cite some of the beatings I had seen and mentioned that many of the offenders were Negro. I also said that the football game promoters had done little to insure a healthy climate at the game, that there were no provisions for riot control and that police were entirely ineffective, if not downright incompetent. What happened? For the first time in more than 25 years of reporting, I loomed as a national hero in the press. Reporters and wire services lifted from the letter the sections which blamed Negroes for the fighting, and dailies ran stories headed, "Negro Blames Own Race For Violence." Was this factor more important than any other, including the fact that in a city with a predominantly Negro population not a Negro served on any planning panel or session prior to a high school game in which a Negro team opposed a white team?

During the Little Rock school crisis, I showed up at a press conference sponsored by the Superintendent of Schools in Little Rock and was asked to leave on the grounds that I had not been invited. Information that I, as a Negro, was not supposed to receive was to be given out. I, a legitimate press representative, was told to my face that I was unreliable, yet not a newspaperman or an editor lifted his voice in protest.

Traveling with the entourage of Vice President Nixon during the 1960 campaign, I was near some of his top aides when his running mate, Henry Cabot Lodge, reiterated his proposal that a Negro be named to the cabinet. I overheard one aide whisper to some wire service men, "Don't talk too loud, Booker can hear us." They were concocting a story so that the presidential candidate could be quoted in a way that would neither back Lodge nor disenchant what he thought was a large Negro following. I asked my publisher to transfer me back to the Kennedy campaign train.

Coupled with this type of experience, a Negro reporter faces the barriers of entrenched discrimination. It took the National Press Club in Washington almost 45 years to elect its first Negro member, national correspondent Louis Lautier, and a few more years to invite its first Negro luncheon speaker, Dr. Martin Luther King. President Kennedy became the first Chief Executive to ask a Negro reporter to a background session and also the first to insist that organizations attached to the White House admit Negroes. Members of the White House News Photographers Association for years barred Negro members. During President Eisenhower's Administration, I protested to Press Secretary James Hagerty about the discrimination but he refused to intervene, claiming that the association, whose members carry special identification to permit them to be easily admitted to the company of the President, was a private group. Finally, at one of President Kennedy's early press conferences, I asked him whether he thought an association attached to the White House should bar Negro members. The President said that he didn't agree with such policies, and in a matter of weeks, the first Negro photographer was able to join the organization. Some other press organizations in the nation's capital which are closed to Negroes, and there are limitations on Negro newsmen serving on radio and television panels. There are still many cabinet and ranking officials who invite only white reporters to background sessions. This policy is also followed by some European, and even Asian embassies.

For a nation's capital, Washington has an undemocratic history. It has always been a center of segregation and discrimination (except for a period after the Civil War) and, while Truman was President, a committee described it as one of the most segregated cities in the United States. Since the city draws the largest contingent of news personnel, it has been regarded as the heart of the profession; many of journalism's big names work in the area. Its racial policies rubbed off on the thinking, the customs and even the writing of the journalists. Few ever protested conditions in the city, let alone the country. It took the Supreme Court, Presidents Eisenhower and Kennedy and the arrival of African Ambassadors to bring relief. It was easier for African diplomats to be featured in newspaper social pages, to buy properties in white neighborhoods and to eat in restaurants. Such privileges continued to be unavailable to the American Negro.

Because the Negro's plight was ignored by the press, the Government and white leaders, most of his gains have derived from outrage at murders, bombings, gunnings and riots rather than an orderly, constructive program to educate, employ and house a deprived people. A threat of racial violence, advertised in the press by either coverage of a speech or evaluation of police department information, attracts more attention that any procedure developed by Negroes, who in most cases are the protagonists for civil-rights gains. This pattern has been shaped by the indifference and the unwillingness of whites to realize the Negro's growing despair. It cost the lives of hundreds of Negroes before the nation became aware of the oppression in the South. It lost the jobs of hundreds of Negro teachers before the United States Supreme Court finally ruled on the issues of wage equalization and segregation. It resulted in the breakup of numerous families, the bankruptcies of businesses, the flight of professionals to safety areas—all because the American communications industry refused to do what it preaches to the press of other countries. It was not courageous enough to campaign for human equality and decency. The press in many ways has been the Negro's worst enemy.

When Negroes in several Mississippi cities attempted to register to vote, certain newspapers printed their names and addresses so that employers could so notice and fire them from jobs as "agitators." Not a press association or news fraternity condemned such a practice as unworthy of the high code of journalism.

From my vantage point, this represents the state of affairs in the world of the press as it moves into a new civil-rights era for which it is totally unprepared and unqualified to report or interpret. No more prepared are most of the American people, who have been lulled by the lack of reporting on this major issue. And what has this lethargy cost in the course of national events?

The Muslims are a good example of an unknown faction of religious holy rollers who skyrocketed into the pages of most newspapers and magazines, got their leaders before klieg lights and became an important cog in the Negro civil-rights front. No reporter had any idea of their size, their treasury, their impact, but they were different. They advocated violence against the white man (whom they described as "devils"), and they constantly derided civil-rights tactics. The cult garnered more publicity in a year than the NAACP had received in 5 years, than the Urban League drew in its half-century of existence. Malcolm X became the symbol the press helped establish. Not content with the coverage in New York City, Malcolm X moved his operations to the nation's capital, on the pretense of wanting to erase juvenile delinquency. Greeted at the airport by a group of reporters, he convincingly made the necessary public relations touch. However, at his first meeting, less than one hundred Negroes (outside of approximately three hundred cult members) turned out to meet the man, whose only cure for Washington juvenile delinquency was membership in the Muslims.

Understanding the intricate and complex activity in our field is a difficult feat for an experienced Negro reporter, let alone a white reporter suddenly pulled from a city desk and told to write an objective piece. Many white reporters have done factual, timely articles; some have consistently covered the field. They constitute a small minority of the profession, however, and few are in the upper editorial ranks. Most of the white reporters, perhaps because of their own upbringing, fail to weigh the zeal, the inconsistency, the hazards and the intense politicking that dominates the real power thrust for first-class rights. Many fail to capture the "soul" aspects of the race revolution, measuring Negro gains in terms of campaigns, jobs and leaders and neglecting to examine the human elements and the violations of constitutional guarantees that press the sometimes-confused Negro along the road. Negroes know that inequality is still their lot and, for many, may continue to be for a long time. Criticism by the press is no excuse to turn or steer from a course. There is always a stand-by—the Negro press.

The Negro press in America ranks with the traditional daily press in America in somewhat the same way Negro baseball ranks with major league baseball. There is no comparison in the size of the institution, the salaries, the over-all performance, even the caliber of players, but there's just enough audience to finance the business, and the business is crusading for Negroes—in a manner. Like Negro baseball, Negro journalism has had its share of stars, some of whom moved upward in the top ranks; it has its history and tradition, and it has a record of accomplishment. It still serves a purpose.

The 1962 Birmingham demonstration provides an illustration of the shaping of press coverage. Such a demonstration had been threatened for more than a year, and the goals were clear-cut: desegregation of downtown stores and counters, hiring of Negroes for upgraded jobs and desegregation of schools. An election took place, and a man identified as a moderate by the press happened to win. Use of the term *moderate* was misleading, in that the difference between Albert Boutwell and Eugene (Bull) Conner in racial views wasn't easily recognizable. A legal snafu delayed the taking of office by the victorious Boutwell, and in the interim, Negroes called for the demonstrations. At this point the press emphasized the views of (1) white liberals who called the move untimely, and (2) Negroes who did the same thing. Both groups described the demonstration leaders as "outsiders" and "agitators."

When the Birmingham city government sought relief by refusing permits and then arrested the demonstrating Negroes for contempt of a court order (which subsequently was voided), the press then highlighted the angle of "mob hooliganism." The national press played the story straight, meaning that it reported a tug-of-war between Negroes and whites, with no emphasis on the denial of constitutional rights. Even with the use of police dogs and fire hoses, reporters' descriptions of the police tactics sometimes omitted any mention of such brutalities. It wasn't the written coverage that eventually turned the tide; it was the photographic coverage—pictures of a boy being chewed by a dog while his police owner held the boy and of a Negro woman, flat on her back in the street, being kneed by a policeman. If there had been no pictures, Birmingham might have gone down in history as a civil-rights defeat. As it was, the riot that followed the bombings of the motel and of the home of the Reverend A. D. King nearly ruined the truce. But did the press question how whites could bomb such strategic centers (the place where Negro leaders met and the home of one) in the heart of the Negro area—unless police protection was lacking?

As an experienced correspondent in the South, I have found that it is the best to refrain from associating with (1) police and (2) most daily newsmen in the area. Their teamwork is an alliance that chokes off any attempt to change either the *status quo* or the use of force in subduing Negroes in and out of jails. The brutality involving sheriffs, policemen and citizens, plus the unjust judicial system (geared to keeping Negroes in their place) make some areas of the South wastelands of despair, poverty and prejudice. Newspapering in these areas is a profession used more to brainwash readership in ways of hatred and prejudice than to revive democracy. Inescapably, if not directly, the white editor has become a backer of the Ku Klux Klan and the White Citizens Council, yet he is a symbol of the free press. Freedom of the press in certain areas of the South is a joke; a cancer has spread throughout the profession. I hope present-day journalism will have a role in remaking of a New South, if Negroes use their influence politically and financially.

A friend of mine often discusses the stereotyped practices of the Southern liberal editors—those who, oft-quoted in the press, are supposedly typical of Dixie journalists. While visiting a southern town, he telephoned the local editor, a former schoolmate, at his office. "Glad to hear from you," said the editor, "Why don't you drop over to see us at home tonight. But come after dark. You know how it is down here."

I remember traveling to a southern city to gather information for a magazine story about a liberal white lawyer. Everything ran smoothly, and the lawyer even invited some white friends to dinner at his home to meet me. The shades were down and the men talked freely—off the record. When the article appeared in the magazine, the lawyer placed an advertisement in a city newspaper, announcing that some of his views had been misquoted.

Another distressing lack of conviction demonstrated by the communications industry concerns the hiring of Negroes. When James Hagerty, former White House press secretary, became news chief for a national television network, he received considerable publicity from an announcement that he was searching for qualified Negro staffers. After conducting a nationwide hunt, in which scores of applicants were interviewed, he finally came up with two, whom he called the cream of the crop. One was assigned to New York City to cover the United Nations while another went to the network station in Washington. In a matter of months, the Negro in Washington had washed out, and the Negro cause was set back, because the pioneer had few qualifications for the post. Few realized that the main concern of the network was to get cream-colored individuals, so that the vast TV audience wouldn't know for sure the men were Negroes; a ticklish problem thus could be averted.

In recent months, the Negro has gained more mention in the press, books, radio and television than ever before. Because images of the Negro have ranged from criminal to agitator, whites in America may wonder how on earth he can ask the right to sit down in a restaurant. Through the years, the communities have been unprepared—their niggertowns seem to have gone mad. Many editors are now discarding the past and groping honestly with this country's racial problems.

Negroes who wish to work as reporters on the daily press must prove they are not militants or NAACP crusaders. "We want reporters," the editors say, "not publicity agents for the radical Negroes." Years ago, a similar controversy raged over whether a member of the American Newspaper Guild could cover business fairly. The press management is so afraid of hiring Negroes who might be outspoken that it has developed a new pimple-raiser. "Negroes get emotional on civil rights," said an editor, "they can't cover any views but those of their own people." Such fears have resulted in few Negroes being able to garner jobs in the communications industry. The quota is small.

The consequence of this discrimination is that the literary Negro, one able to articulate honestly and objectively, has been forced to seek other employment. There is a dearth of Negro writers, not because they lack capability, but because they have been denied opportunities on the newspapers and the magazines. For a long period, therefore, the views and opinions of only a handful of Negroes have been known to Americans.

One of these days, the Negro press will be out of business. But it won't be for a generation or so. Upper-class Negroes look askance at the motley collection of news and advertisements in Negro publications. The Negro press, therefore, is turning to the middle and lower classes for support and patronage. It will continue to try to be the voice of the people inhabiting the ghettos in the cities with the poorest housing and the menial jobs. As long as the voice is strident, clear and militant, its function will be valued.

The changing of roles, is perhaps most difficult for prosperous Negro publishers. They must embark on an effective program of good, solid journalism. The Negro press formerly operated on a national basis. Newspapers were distributed from coast to coast; they boasted wide circulation, talented staffs and fluent editorial writers. Even the major civil-rights leaders consulted with the publishers before launching a national campaign, because it was the Negro press which provided background for the activities, covered them, publicized them and reached the masses. The Negro press set the pace; it was virtually the sole channel of communication during the bleak years. Even without advertisements (many companies deliberately chose not to advertise in Negro publications because they feared any expansion of militancy), the Negro press grew big, strong and articulate. It was the only mouthpiece to Negroes who patiently waited for a weekly newspaper to "find out what *really* went on," after scanning the daily press.

The Negro press deserves a lion's share of credit for its contribution to Negro advancement in America. Its editors railed and protested against injustice when other media were silent; its reporters searched out stories of discrimination and deprivation ignored by our colleagues. "All mouth," a reader once told me, "All civil rights. Hell, I can't even get the weather from your paper."

But that was the way it was. Civil rights was the sole subject of our Negro beat. In between a spicy divorce or crime story to sell the organ, we headlined notorious examples of discrimination. Consistently, regularly, our press smacked at the hypocrites, swore at the Dixiecrat, frequently lambasted the white liberals. An expert once attributed the role of a "straw boss" to the Negro press because it maintained a policy of militancy and aggression, while at the same time it debunked the conservatives, the moderates, the gradualists. It set the pace with its editorial view. There were setbacks, of course.

During World War II, a Negro newspaper led the drive for Army integration. When Negroes were rustled from engineer divisions to prepare for front-line duty, the GI's raised hell. Many argued that the editors should be trained for the infantry "if they wanted to die as soldiers."

Keeping vibrant the Negro's toughness and courage was a thankless role. Whites generally referred to the Negro press as "trash" and "gossip sheets," but they never got the message; they never understood its role. The press boasted editors who could easily rank in America's Hall of Fame. One in particular, Harvard-trained Carl Murphy, for years editor of the Baltimore *Afro-American* newspaper chain, was a shrewd, bold chief who assigned staff men to major stories in every part of the country. Fearless and uncompromising, Murphy developed many topflight Negro reporters who later moved into the ranks of daily journalism. They included Carl Rowan, now director of the USIA, and William Brower, long-time reporter on the Toledo *Blade*. The *Afro-American* became a symbol of aggressive journalism, and during World War II, some prominent government officials reportedly sought to halt its publication because of its unending fight against discrimination.

Any civil-rights explosion in the South was a homecoming for the finest in the Negro press. Reporters converged on the trouble spot, knowing that they could expect little protection from police. But they reported the news without benefit of risk insurance or even an editor's blessing. One of the bravest men who ever roamed the news front was the late Alex Wilson, a reporter for the Chicago *Defender* chain.

A tall, gangling man, Wilson gained international recognition when he covered the Little Rock school crisis. Moving onto the scene when the Negro children entered Central High School, Wilson was attacked by a mob of whites. During the melee, his hat fell off. When he stooped to retrieve his hat, he was kicked from behind. This occurred five or six times, but Wilson refused to run or walk without his hat on. In the midst of the turmoil a photographer snapped a picture of him that was used by newspapers throughout the world. "Never be afraid around hoodlums," Wilson told his fellow scribes after the incident, "I haven't learned to run away." Several years later, he died from what friends say were injuries received during this experience.

As the civil-rights era wore on, the clamor for integration and the broadening horizon of opportunity changed the picture. The powerful Negro newspapers bowed from the national market and turned their attention to the immediate regions or cities. The magazines *Ebony* and *Jet* took over the responsibility of informing the Negro people of the national scene. The catalyst for this shift of emphasis was a broadening base of operations, which found the Negro press unable to keep up with the fastbreaking and spreading civil-rights activities. Along with the NAACP and the Urban League, the Negro newspapers, champions through the dark ages, found themselves no longer in the driver's seat, no longer the generals. Staffs were too small and untrained, and more and more the daily press moved in to cover the national civil-rights stories, leaving the Negro papers with the mopping-up operations. "We couldn't change gears," an editor told me. "We've already worn out our staff. We'd burn out the engines if we kept up the tremendous pace. We just had to re-evaluate our program."

The increasing complexities of the metropolis have precipitated the biggest crisis for the Negro press. Its long history has been dotted with courageous men and women who covered the big civil-rights stories, but no assignment has been as demanding as that now required for first-rate metropolitan coverage. The problems of urban Negroes include employment, housing, welfare, unemployment compensation and health—all areas demanding high technical knowledge and skill in interpretation. To augment the strong citizenship requirement of what is called the "New Negro," our press must focus attention on opportunities for more training to secure better employment, ways to teach migrant families how to use facilities of the city, campaigns to influence city officials to develop constructive relief programs (so that our people will not constantly remain on the dole) and projects to improve health and educational facilities in our areas. These are not the spectacular, sensational stories which sell newspapers, but they will make the press useful in the years to come. More than any other institution, the Negro press has the function of bringing lower-class families into the upper strata of civilization.

Can the Negro press accomplish this job? Time will tell, but the trend toward performing more service for the communities is moving slowly, too slowly to keep up with the pace of the social explosion. Among editorial circles there is an argument over whether the press should be geared to entertainment or to service, whether it should focus on the exotic life of stars, personalities, society queens and cultists, or whether the emphasis should be aimed more toward uplift projects, self-improvement and educational campaigns and inspirational stories to revive our discouraged populace. The decision is not an either-or proposition; we have to do both, but there must be enough service endeavors to make an impact. The "gut" issues of Negro survival must be tested. Lack of sufficient programming is enough for some critics to accuse the Negro press of exploiting their communities. In Cleveland, white pastor John Bruere charged that the Negro paper, the *Call and Post,* "inflamed racial prejudice and ran unscrupulous religious advertisements." On a radio program, he said the paper carried ads in which "religious adventurers offered to evict demons from people's innards—in return for donations—and which even offered lucky numbers for people to gamble on so that they could pay off their debts." Joining in the attack was Negro Councilman Leo Jackson, who in a speech on the Cleveland City Council floor, charged that the newspaper "resulted in the fleecing of many poor and ignorant Negroes." Later, the newspaper publisher, William O. Walker, first Negro named Ohio Industrial Relations Director, a state cabinet post, denied the charges and showed that the newspaper had campaigned for many worthwhile causes.

It also could have been pointed out that in years past, many downtown stores and major industries had refused to advertise in the Negro press. Financial income has stemmed more from circulation than from advertising. Now that the first civil-rights battles are over, an improvement in the relationship with downtown business would help the Negro press meet its budget and hire more qualified staff people. The mopping-up phase will be vexing, but teamwork with the Negro press will help cities handle the new problems of realignment of a disadvantaged people. Many businessmen, as part of the power structure, have been reluctant to advertise in the Negro press because of their desire not to be involved in any militant struggle, possibly directed against themselves. A change in attitude among the businessmen and among the officials of press associations and journalism schools would send a fresh breeze into the ranks of the Negro newspapers and encourage them to continue along the road to winning eventual freedom for every Negro.

# ★ ★ ★ 11 Mississippi

"In Mississippi, the face of Christ on the Cross resembles Hitler. Christianity is as impoverished as the people. Get the hell out of here before you become a Communist."

These lines on note paper stand out as a grim reminder of past trips to Mississippi, usually to investigate a murder of a civil-rights hero, spokesman or a Negro who stood up for his rights. The pattern was always the same—a finding of justifiable homicide or accidental or suspicious death. I can remember no action in any case that brought a conviction, but the words of a sheriff still burn in my ear, "Get the damn corpse in the ground before we beat some nigger's ass." Mississippi is still that brutal.

Any Negro traveling to the state is suspect and can be accused of being an extremist or an agitator. The procedure is to arrest a man for a traffic violation (always far-fetched, yet a charge you can't argue about) and haul him off to a justice of the peace, the sheriff or jail. From there on it's barbaric. Typical is this case publicized in 1963 by the Mississippi Advisory Committee to the United States Commission on Civil Rights:

On . . . about 11:30 a.m., I . . . was trailed about 3 miles by a highway patrolman, immediately after leaving . . . knowing that I was being followed, I took extreme caution in my driving.

When the officer decided to stop me he blew his siren, and I pulled to the side of the road and stopped.

At this point the officer got out of his car, walked to the rear of my car and demanded that my friend remain in the car and I come to the rear. When I approached the officer he asked me for my license. As I began looking through my belongings for my licence, I asked the officer what were the charges, the officer replied, "Nigger you keep your damn mouth shut, I'll ask the questions." At which time the officer raised his blackjack and began hitting me on the head and the shoulders. In an attempt to protect myself from him, I threw my arms up. The officer, still trying to hit me on the head, demanded that "you move them damn arms, boy, move them, God damn it."

Because I did not move my arms from around my head, the officer drew his gun and declared, "Damn you, nigger, I'm going to kill you." I begged him not to shoot me, and he told me to "Shut up nigger" and hit me, with his gun on me, declared, "I will make you move them arms, nigger, put your arms out here" at which time he handcuffed me and hit me several more times, pushed me to the side of his car, opened the door, pushed me in, hit me on the head and told me to "Sit there you black b—— and shut up." The officer then walked over to my car, where my friend was sitting. With his pistol in his hand, he pulled the door open and demanded that he get out and get in the car. When the officer got in his car, I informed him that I had dropped my wallet, and asked him could I get it. At that moment, again he began hitting me as he was saying, "I thought I told you to shut your damn mouth." "Move your hands, you damn nigger, God damn it, I'm going to kill you." After he had finished beating me, he placed his gun under his left leg and proceeded to drive.

On our way to the police station he asked me "Where were you going, boy?" I told him we were just riding. Then he asked me "What are going this way for, boy?" I told him I had planned to visit some friends, where he said, "You are telling me a damn lie, boy" and then asked my friend where he was going. My friend said he just came along with me, then the officer asked "You mean you just go along with people, without knowing where in the hell you are going?" In reply my friend said, "He is my friend—I don't have to ask him where he is going; if he was a stranger I would have."

When we reached the station he demanded us to get out of the car and head for those two doors on the right, he was walking behind us. Upon entering the building, he demanded my friend to sit down in the hall and continued to trail me into the clerk's office.

Before we had reached the center of the room he began hitting me with his blackjack on my head and arms, as he was saying "Boy, I am going to kill you," "this damn nigger scratched me," "I'm going to kill this nigger."

There were eight or nine other men in the room, and I pleaded with them to stop him from hitting me, but not a one said a word, as the officer continued his inhuman attack.

When the officer did stop, I asked to use the phone and was told by the officer, "You ain't using nothing." The desk clerk, wearing glasses, took a leather strap out of a drawer (A brown strap about 4 or 5 inches wide and about 2½ or 3 feet long) and said, "Let's take him down." When my friend got up to come along, he was told to stay there.

The officer that brought me in, the desk clerk, with the glasses on, the warner [sic] and two other men escorted me to a little room in the building where the cells were.

With the five men standing around me the clerk said, "Drop your pants, nigger." I did as he said, and some of the other men began instructing me how to lay across a chair. My hands were handcuffed around the foot of the chair as I lay across the back of it.

After I was in a position to please them the clerk said, "If you holler, nigger, we will kill you." The officer said "Nigger, we are going to tear your a—off," and hit me again on the head with his blackjack. As all of them took turns beating me with the strap I could hear statements as, "Let's kill this nigger," "This nigger knows what he has done wrong—a nigger going to hit an officer."

This beating continued while two men held my legs and one my hands.

The officer asked the jailer did he have anything to keep me from swelling? In reply the jailer stated he had some whiskey and poured some over my back and legs.

During that time the clerk said, "Get up nigger, you are lucky you are not dead." As the other men began leaving the room, the officer said, "What is your name, nigger?" When I told him my name, he said "Wipe the whiskey on your a—nigger and pull your pants up."

After I had dressed, the jailer carried me to a cell. I again asked to use the telephone, but he said, "No, not now, maybe later."

During my 28½ hours in jail I asked the jailer four times, each time he brought my meals, to let me use the phone, and he said, "Later."

Eluding law-enforcers is more of a challenge for a law-abiding Negro citizen than it is for a white violator. Negroes wear chauffeur caps and sit in the front seats of cars to give the impression of being "Mr. Charlie's boy." Prominent Negroes travel at night to escape harassment. Negro women are used as spokesmen for detained groups because they hold charm for southern officers. All this is public knowledge in Mississippi, and Federal authorities have long been aware of the conditions.

Mississippi could easily rank with South Africa, Angola or Nazi Germany for brutality and hatred. The average American has no idea of what life is like for Negroes in Mississippi, Alabama, parts of Georgia, South Carolina, northern Florida and Louisiana. American newsmen travel to Haiti, Cuba and other global dictatorships and write gripping stories of fear, terror and hate, but few go into these Deep South states and picture the Negro's existence.

Having lived in the North all my life, I was impressed when I first visited Mississippi in 1955 as a reporter to cover the opening of a vote registration drive. A mass meeting in all-Negro Mound Bayou featured Congressman Charles C. Diggs and attracted some 13,000 Negroes from the Delta area. It was a camp meeting, a big production for a Mississippi Negro group headed by Dr. T. R. M. Howard, a colorful physician with a booming voice.

One of the most unusual men at the meeting was the Reverend George W. Lee, a tan-skinned, stumpy spellbinder. "Pray not for your mom and pop," he urged the crowd, "They've gone to heaven. Pray you can make it through this hell." A religious powerhouse, Lee pastored four churches in a nearby county, operated a grocery store and a printing shop. Unlike his brethren, he preached well beyond the range of the Bible and Heaven and the Glory Road. As one of the vice presidents of the Mississippi Council of Negro Leadership and a member of the NAACP, he sermonized about voting and eventually electing a Negro congressman —an idea that caused whites to fear such a political triumph because of the predominant Negro population.

"Do you believe you can elect a Negro?" I asked Lee. "Some day," he said. "Maybe my grandchildren will. But Negroes in Mississippi, and white folks in Mississippi, need something big to shoot at or they don't get excited."

Backslapping the Delta farmers and giving each a sample of his fiery civil-rights message, Lee electrified crowds with his down-home dialogue and his sense of political timing. Flying back to Chicago to write my first dispatch, I thought of the eventual political future in Mississippi. Someday enough Negroes would be aroused to register and vote. Lee had the Christian principle of helping his fellow man and seemed to do wonders with the cotton farmers, many of whom didn't seem informed on national affairs.

My image of Mississippi faltered several weeks later, and this article appeared in the *New Leader* under my byline:

Near midnight on May 7, 1955, the Reverend George W. Lee was driving home in Belzoni, Mississippi. He had just gotten his pressed pants from a tailor shop in readiness for preaching Sunday. As he drove along Church Street, nearing the Negro ghetto, a convertible pulled up beside him. There was a shot, then a second shot. Reverend Lee's car spun crazily from the dirt street, swerved across a walk and crashed into a shanty house, knocking the structure from its foundation and almost scaring to death the occupant, midwife Katherine Blair.

His face partially blown off, Reverend Lee groped from his wrecked car and staggered blindly. Two Negro taxicab drivers ran to him and helped him into their cab. He died on the way to the hospital.

Called to investigate, Belzoni Sheriff Ike Shelton took one look at the lifeless body and pronounced the death due to a concussion from the traffic accident. But widow Lulu was not so sure. Despite Sheriff Shelton's attempts to persuade her to turn the body over to a Negro funeral home without the benefit of an autopsy, Mrs. Lee summoned two of her husband's best friends, Dr. C. C. Battle, a 28-year-old Indianola physician and Dr. Cyrus Walden, a Yazoo City surgeon. Their examination disclosed a number of lead pellets about the minister's face and head. One shot had passed through the neck at the throat, accounting for the fact that the minister was unable to talk en route to the hospital.

Meanwhile, since Belzoni telephone operators found it necessary to inform would-be Negro customers that all long distance lines were tied up, certain Negro leaders decided that the best way to break the news blackout was to organize expeditions to distant places. They agreed to send a carload of citizens to Dr. T. R. M. Howard in Mound Bayou, and to Dr. A. H. McCoy, state president of the NAACP in Jackson.

Shocked at the news, Dr. Howard immediately telephoned Detroit Congressman Charles C. Diggs (who two weeks before had addressed a 13,000-person Council meeting in Mound Bayou which was attended by Reverend Lee). Diggs notified the White House as did the New York NAACP office, which Dr. McCoy had contacted. Later Dr. McCoy, after making a probe of the death car and finding lead pellets in a front tire, asked Mississippi Governor Hugh White to order an investigation of the killing. He was informed that the Governor "pays no attention to NAACP requests."

As a result of the national publicity given to what he and Dixie dailies reported originally as a "freak accident," Sheriff Shelton decided to send the gathered evidence to the Federal Bureau of Investigation laboratory. The autopsy report came back several days later. The conclusion: death from a hemorrhage and asphyxiation, evidence of lead pellets. Taken aback by his error, the sheriff theorized that Reverend Lee, being a "ladies man," was probably killed by a rival. Painfully, however, he ordered a new investigation—Mississippi style.

"Reverend Lee was a warrior," charged Dr. Howard. "And he was murdered because he refused to put down his arms in this civil-rights battle. He was murdered because there are people in this state who oppose our having every advantage of citizenship. Reverend Lee died not as a cringing coward but as a hero. His death will be long remembered in this Delta land. He did not die in vain."

The funeral of the Reverend George W. Lee, held in Belzoni, was the turning point. I sat with wet-eyed cotton farmers, with whom I had one thing in common: we all wore old clothes and unshined shoes—but mine were to conceal my identity. What intrigued me was that most of the Mississippi Negroes believed that they were inferior, that they should have inferior schools, that the white man should rule them, that they were still slaves. Even at the funeral, I heard Negroes whisper, "Reverend Lee did wrong. He shouldn't have tried to go against the white man."

There were the tears and the beautiful singing—always the hallmark of a struggle and pain—but there also were whispered expressions, such as "Lord, I'm glad Reverend Lee's gone. He done got this white man evil." I became very discouraged at what I thought was a promising civil-rights campaign.

It was fairly evident to me that the white man was supreme in Mississippi—and this was the first time I ever believed it. I thought the stories and reports of white supremacy were tomfoolery. At the funeral a white detective walked through the crowd without touching a soul. A pathway opened automatically as if the Negroes, even with their backs turned, could feel the presence of an approaching white man. Not a Mississippi Negro would look a white man in his eye. The eyes were always shifting, voices quivering and faces trembling. "Yas sah, boss," they readily responded. Even when one of the militant Negroes talked with a confident tone, the appearance of a white man drastically reduced his word output and degree of fluency. This fear reached every Negro, even little children. A friend told me how 6- and 7-year-old Negro children would jump to their feet at school when the superintendent or any other white visitor came into their room. The Negro community was a hodgepodge of schoolteachers, ministers, a few businessmen and cotton farmers (the predominant occupational group in the Delta). The schoolteachers were ineffective, many being too frightened even to join organizations. The ministers stomped, shouted about Heaven and ate chicken dinners on Sunday. Few of the business people became involved in civil rights because of the fear of reprisals from downtown forces. The cotton farmers, a tough, hardy lot, were the backbone of the Delta. But some of these muscular men shook at the thought of walking into a county building and saying, "I want to vote." I knew of a family that had considerable real estate, but the mother refused to buy a family car for fear one of her sons would be arrested and hurt by police for nothing.

The fear of the white man was not unfounded. These Negroes knew of the cruelties, the lynchings and killings even of members of their own families. There was no court of law, no justice, no policing, not even a minimum standard of decency. What counted was skin color, and justice was dispensed in varying degrees based on color. Thus, a full black had no rights and little reason to live in Mississippi. A light-skinned Negro always had contacts—his white parent and relatives.

There was a lethargy among Negroes that I couldn't understand, except that they just didn't give a damn about freedom or had been brainwashed over centuries of deprivation. The murderers of the Reverend George W. Lee were never found; in fact, I don't think law-enforcers even tried to find them. Few Negroes could appreciate the significance of a government standing idly by as a minister was killed by mob action for attempting to carry out his rights. The refusal of the local, state and Federal officials to seek justice in this case mirrored the hypocrisy of democracy in the South. The first doctor on the scene, Dr. Clinton Battle, told me how a Mississippi-born FBI agent laughed so much in his face in his Belzoni office that he had to be given sedatives. He laughed because Dr. Battle said he expected the FBI to find the killers. Even now, Dr. Battle, an exile from Mississippi, says, "I shall never forget the night of the slaying of the Reverend George W. Lee. When I located metal fragments in the minister's neck, the chief of police stated that the metal was dental fillings. The FBI reported the metal as No. 3 buckshot from a sawed-off shotgun."

In the intervening years, many leaders in the Mississippi civil-rights movement were killed or chased from the state by mob action, while not a Federal department or agency did much to stem the angry tide. The civil-rights movement grew, and more Negroes started revolting, protesting and challenging their way of life. This is the untold story of the ferment in Mississippi. It is untold because the freedom fighters were Negro, and they fought the Establishment in Mississippi, which used racial terror as a weapon inside the state and public relations tactics outside.

Firearms, protection and security are ingredients of a successful civil-rights program in Mississippi, as they are in many other sections of the Deep South. The Negro social reformer must defend himself, because he has no protection from police, sheriffs or state troopers. He must be ready to die at any moment. Some have died in the first century of American freedom, hunted down and killed like squirrels on a hunt. The reason many more Negro civil-righters are not killed is because they are armed to defend themselves and their families. In recent years the government has seen fit to move into the picture.

A good example of the security was that employed by Dr. Howard, the outspoken civil-rights leader who lived in all-Negro Mound Bayou. A prosperous physician and director of a hospital, Dr. Howard owned a beautiful farm home with a staff of servants, chauffeurs and farm workers. Because of his civil-rights activities, he was forced to keep armed guards at his home and to travel with an armed chauffeur. He also maintained a cache of rifles and pistols. Dr. Howard carried a pistol strapped to his waist, and even Negroes who went near the physician were frequently searched. His security program was a model of dispatch and efficiency.

When Dr. Howard first went to Mississippi and established a hospital in the Delta, newsmen wrote articles on his project and cited the physician as an amazing medical man. However, when Dr. Howard became outspoken in civil rights, the same newspapers described him as an extremist and an agitator.

As Dr. Howard developed a reputation for organizing Negroes in the state, he became hated and received anonymous threatening letters, telephone calls and personal accusations. Banks, savings and loan firms and businessmen pressed him for immediate payment of bills or loans. He was harassed by health inspectors and county agents. His wife and child were constantly exposed to tension and terror. But for a decade Dr. Howard stood his ground, outspoken, fearless and cunning. He awakened many Negroes to a future in Mississippi—if there was co-operation and a sustained fight.

One of the remarkable attributes of "Doc" Howard was his ability to inspire the Delta folk. He frequently told about the Mississippi farmer who was charged 25 cents for a suburban phone call in New York and complained to the operator that he "could call hell and back for that price in his state." Snapped the operator, "Well, that's a local call." I can remember him telling the joke about a dark-skinned foreigner walking into a Jackson, Mississippi cafeteria and being told by a waitress that they didn't serve Negroes. Said he, "I don't eat Negroes." Or I can see the tall, broad-shouldered physician with his arm around a Delta mother, "Sis Lou, you're a mighty healthy woman to raise some eight kids."

These qualities made Dr. Howard a sectional hero, and with his surgical skills, he became part of the Delta's folklore. When Emmett Till, a Chicago youngster, was slain while visiting his grandparents in Money, Mississippi in 1955, Dr. Howard proved his worth. For one reason or another, the State had found no witnesses to the slaying and had no knowledge of the site of the murder. On the first day of the trial, a Negro plantation worker walked and rode some 80 miles to Dr. Howard's house and in his front room told him a harrowing story: Three or four Negroes had seen the boy, tied up in the back of a truck, being hauled into a barn on a particular plantation. Later they heard the boy scream in agony, then saw the truck come back out of the barn. A Negro helper was on the back of the truck. All of these individuals were available.

Excited by the news, Howard called in eight reporters, including four whites, to tell them about the development. Although the reporters had agreed that they would not write the articles for a day, to allow sheriffs to investigate, one of them tipped off someone at the plantation where Till had been seen, and several of the Negroes were not found until after the trial. Two witnesses, Mandy Bradley and Willie Reed, were located and testified at the trial, but the all-white jury, after a round of cola, freed the two defendants in record time.

Years later, a white minister in a small Mississippi town told me the story of the Till boy's murder. One of the murderers, who lived in his town, got drunk one evening and told a deacon what happened, episode by episode. Late one night four whites had kidnapped Till at gunpoint from his grandfather's farmhouse. He was beaten and shot to death. They then tied his body to the wheel of a cotton gin and dumped it into a nearby river. The account spread rapidly throughout the state. Police knew what had happened, but according to unwritten law, there is no penalty for a Negro death. This has been the law of the jungle in Mississippi since Reconstruction. While I was traveling to another Mississippi town to probe the death of a Negro principal, a white man, evidently mistaking me for a member of his race, said, "Why is everybody so concerned with the death of this nigger. Hell, they just pulled a nigger body from the river yesterday, and no one even claimed the body. His head had been smashed in."

Dr. Howard's intervention in the Till murder case, coupled with his exposé of conditions, alarmed white officials, and they openly sought to chase him from the State. The harassment increased. Damage suits were filed against him by business firms and Negroes, all to be heard by prejudiced judges. The state had openly established a committee, employing agents and Negro informers to gather information for war on the civil-rights fighters. Phones were tapped and police distributed bulletins on civil-rights leaders as if they were "wanted—dead or alive." On speaking missions in the North, Dr. Howard blasted Dixie white supremacy and kept the state in the headlines.

Mississippi Negroes—at that time—were fearful. But when the freedom fighters launched their remarkable campaign, the Negroes of Mississippi began to defy the white supremacists. They started protesting the brutality and asking why they couldn't vote.

They began to point out Uncle Toms. They started attending civil-rights meetings and listening to the speakers. They learned that the Negro was on the march in every state except Mississippi, and they became angry. A social revolution was taking place.

In a few months, a civil-rights network covered Mississippi.

There were no areas in which Negroes could be attacked, assaulted or killed without someone learning about it and reporting to a central headquarters. Once the report was made, investigators moved in to gather the facts and telephone them to Northern Negro newspapers and United States authorities. The constant publicity kept Negroes aroused and ready to contribute to causes in Mississippi; it kept the freedom fighters confident. It kept bigoted officials on the hot seat.

Then misfortune came. The pressures had destroyed the tranquility of the Howard household, and Mrs. Howard was a nervous wreck. Howard had been warned he had a $1,000 price on his head. Said Dr. Howard, "I feel I can do more alive in the battle for Negro rights in the North than dead in a weed-grown grave in Dixie." Losing some $100,000 in disposing of his properties, Dr. Howard moved to Chicago, where he established a practice on the city's South Side.

But Dr. Howard's strong image remained to agitate the Delta land. Many cotton farmers had heard the message, and the territory was in ferment. The NAACP was sponsoring vote clinics in the heart of many Negro counties, training scores of sharecroppers to pass voting tests. In one class, held at night in a lonely farm house, approximately 125 persons showed up. One individual commented, "When I get on the voting list, it'll be the happiest moment of my life."

Typical of the new voting recruits was middle-aged Jodie Glenn, a Minner City farmer. Because of his father's deathbed wish that he "not stir up white folks" and lose the family's 40-acre farm, he had never tried to vote. Now, accompanied by his brother, Jessie, he walked into the Leflore County Courthouse in Greenwood and attempted to register. Several days later, a white delegation visited his home and hinted violence if he insisted on voting. Retorted Glenn: "I want to become an American citizen, and I'm not afraid."

Such courage was widespread in Mississippi despite the terror, the intimidation, the financial pressure and even death. As scores of prominent Negro leaders fled for their lives from the state, others quietly took over the leadership, despite the penalties. In Vicksburg, undertaker George Jefferson, because he signed a NAACP school-integration petition, was denied loans for a $200,000 housing project. In Yazoo City, the Reverend Thomas Allen bought four tires on credit from a white dealer. When it was discovered that he was a militant Negro, the dealer jacked up the car and took the tires. When Jackson postman James A. White refused to halt his work with the Progressive Voters League, creditors demanded immediate payment of all his bills. One leader was pulled from his car by a sheriff and told, "You're just a nigger despite this car. You ain't got any more rights than a field hand." Violence was everywhere and many incidents were not reported. In Cleveland, Mississippi whites burned a Baptist church because its minister, the Reverend E. C. Smith, allowed the NAACP to meet there. (The White Citizens Council met in the United States Courthouse). In place of the spasmodic Negro killings, a wave of "legalized violence" began, waged by law enforcers who beat Negroes at will. A young college student in Cleveland was clubbed by a cop because he was standing in the doorway of a home and didn't move fast enough. The courts provided little protection. Lawyers turned down cases when the only witnesses were Negro and the opponent was white. "A Negro's word in court means nothing compared to a white person's."

Against this backdrop of terror and intimidation, Negro freedom fighters turned courage into dividends and began to topple a racially corrupt state. One of the biggest worries of Negroes was the fear of friends turning over to state officials confidential information about militant groups. As a result, photos of delegates and membership and financial records were banned at NAACP state meetings. There were setbacks because of "sell-outs." At a top-level meeting in Jackson to plot a bus-integration suit, it was agreed that two college students would board a certain bus at a certain time and place. At the given time, the bus failed to show up, and two white cops patrolled the area. The "testers" could easily figure that one of the five Negro leaders had tipped off the whites. There was a constant tug of war between paid Negro agents of the state groups and informers for the police, as they sought to worm into the confines of the Negro operation, touching off intrigues and counterintrigues. One of the quickest ways to eliminate a suspected informer was to have an NAACP membership card sent to his work address. Delivery always brought a request for an explanation, and invariably suspicion between employer and the Negro developed. In another city, a Negro minister who was anti-integration in his views and who used his influence to fight the NAACP, became exceedingly powerful in halting the tide of liberalism. It was agreed that Negroes would have to know and understand him better and possibly develop a new religious leader to offset the effects of his attitude. Cards for an NAACP meeting at his church were sent out, although no meeting had been scheduled and the minister was not an NAACP member. The minister thus was forced to make a statement in the white press that no meeting was scheduled and that he didn't believe in the NAACP. As a result he lost face with the Negroes.

In the 1950's most of the Negroes backing civil rights were in the low-income levels, except for a few independent leaders. Most professionals would have nothing to do with the crusade. When I covered a lynching in a certain city a very prominent family, which owned drug stores, shops and a business building, refused to allow a photographer and me to stay in its home. The family claimed that it "couldn't get involved in civil-rights fights." "Why?" I asked. "You can't win," one of the brothers, a doctor, replied, "Too many whites. Go along with them." Many other professionals in Mississippi and in the Dixie Black Belt ignored the call of the crusade. "Teach the lowly how to keep clean," one said, "and you'll do more in a year than in raising all of this hell in fifty years." "We've been living well," said a principal, "We've had peace. Why start agitating?"

But the surge of the sit-ins, African independence and the emergence of youth served to challenge the Negro conservatives and practically remove them from positions of power within their community. This is the great transition in Mississippi, which for years contained the peaceful Negro giant. Now he is aroused, in Mississippi and in the other Deep South states.

From fear to courage, from cowardice to awareness has been the path of the Negro in Mississippi, but he is a long way from the promised land. Restrictions on voting keep political strength at a low ebb. In two years, civil-rights organizations reported more than fifty incidents involving attacks of vote registration workers, would-be voters, or militant Negroes. Numerous shotgun assaults and dynamiting of homes occurred.

Yet while Mississippi whites openly rant at the thought of integration, the "twilight mixing" in the state is disgraceful. In many cities, Negro women complain that they face open courting on streets from white men, but there is no means of appeal for relief. In one city, a mayor's son contracted VD. As a result, a Negro house of prostitution that catered to whites was shuttered. Many Mississippi towns have imposed an 11 p.m. curfew, which is enforced in a way to keep Negroes off the street after dark. Throughout the state, there is criticism of Negro schools. Classroom populations in many areas are as high as seventy pupils, with several grades in the same room. There is always a shortage of supplies. Said one teacher: "A Negro high-school graduate here isn't equivalent to a sixth-grade student up North."

Mississippi whites walk the chalk line in opposing the slightest evidence of Negro progress. Said a Negro: "These peckerwoods have gone mad. Every white man in the state is deputized, while Negroes can't get bullets to go hunting. They act like the Union Army will be coming in soon."

The whites' fears were justified when troops were forced to move into the state to insure the enrollment of James Meredith as a student at the University of Mississippi in 1962. There was world-wide reporting on the rioting, including the two deaths, but few reporters stayed long enough to probe deeply. Most couldn't understand why a Negro was so interested in going to an institution at such an awesome cost. The point was that Meredith's enrollment was another step forward in an agonizing struggle.

Advances in Mississippi will come at the point of a gun or with a bashed-in head.

Almost a decade ago, a Negro school principal was mysteriously killed near Clarksdale, Mississippi. His body was found floating in a pool of water. Negroes whispered he was murdered because whites thought he was a member of the NAACP—it would be heresy for a Negro educator to accept employment from whites and then betray them by becoming a part of the civil-rights movement. There was little investigation of the case.

At a funeral home a few days later, I talked to his widow. "He's gone," she kept saying, "That's all I know. Somebody got him."

Shortly afterwards, a young, energetic Negro walked into the funeral home and stood silently next to the casket. He turned, saw the woman and me and came over.

"I'm Medgar Evers of the NAACP," he introduced himself.

"Lord, get him away!" the woman shouted, "I don't want to talk to him. I don't want him here. Get him out of here."

The widow was hysterical. She kept screaming, "Get him out of here. They got my husband killed, and now they're going to get me killed."

Evers was a new NAACP man in Mississippi. He had been assigned to investigate the case, but the widow's actions unnerved him. "Take it easy," I cautioned him, "The woman's angry, heartbroken and disgusted. It could be that her husband quietly worked with the NAACP."

From that baptism, Evers struggled to organize a civil-rights front. He investigated every racial crime. Although arrested several times, he refused to quit. He was easily the outstanding Negro crusader in the state—aggressive, uncompromising and ambitious. Negroes accepted him as their new leader. In June of 1963, Evers returned home after a round of conferences and was shot to death as he emerged from his car in the driveway. His body lay sprawled on the cement. His children stood in the doorway and watched as he tried to struggle to his feet.

The death angered Negro Americans more than any earlier Mississippi crime. The FBI snared a suspect and charged him with the killing. Instead of demoralizing Negroes in Mississippi, the wanton murder solidified them. No longer were they asking, "How long, oh God?" Negroes were itching for revenge, not in murders but with a growing number of new voters.

# ★ ★ ★ 12  Slums, Poverty and Crime

The Negro slum is a picturesque locale in literature. Authors and script-writers long have profited from stories of the ghetto; sociologists have won recognition from accounts of the human deterioration and rental and credit merchants have developed unrestricted trade.

For everyone else, the Negro ghetto is a money-maker, a launching pad for politics or business, a base for a notorious crime syndicate. Few Negroes make money out of segregation. In only five cities in America have Negroes harnessed the political power to elect a congressman. In many ghettos, Negro racketeers have lost control of their operations; most now work for the white kingpins of vice.

The Negro ghetto now stands as the last remaining vestige of mass exploitation, poverty and crime in America. In it, few Negroes have lifted their voices for reform. The residents are poor, hungry, tired and disillusioned. Fifteen years ago, as a young reporter, I moved into a slum section of Cleveland, Ohio, anxious to gather material for what I thought would be a novel. After experiencing two months of living in an old tenement house, patronizing cheap down-and-out eateries and huddling close to a pot-bellied stove in near-zero weather, I was ordered by a physician to move elsewhere. I had contracted pneumonia.

In that short period, three individuals stood out as the survivors of the slum. Here is what I wrote about them:

The street below Uncle Abe's window was his world—the only community he had known in the last 8 years, the only people he saw, the only landmarks he diagrammed in his mind with a carpenter's skill. He knew the big gray tenements with roofs that sagged in the middle because of age; the tavern across the street with the heavy, iron grating to keep drunks from breaking the glass; the high, pointed steeple of the church with one of the arms missing from the cross; the people, hard-faced and cold, trudging to and fro with lunch buckets or shopping bags—some with live chickens tucked under their arms for Sunday. From the simple details, Uncle Abe gained satisfaction that he was an authority on the section, like a wrinkled oracle, sitting high on a throne. He knew precisely little things, such as the days the garbagemen rolled their big white trucks down the street, leaving a trail of overturned cans along the curb; or insurance payment dates of collectors, who tramped the street with black books and talk of money for lavish funerals; or pay-days of muscled longshoremen who lived in the block, who would get drunk in the tavern, come outside, slugging one another, to end up sprawled on the church steps.

This was the end of the road for humanity, the section that turned nobody down because of a prison record, an illegitimate child, or a common-law wife. This was the outpost for families who trekked from the South for freedom; for the old people, who knew the dangers but had become resigned to the fate of never being able to leave; this was the section that was dominated completely by racketeers, gamblers and pimps, whose only standard of living was making money, lots of money in any fashion or form, driving big cars and running with pretty women. The odds that families could leave the section and preserve their decency were as high as chances for hitting policy numbers or winning money with loaded dice. After a few months of struggle, bad whiskey and inducements by dollar-a-week budget stores, families gave up—turning to symbols of success such as Buicks, television sets and fur coats. Instead of leaving the section, families then became prey for the notorious "Underground Railway," a bill-collection agency that hauled people into court when they missed a single payment, stripping them of the luxury items and selling the few possessions at public sale. Disillusioned, families became more desperate and their standards would drop, till they were finally and firmly gripped in the octopus of the neighborhood with its rent barons, chiseler merchants and credit taverns.

Uncle Abe knew that he would stay in the section throughout his remaining years on earth. Once he was big and strong, with a carpenter business, a house of his own, a garden and a car. He had been a deacon at the church, a voter and an upright citizen. Now he was poor, in bad health, a forgotten man in a forgotten area. There was no one to whom he could tell his troubles, no one from whom he could ask counsel. Sure, there were preachers, social workers and old-age pension people, but they were mechanical, heartless in their contacts. Fat preachers who drove around in shiny cars, taking huge hunks of poor people's money as a sort of railway fare to heaven. Moaning deacons and trustees drooping over bars at taverns on weekdays and crying on Sunday for the Lord to save them. Big-chested social workers who came marching into the section with books and charts, keeping records of the people as if they were guinea pigs, asking questions about how many times they went to bed with women, or had had VD, or gave birth to children. Pension people who deducted allotments because they said the governor wanted to have a surplus in the budget when he ran for re-election.

Consequently Uncle Abe was a cynical, stubborn, blustery old man, with his own queer doctrines of life; his philosophy was patched together from incidents of window watching, overhearing conversations, and reading the few newspapers he managed to get his hands on.

Rocking in his creaky chair by the window, Uncle Abe watched the children romp up the sidewalk on their way home from school. One extremely thin boy was chasing two girls who were outdistancing him, to the delight of the other children.

It made Uncle Abe happy to see children, and their laughter brightened his day. A few stragglers in front of the tavern were eying the full-bosomed high school girls. Occasionally, one of the girls would turn around and grin but keep on walking. A lot of the young girls had babies of their own.

Uncle Abe straightened in his chair as best he could, and bent over closer to the window. A car was pulling up in the parking space in front of the house. It was Turner's regular parking space, but his car was cream-colored with white-walled tires. This car was green and longer than Turner's. A colored man got out of the front seat and opened the rear door. A white lady holding a pair of funny glasses and wearing a brown suit emerged, and the two began walking toward the house. Instantly Uncle Abe began turning pages in his mental diary, trying to find some recollection of the two, but there was none. They were newcomers. They were strangers. They were bringing trouble to the neighborhood. Something was wrong, and Uncle Abe sensed it. He could tell by the knocks on the inside doors and the whining of the wooden floors. What did they want? The last white woman who came here was looking for a maid who had stolen a diamond ring and vanished. Afterwards, gangs of detectives and policemen came, searching every flat, turning over beds, jumbling drawers. The following day, the white woman found the ring in her bank vault. There weren't many visitors coming to Potato Flat, except television or used-car salesmen, bill collectors, or red-coated women selling Bibles.

The loose boards on the steps groaned, and Uncle Abe winced. The pair was climbing the stairs. When he was positive, he reached into the table drawer to make sure his gun was there. Meddlers, Uncle Abe rated them, just plain meddlers. When he heard the knock at his door, he braced his back against the worn leather chair, turned his head and waited, determined not to speak. With the second flurry of knocks, he scowled and cursed to himself, but he didn't answer.

There was a pause and Uncle Abe looked down at the street. When he turned around toward the door again, he gasped.

There was a black man, with a chauffeur's cap, standing inside his place a few feet from the door.

"Just a minute, buddy," he heard the man say, tiptoeing toward him. "I hate to interrupt your nap, but my boss lady wants to see how you people live. She's got a lot of money, buddy. Fat with dough."

Uncle Abe glinted his eyes. The man had a slick look in his face. He wore yellow shoes that flashed as much as his eyes.

"I ain't no trouble, partner," the man said, holding his hands out to show he didn't have a gun. "I just drive for the boss lady. I live around here, so I know the score. You know we colored folks got to stick together."

"What you want?"

"It's like this, partner. We read how you folks been beat over the head and busted down to size, and the boss lady, well— she's kind of het up. She wants to bruise a few of the big shots' knuckles for letting you folks get treated rough."

Uncle Abe wondered what he was talking about. Nobody had been beaten around here.

"Get me, pal," the man gently slapped Uncle Abe on the back, grinning from one end of his large mouth to the other, "Boss lady's kin to some important people across town. She come over on the Mayflower or Queen Mary, let me tell you."

"What's this all about? This house ain't on display."

"Sure, partner, I dig you perfectly. You ain't for a lot of mouth. You wants some foot lifting up and down. I get you perfectly. Tell you what. I'm gonna ask the boss lady to duck inside and see for herself." He leaned near Uncle Abe and whispered, "This place ain't bad as mine. You got bigger rooms."

"Now just a minute. . . ." But it was too late, the man had eased out of the flat.

There sure was a lot of attention on this particular house in the past few days, thought Uncle Abe. A lot of meddlers.

The colored man came back into the room, bowed low, swinging his hand down as if he was trying to show Uncle Abe the top of his hat. "This is Madame Lillian F. Franks. She wishes you to know that she is a friend and once made a trip to Africa."

Uncle Abe felt his heart skip a beat. The lady stood erect, holding the funny-looking glasses, which she set on her nose. She didn't bow down going through the door and almost struck her head.

"Positively disgusting," she said, with one glance about the bedroom. When she spied Uncle Abe in the rocking chair by the window, she said, "Excuse me, young man. I'm not referring to you."

Uncle Abe shook his head up and down.

"I'm chairman of the Housing Committee of the National Federation of Women's Auxiliaries. I'm so disturbed about what I read in the newspaper this afternoon, I just had to come over here."

"You folks rated the front-page piece in the paper today, partner," the colored man said, sitting down on Aunt Helen's valuable trunk, "Shows you got a lot of pull somewhere."

Uncle Abe bent his head sideways to hear better. "Ain't nothing bad?" he asked.

The white woman was wandering through the place as if she were some type of inspector. The colored man winked, "Same old stuff," he said, "only this cat that owns the place ain't paid off, and City Hall got a rope around his neck. The cat pulled down a few thousand profit in a couple years, and the boys downtown want their cut."

"Tom, ask him how many people live in this place."

Uncle Abe thought for a while. "Too many."

"He says they's people here from the basement to the rafters, sleeping on one another."

"Terrible," the white woman said. "We must pass a law outlawing such houses."

The man got off the trunk and came over to the window.

"Say, you know the number today? I got 82 cents on eighty-two."

Uncle Abe shook his head. The man was beginning to sound like a suspicious character.

"Ask him about sanitary facilities, Tom."

Uncle Abe kept shaking his head.

"Out of work," the colored man told her.

"Positively revolting in this century. Ask him how soon they're going to leave this house, Tom."

Uncle Abe lost his voice, but shook his head violently.

"Ain't leaving," he said stubbornly.

"He says he doesn't want to leave, madame."

The lady walked over to the rocker. "Sir, you do not know what is good for you. Tell him, Tom."

The colored man nodded his head.

"This is a horrible place for people to live. And imagine, the city's just getting around to tearing it down."

"I ain't leaving," Uncle Abe said determinedly, "You ain't making me leave."

"Tom, don't you know of some decent house where this man can live?"

The colored man nodded his head, "Right across the street from me there's a house with two rooms vacant."

"I ain't leaving."

She opened her pocketbook and held the glasses close to her eyes as she looked into the purse, "Tom, do you have a dollar bill?"

Winking at Uncle Abe, the man reached into his pockets and withdrew a bill. "Yes, ma'am," he answered.

"Give the gentleman the money, and I'll repay you later. We'd better leave now, Tom."

The lady went out, followed by the man. He stuck his head back into the doorway and said, "She got money, partner. I told you."

For what seemed like hours, Uncle Abe rocked by the window, letting the incident toss in his mind. The street lamps came on, and the men across the street by the tavern leaned against the posts and fences. Like the mouth of a giant fish,

the tavern door flicked open and shut. Turner had parked his
car, waved to him and come inside. The Johnson kids had
played in the street and come inside. The Fleming boy had
come home from college. In a little while, Aunt Helen would
be home and she would put him in bed—away from the violent
scenes of the night. He loved the day but hated the night, with
its darkness and shadows. Night was like a huge monster that
swamped the light of the sun, crawled down over the earth,
shutting off the brilliance and sparkle of day. Man, even with
his searchlights, neon lights, electric lights, hadn't outwhipped
night; it reminded Uncle Abe of the all-powerful disease of his
own case. Doctors blamed his crippledness on working too hard,
said his strength was used up and there could be no recovery.
Aunt Helen said it was because he didn't go to church and get
on his knees and pray to God. All Aunt Helen's prayers, all her
minister's prayers and all the church people's prayers for twenty
years hadn't helped. Through the years, Uncle Abe felt his
strength waning—felt himself getting weaker and weaker.

"You come out or I'll bash your head in," Potato said angrily
from his post atop the leaky stool in the cellar privy, "Can't an
old man sit down without being bothered. Can't an old man be
in peace once during the day." Potato panted like a tired old
dog, peering at the slit of smudge under the tub. "Come out
and I'll pound the daylights out of you, grind your head against
the rough boards, smear you into a yard-long stripe. Sick man
being agitated, sick man being bothered." Running along the
edge of the tub toward the rotten sideboard was a fat cockroach.

Potato bent over closer to the floor, watching the cockroach
run. Any other night at eight he'd be drinking wine at Joe's.
Now look at him. A shame when an old man gets stopped up
and got to take caster oil, milk of magnesia, mineral oil and
three sixes. Old man gets sick and there ain't no one to look
after him. An old man got to struggle along by himself, hoping,
figuring what comes next.

A privy ain't the best place for an old man to kick off in,

either. Not a privy with plaster suspended by dried-out wall-paper, and bugs peeping out of holes and water puddles all around. You got to cross your legs, smell stench from broken sewer pipes and see by a 20-watt bulb—not enough light to find Heaven, even see the chariots coming. A privy like this makes an old man see just how empty life is, how meaningless, how useless to struggle. A privy like this makes an old man downright sour and disgusted. But this privy is a lot better than most. Take the one in the tavern with the greenish colored stool and the tin can you got to pour water with to make the stool flush. Or the privy next door, which six families use, that's cracked down the middle and runs water all over the floor. Or the one at the settlement house that's got a white tub over the stool that leaks on you when you sit down. Potato Flat has a nice privy compared to many, and Potato Flat's a nice tene-ment compared to many. Potato Flat has been a kind, old place for an old man. Ain't many places where you don't have to pay rent and get a room to cook and sleep in. Ain't many places with a big pot-bellied stove which you can set next to your bed and lay your feet on in the winter. Ain't many places where you don't have a four-eyed landlady always sticking her nose in your room to see if you're sleeping with a light on or washing socks in the trash can.

And to think that the city's tearing down a place like Potato Flat because it's dirty and unfit for people to live in. Tearing down the cellar room and the privy. Potato groaned and got to figuring where he was going to live. What was he going to do? He had to start packing his stuff in the duffle bag and get out. Everybody had to get out. Turner and the Johnsons with the two bad kids, and the Flemings and Uncle Abe and Aunt Helen. Everybody had to get out. Scram! Just like the city says. Get out! Scram!

Where was Potato going? Not to the Salvation Army where the old men have to sing hymns before they can eat and have to listen to bands playing *Nearer My God to Thee* before they can go to bed. Not to the municipal flophouse either, where colored men are stuck in the dirtiest corner of the rambling house and given porter work during the day for meals.

Potato looked at the patched ceiling and saw a spider swing down from a dusty web, down the silked string, down, down, past the 20-watt bulb, down, down, and then the cockroach was racing toward the tub. That's right, Mr. Spider, you chase him out of here. The cockroach made it to the tub before the spider soared from his high vantage, and Potato leaned down, lower, lower. All at once, he felt his body moving forward. He tried to grab himself, grab the tub, grab the wall, anything but it wasn't any use. He was falling from the seat, tumbling over.

God damn that cockroach, he cursed. His head splashed water out of a puddle and his fingers ground against crumbly wood. From where he lay, the bulb seemed like a dull star, miles away. A colony of brown bugs began migrating from the inside rim of the tub. The four windowless walls seemed like the sides of a dark pit. Potato thought of a grave, any grave, his grave. He glanced under the tub and could see better, clear to the sideboard, where the cockroach was squeezing through a crack in the wall.

Hosea dug into the mound of cornflakes, scattering them across the bottom of the bowl. It would taste better if there were more milk and sugar on the cereal, but his father had used the last-remaining milk in the bottle and the sugar was gone. To ask for more would only invite trouble. It wasn't much of a breakfast, just cornflakes and a slice of stale bread, but what could you expect with Josie mixing the meal? She didn't know as much as Mother. She was so busy trying to primp for school, making ugly faces at herself in the mirror propped in front of the dressing table, while he, his brother and their father were seated at the table. No one really wanted the meal, including his father, who always liked coffee for breakfast but who drank milk instead.

"Hurry up now, let's get out of this house," his father said.

While he was going to the bedroom, Hosea stuffed the bread into his pants pocket.

"Where's Mom?" he whispered to Jeremiah.

Jeremiah balled his fist and put it over his eye.

Dad came out of the bedroom, adjusting his bow tie.

"Hurry up there, boy," he warned Jeremiah.

"I ain't hungry," said Jeremiah.

"Then get up and go to school."

They met Mrs. Fleming in the hallway. "Is your father home?" she asked.

"Yeah," answered Hosea.

"Is that the way you answer someone?"

"I mean 'yes sir'—yes ma'am."

Hosea grabbed Jeremiah's hand and shot through the hall—'way before Dad or Josie could get to the door. They clambered down the front steps of the house and ran. Dad was always whipping Hosea about respecting grown-up folks.

"Where's Mom?" Hosea asked as they got to the corner.

Jeremiah was out of breath. "Gone," he answered.

"Gone where?"

Jeremiah shook his head.

Hosea stopped and grabbed Jeremiah's shoulders. "Now look here—don't be holdin' anything back on me," he said fiercely.

"I ain't," Jeremiah said meekly, "She's just gone, that's all."

An arm slid around Hosea's neck, he felt himself being lifted backward. "Jumping little boys, huh!" he heard a snarling voice, "I'll show you."

Hosea toppled backward on the pavement, Angered, he flipped over on his belly and struggled to get to his feet. He glanced up at a boy twice his size.

"Come on, sissy," the boy said, putting up his fists, "Don't you like it?"

"He's my brother," Jeremiah protested.

The boy shoved Jeremiah away, "I don't like his looks. He's one of them smart guys."

School kids were gathering around Hosea and the bully, shouting and waving books. Hosea fingered in his pocket. At that instant, the boy whipped out a shiny object and gestured menacingly with it.

"Try some dirty work," he said.

Hosea saw the flashing switch-blade knife.

"I ain't done nothin' to you."

"You gonna quit being so smart, picking on little kids."

Hosea hung his head, "Yeah."

"Yes sir!"

"Yes sir," Hosea repeated.

The school kids hollered, "Sissy!" and set out behind the bully, leaving Hosea and Jeremiah walking alone.

"When I get big, I'm gonna get a gun like Turner. Ain't nobody gonna bull me," Hosea said.

"Turner got a gun?"

"Three of them, and they shoot real bullets. That's why nobody don't ever bother him—not even policemen."

"I wanna be like Turner too."

"I been telling you all along. But you ain't said about where Mom went."

"Daddy hit her in the mouth last night and put her out of the house. He made her cry, too."

Disconsolately, Hosea jammed his hands into his pockets. He felt the bread he'd put there while sitting at the table. Turning his pocket inside out, he dumped it out.

"That boy break one of your bones?" he heard Jeremiah ask.

"Ah, no. My bones are strong—that's bread."

Jeremiah shook his head as if he still didn't believe what he was saying. Young kids don't think like men.

Some boys were gathered in front of a small grocery store. A cat was asleep on top of a pile of apples. The boys were trying to awaken him. A man came up and chased them away.

As they approached the school, the sidewalk and yards became thick with children. Hosea took Jeremiah's hand and sliced through the wall of children into an opening. He stepped off the walk and was in the street.

"Hey, shrimp! Get back on the sidewalk," a voice ordered. Hosea made an attempt to run, but cars were going by. He felt someone grab him.

"You know better than this." Hosea looked up and saw a dark boy with white straps crossing his shoulders and chest. He was the captain of the safety patrol. He took out a pad.

"What's your name?" he asked. "You'll get the damndest beating you ever got."

"Hosea and Jeremiah Johnson," whispered Hosea.

"Take these kids and go to the office," the captain barked at his aide, a squatty fellow.

"Let 'em go themselves. They can't run away. Who's gonna be here with you if I go?"

The captain turned to the boys, "Report to the principal's office as soon as you get to school."

After crossing the street, Hosea whispered to Jeremiah, "Let's quit school and run away."

Jeremiah looked puzzled. "How we gonna eat?" When Hosea didn't answer, Jeremiah added, "I'm hungry now."

Hosea thought of the freight house and the big wooden cars that, loaded with oranges, apples, and watermelons, rolled up close to the terminal. "I know where we can go."

They bucked the kids hurrying to school, darted into an alley and ran. They sped on along the narrow, winding passageway, through a channel of smelly garbage cans. Hosea looked back and could barely see the towering chimney of the school. When they came to a wide street, they were tired from running so hard and sat down on the curb.

"I'm hungry," Jeremiah reiterated.

A big truck loaded with crates of vegetables rumbled by.

"The market's nearby. I'm gonna show you how to get a bellyful, then we can hop a train," Hosea said.

"Hop a train?"

"Sure. Go somewhere."

"But you leaving Turner?"

Hosea hadn't thought about that. But then Josie had started seeing Turner. Anyway, they didn't have much to look forward to with Mom gone.

"You know," Hosea said, "I can drive Turner's car. We can take his car. We don't have to catch a train."

They got up and walked past several stores, looking in the windows at shirts, sweaters and pants. The sweet scent of cookies and cakes filled the air from the small bakery. On the corner, an old man selling newspapers stared suspiciously at them.

The market was filled with people filing through the slim lanes, looking at fresh vegetables and fruit piled up in the stalls. A wrinkled old lady sat on a stool amid baskets of apples.

Hosea went up to her. "Can we run an errand for you, lady? We're hungry."

There was a glint in the old lady's eyes. "Nope. And don't be hanging around this place to steal my fruit."

Hosea measured the distance he would have to run if he stole some apples. It was too far and men who would chase him were around.

He took Jeremiah to the rear of the market where the big engines pushed freight cars up to the loading platform. Huge Negro men stripped to the waist were carrying bags of potatoes from a freight car, stacking them up on the side.

He and Jeremiah watched for a long time. Then the men began carrying off crates of oranges. One of the men stopped near them and lit a cigarette.

"You got any jobs?" Hosea asked.

The man blew out the match, peered down at him. "Boy, this here work damn near kill you."

"I've got plenty of muscles."

The man grinned. "You better get a gal then."

"You know where we can get something to eat? My little brother here is hungry."

The man ripped open a crate of oranges and gave each of them two. "You better get the hell out of here now, 'fore boss man come around."

Hosea thanked him. "But we want to hop a ride in one of these trains."

The man let out a loud roar. "This here car ain't got an engine in front of it. You better book passage on a train that's going somewhere."

"Where's that?"

"Down at the station. But you need money—lots of cold cash." The man walked away, laughing.

Hosea bit into the orange.

"I know where there's some money," Jeremiah said.

"Where?"

"Home. I saw it."

"How much?"

"A lot of money."

"How much?"

"I don't know."

"There's no money around the house, except for what Josie might have in her pocketbook. And she's got that in school."

"I want to go to the bathroom. Let's go home."

"Okay," Hosea said reluctantly. "But when we git home we're picking up our clothes now and leaving."

By the time Hosea got to Potato Flat, his feet ached so much he thought that it would be best to postpone his leaving for a day. Uncle Abe waved to him from his second-floor window, and Hosea waved back. Uncle Abe was a nice kind of man; he never told anybody about what he saw in the street. Once he had given Hosea a nickle.

"Turner ain't home now," Jeremiah said, noticing that the car was not parked in its usual place.

Hosea slipped through the front door, then stuck his key into the lock of their flat. Cracking the door a bit, he saw that the kitchen was empty and strode into the room. Apparently he had shut the door harder than he realized. There was a rapid series of sharp steps sounded in the bedroom, accompanied by a startled, "Who's there?"

He struggled for the door handle.

"Gracious goodness!" Hosea heard, "What are you doing here?"

Hosea was frightened. He braced himself for a flurry of scorching words and the eventual licking, as sure to follow as the night. When he turned around his eyes were focused to the size of balloons. His throat was choked up, and tears were on his cheeks. Standing in the doorway, dressed in a new brown suit, with two traveling bags at her feet, was his mother.

Jeremiah broke the silence. "Mommie!" he cried and ran over to her, "We were running away because you left."

Hosea stood near her as she fondled Jeremiah, caressing him and rubbing her fingers over his woolly head.

"You leaving us?" asked Hosea.

There were little flecks of water in Mom's eyes. "Kids, I'm going to New York, but as soon as I get a place to stay, I'm coming back for you. I'll borrow some money. I'll do anything to get you away from here."

"Did Daddy hurt you, Mom?" asked Hosea.

"He's all right. Respect him and do what he says."

Jeremiah scampered into the back room, leaving Hosea and Mom alone.

"Mom, someday I'm gonna get even with Dad for what he done to you."

"Young man, you'll do nothing of the kind. You'll take your younger brother and go right back to school. I want you two to grow up to be fine young men."

"Yes."

"Yes, 'Mother,'" she corrected him.

Jeremiah came back into the room. Mom kissed both of them.

"My train leaves in half an hour. Jeremiah, you go with Hosea right back to school. Be good boys for Mom. I'll be seeing you in a couple of days."

She kissed the two boys again. This time there were tears in her eyes. She waved as she rushed out of the flat.

Jeremiah cried after she had gone, but Hosea's eyes were dry.

"Where's the money?" he asked Jeremiah.

"Mama wants us to go to school."

Hosea began searching the front bedroom. He pulled out drawers of the bureau, ran his fingers along the sides, the corners. He checked the bed, examining the mattress. He opened the clothes closet and searched his father's suits. When he had finished he had 20 cents—a pretty good sum.

He went back into the kitchen and found Jeremiah standing over the family trunk. Hosea went over and saw what Jeremiah had been looking at. It was a brown package. Taking the bag, Hosea opened it and looked down. His mouth dropped open. There were more green bills and silver coins in the bag than he'd ever seen in his life. He flicked out a bill. He saw that it was a hundred dollar bill.

"It's real! There's millions!"

"Dad said it's for Josie's college."

"Huh!" Hosea said, stuffing bills in his pocket. "We're gonna duck the rest of this money. Then we can run away."

"I'm hungry."

"Aw nuts!" Hosea said. "You can get anything you want to as soon as we hide this money in the cellar."

The Negro ghetto is not gay and carefree. The majority of Negroes in the United States are closer to slums, poverty and crime than they are to suburbs, comfort and work. The slum is the workshop of the Negro, despite the optimists who speak of Negro progress and the comments of some who refuse to face the fact that the end results of poverty are finally overtaking the posture of my people. Our thrust now, far from being a drive of skilled and qualified troopers, is a desperation assault in which many of the attackers will fall before they achieve opportunity—never to benefit from the gains.

The ghettos, with their atmosphere of failure and defeat, will become the testing ground for the New Negro's versatility. For the first century of freedom, much of our leadership focused on civil-rights inequities that blotted out hope for a full life. Concentrating on the regaining of a basic dignity, we used integration as a catchword to arouse interest and to put white America on the defensive. In the second century, we must buttress this new dignity with education and training to prepare our people for a much more fruitful life, both in and out of the ghetto. In other words, with a high percentage of Negroes in the ranks of the untrained, unskilled and uneducated, the success of the drive in the years to come will be judged by the gains made in utilizing new opportunities and rehabilitating the masses. How fast the ghettos disappear will be determined more by how soon Negroes can be trained and qualified to take their place in society.

In the long run, the existence of the ghetto will be more attuned to the Negro's desires than the force or compulsion of society. Segregation by race will ultimately be erased, but the barriers based on income and skill could be equally devastating in separating Negroes from whites. Many of the Negroes who parade to demand city hall jobs will find themselves qualified only for maintenance positions. Many of the Negroes who sit in restaurants will find themselves unable to afford the price of a meal in such settings. Many of the Negroes who fight housing bias will find their wages insufficient to handle the mortgage payments in mixed communities.

This is a grim prediction. The elimination of the slums and the integration of people who have long been accustomed to slum existence will require an entirely new community approach and possibly create serious hazards to healthy race relations. It is a job so tremendous even social workers privately admit that the end is not in sight. One told me, "There just isn't a solution. When man solves the problem of poverty and slums, forget it. We'll have a nation of little Jesuses." Another said, "We'll have communism."

To visualize how much the Negro is on the bottom in America, study the statistics of the big cities after the transformation of the face of this nation caused by what the National Urban League calls "one of the great population changes in modern history." In a half-century, the predominant Negro population in eleven southern states, mostly in rural areas, shifted to the cities of the big industrial states, almost half in the North. With the migration from the Dixie farms came heavy costs in terms of family dislocation, pauperism, crime, delinquency and urban blight. Up went expenditures for public welfare, relief, aid for dependent children, unemployment compensation, welfare, the courts, prison upkeep and anti-juvenile delinquency projects. In past years, little was spent to salvage the Negro. As a result, the drain for these welfare services is now staggering. Even with the national, state and municipal governments defraying considerable costs, few areas have developed constructive programs designed to retrain or to help victims of the economic oppression find their way into society.

A few years ago, Washington civic leader Bertha Lomack, writing on the subject of Negro juvenile delinquency, said:

> Any fruitful discussion of juvenile delinquency among Negroes requires an understanding of the problems of the Negroes in the United States, for the problems of juveniles cannot be isolated from the problem of Negroes in any other age group. This requires an analysis of the sociological factors which greatly influence these problems. There are those who view the Negro as subhuman, criminal, ignorant, immoral and unmoral, fearful, irresponsible, slack, ugly, susperstitious and evil, noncontributing to society, aggressive, poverty-stricken. They see Negroes as inherently inferior without considering the societal cause of behavior.
>
> Negroes have suffered generations of living in dilapidated ghettos, of poor schools, few job opportunities related to educational levels, little opportunity for job promotions, the tragedy of old clothes, ugly surroundings, second-class citizenship in a country which everywhere proclaims belief in the equality of opportunity denied him.
>
> He finds himself portrayed to the world as disinherited and dispossessed or as a buffoon as in *Porgy and Bess, Amos and Andy* and *Imitation of Life*. These romantic presentations portray the weak, immature, child-like Negroes who get drunk. They do not

show the community power structure which controls them and the part the liquor store operators play in it or the profit they derive from it.

These handicaps have caused distrust, frustration and conflicts in the Negro home, which results in the destruction of the family. The child, mother and grandmother have lived with these conditions. What would be the expectancy for the making of a good citizen under these conditions? The Negro exists in an angry, hostile world. It is a constant struggle for him, knowing that the odds are against him as to achieving his place in the body politic—a high status and a job. Some of the youngsters never had the chance.

As a Juvenile Court project study of the District of Columbia reported, "Any juvenile delinquency is too much juvenile delinquency. Hundreds of millions of dollars are expended each year in this nation for police forces, juvenile courts, detention facilities and training schools. Millions of man-hours are devoted to the apprehension of delinquents, to their adjudication, to their probation services and to their rehabilitation in training schools, and millions of hours are lost from schools and from homes by the delinquent children. The expenditure in money, man-hours and lives attendant to juvenile delinquency is phenomenal and it probably is best that we never know its magnitude."

The fact that the Negro juvenile delinquency rate is far out of proportion has been known to Negro leaders for years, but it is now so critical that community officials are beginning to take notice. Appearing before a House education committee in 1961, Abraham Ribicoff, Secretary of Health, Education and Welfare, testified:

But in recent years the problem (juvenile delinquency) has shifted to the "new migrants" and new marginal groups within the American scene: the urban-drifting Negro, the Mexican, the Puerto Rican. Such groups suffer from social and economic barriers, concentration in deteriorated living areas and cultural segregation. Thus, although Negroes represent about 10 percent of the total population of the Nation, they contribute nearly twice that much to the delinquency rate. In some large metropolitan areas, the disproportion may range as high as three, five or even eight times as high as the contribution from whites.

If jobs are scarce, schools appear meaningless, communities are poverty-stricken and disorganized, families are disrupted and advancement is barred by ethnic barriers, then a sense of the meaning of a conventional way of life disappears altogether. When access to a whole range of opportunities is denied, withdrawn or unattainable, and when these barriers are visible and the frustrations are shared, there then develops a wholesale loss of support for a law-abiding way of life.

Under these conditions, law violation becomes, not the isolated outburst of a disturbed child but a way of life, supported by a set of attitudes which engulf otherwise normal, healthy productive youngsters. Delinquency is group-oriented, hostile to all aspects of convention and may become very sophisticated. It is, in short, a system of beliefs and values with a strong and stable tradition of its own, and its power goes beyond the individual, or even the family, whose good motives to do well for its children have little material to work with.

It is, of course, in such groups that delinquency is most serious. It is here that we find the "bopping" or fighting gangs which have become notorious. But even when the drama of gains is absent, delinquency, even if quieter, forms. Theft, larceny and assault pile up on the police blotter, if not in the headlines. Drug addiction, prostitution, alcoholism and other signs of crippling despair signify retreat from life and feed the income of the organized criminal. Here is community life wholly out of control, community failure in its purest form.

Such grave trends should make it clear that the problem we face outruns the effectiveness of our control, enforcement and correctional efforts. Even with increased emphasis in these spheres, we are dealing with the end results of delinquency—not the sources. Our concern must therefore broaden to include the field of prevention, and this means a concern with the effects of widespread changes in the social and economic life of our society.

Such an approach to the problem has been advocated by National Urban League Director Whitney Young, who said, "To correct the problems, the co-operative effort of many social agencies, both public and private, in a massive "crash" attack on the problem is required. Such a crash program, sustained for a reasonable period of time, will realize savings of millions of dollars in the cost of welfare services and public hospitalization. Such a program will reverse the widespread social deterioration of urban families and communities and also help us to develop the tools and understanding which will prevent the development of such deterioration in the future."

Whether this program has merit will be determined, but certainly the Kennedy Administration, with its pioneering projects in anti-juvenile delinquency, manpower retraining and domestic peace corps, moved front-line assistance into strategic areas in the big cities. Coupled with its civil-rights program and an emphasis on human welfare, the Administration has promoted new hope and enthusiasm among Negroes.

But the engineering alone is not enough. The mechanism, the programs or the projects need the combined efforts of Negro organizations to shove them into orbit and within sight of our demoralized mass. This is a role for church, fraternal, civic educational, religious and civil-rights groups. Only in recent years have Negroes themselves faced up to the proposition that their world is second class and that the distressing dilemma of slums, poverty and crime is mounting around us. Many civil-rights leaders of my acquaintance privately used to say, "Don't worry about crime. We can't do anything about it. Close your eyes to it and fight for integration." Others alibied, "City officials are responsible. Negro crime is a city problem, not a racial problem. Still others: "If we had integration, all of this would not have happened."

Today the Negro's civil-rights victories are warped by the damming up of the casualties. The slums have a message and gospel of despair. Misery, poverty, sickness and crime abound. Fighting to make a way out of the ghetto, Negro leadership has ignored this mountain of hopelessness. If many Negroes are to take advantage of the civil-rights victories, our leadership must return to the ghettos and fight hand-to-hand to eliminate the conditions, inspire the youth, train the parents, improve the schools and make the slum a better place to rear our next generation. This will not be easy. Much of our leadership would prefer the headline showmanship of the suburban class. Those who choose the slum as a laboratory will find ignorance the major foe, but even though gains will be slower, in the long run, the campaign will have a lasting effect on race relations. Eliminate the slums and their evils, and the Negro gets a better chance in life. This is the New Frontier for the Negro.

# ★ ★ ★ 13 VIPs and Not

Once, when my wife and I were leaving Robert F. Kennedy's home in Virginia, I told him he shouldn't stand on the front porch and bid Negro guests good-bye, that real estate specialists would downgrade the value of his house. Kennedy looked pained, even though he realized that the remarks were partially in jest. I had the feeling he caught some of the irony in the statement.

Often a target of criticism from Negroes, white Southerners and even Northerners, Attorney General Kennedy, nevertheless, is a cabinet member who has won quite a bit of affection from my people for his actions, especially those designed to improve the conditions in the South. Billed as an aggressive, sharp executive, who didn't know the meaning of "No," the AG moved into the Department of Justice and started the fur flying. Justice was a lily-white department with few Negroes on the employment rolls and little action in Southern civil-rights cases. Under the Republicans, Attorney General William Rogers shuffled a number of papers on his desk and moved in only a few cases. During the 1960 campaign, when I traveled with Vice President Nixon, I noted that Rogers stayed in his travel compartment on the campaign train throughout the South. Kennedy got the department moving in civil rights, for perhaps the first time in history.

In the one hundred years after the Civil War, the Department of Justice did little to enforce law in the South. Negroes were lynched, beaten and deprived, in some instances, of every constitutional right. Over-all, this slumber lasted, I would say, until the

Medgar Evers killing in 1963, when the FBI raced out and in a matter of days snared the killer. In some earlier cases, the FBI had fingered the killers, but there were no indictments by Southern grand juries. The Department of Justice waited until public outrage had subsided before dropping anything relating to a federal violation.

Of all the Kennedy Administration policy-makers, the Attorney General was the champion of civil-rights progress, but even he fell short of the mark Negroes expected. As a white American and a member of the majority, he is caught in the web of circumstance. He doesn't shoot from the hip as segregationists in the South believe, but neither is he as spineless in civil-rights matters as some of his predecessors.

Robert Kennedy became perhaps the first American white man really to impress Negroes with his civil-rights actions, leaders and followers alike. For the New Frontier, the Attorney General was the messenger, the wonder boy, the crusader to Negroes. No individual, including the late FDR, gained such billing and a respect. Not even his brother rivaled him in popularity among Negroes during the first years of that Administration. It can be said that Negro leadership feared the tough-talking AG who, shortly after he assumed office, took on union boss James Hoffa. Many educated Negroes sought favors, jobs and trips, gushing adoration for the Kennedys, who seemed to pick Negro entertainers as frequent party guests.

The Kennedys' bubble expanded.

Encouraging a vote drive in the southern states, Robert Kennedy spoke out in forceful language of his intentions to carry out the letter of the law in every field, including civil rights. As the majority of the Negro groups concentrated on Southern vote-registration drives, CORE's James Farmer, already a pro at promoting sit-ins, conceived a Freedom Ride from the nation's capital to New Orleans to test interstate bus transportation policies. Farmer brought 15 white and Negro volunteers, selected from a field of more than three hundred throughout the country, to Washington for an intensive 3-day training course. Plans called for whites and Negroes to sit together and to use facilities interchangeably. Whites were to barge into Negro rest rooms and stand at their lunch counters, while Negroes pushed into the main bus terminal facilities.

Unable to dissuade Farmer from canceling such a plan, certain Negro civil-rights leaders publicly attacked the project as fanatical and unwise. Some government aides passed the word around conservative Negro quarters that the project was "Red-oriented." Southern senators and newspapers had a field day arousing the passions of whites in the areas to be visited by the group.

But the Freedom Riders got on the buses and rode. A bus went up in smoke, and riders on a second Freedom bus were badly mauled outside of Anniston.

Farmer wasn't on either bus. His father, a former college professor, had died in a Washington hospital a few days earlier, and Farmer had to return to arrange for the funeral.

The morning after the first Freedom Ride, while I was eating breakfast at his home in Birmingham, the Reverend Fred Shuttlesworth called me to the telephone, "The Attorney General wants to speak to you."

Why joke at such a crucial time, I thought. Completely disorganized now, with half of their number smoke-drunk from the bus burning, the Freedom Riders had yet to decide whether to continue to Montgomery in the face of hatred. I picked up the phone. It was the AG.

"What are you doing down there?" he asked.

"I'm a reporter. Remember?" I answered.

"What's it look like?" Robert Kennedy asked.

"These people are in trouble. They need help," I answered.

Later, I gave Shuttlesworth the phone, and he chatted with Kennedy—the first communication in modern civil-rights history between a cabinet member and the leader of an integration effort in the South. From the tone of the cleric's voice afterward, I assumed the AG had conveyed words of encouragement. A few minutes later, the Freedom Riders voted to continue, and we prepared to leave Birmingham.

The Freedom Ride fizzled in Birmingham. Two bus drivers walked off the job rather than transport our group. Two flights were canceled after bomb threats, so we huddled in the airport lobby with a few state police holding back an angry crowd. Finally, at about 11:00 p.m. John Siegenthaler, the AG's assistant, flew in, and we embarked on a plane to New Orleans, thus ending our Freedom Ride.

Peace was not to come. Immediately a new group of Negroes rallied and announced that they were picking up our trail and continuing on to Montgomery, Alabama and Jackson, Mississippi. At this point, the AG intervened to urge the Negroes to cancel, advising that negotiation would effectively solve the problem. The answer he got surprised the AG. He was turned down, and the rides continued. More tension, more friction and more violence ensued, but weeks later, the government intervened to attack the problem of segregation in interstate travel.

The intervening months erased the Kennedy infallibility as far as Negroes were concerned, and the Attorney General loomed more as a human being—a white man caught in a web of racial passion and prejudice, but a white man who had a sense of fairness and decency. I heard him background many cases, from Albany, Georgia to James Meredith, from Mississippi voting to the Birmingham demonstration. "Come up and see me," he always said when I encountered him at a press conference or hearing. "For what?" I'd throw the needle, "For you to tell me to have Negroes quit this or that?"

He'd grin.

I admire Kennedy in many ways. He encourages a healthy relationship in which a Negro and a white can speak frankly and to the point, disagree and yet avoid emotionalism. Whenever I become angry at the Attorney General I remember a visit to his home. One way to test a family's democratic tradition is to encounter the young children. If a Negro finds a white child backing off or blurting racial terms or feeling uncomfortable, it can be assumed the child's experiences have not included acquaintance with a colored person. If the experience is limited to a maid or chauffeur, the child probably will assign you to that category and make some comments in that direction. But that night the AG's children went over to a Negro couple and asked the man to read them a bedtime story. It was a beautiful glimpse of democracy. I knew that the principles of the AG's struggle in civil rights had either rubbed off or had been there a long time.

John F. Kennedy was not my sentimental favorite prior to the 1960 Democratic convention. During the primaries, I had favored Minnesota Senator Hubert Humphrey, a liberal who had been a devout civil-rights advocate for as long as I remember. Hailing from a state where Negroes form a small percentage of the population, Senator Humphrey nevertheless was outspoken on the subject. When he entered the primaries, his campaigners had little money, and perhaps a minimum of political skill. I feel that if civil rights is as important as we Negroes say it is, we should also think in terms of principle. We should respect a man's record. It saddened me to see Negroes go against Senator Humphrey and flail him as "a bigot," while at the same time hailing Senator Kennedy as the new champion of freedom. Frankly, I had no contact with Senator Kennedy during his years on Capitol Hill, and I don't believe many other Negroes did, except those who tried to get on his payroll for the campaign.

My second choice for the Democratic nomination was Senator Stuart Symington, a man I respected for his record even though he was from a border state. As an industrialist, he was one of the first to back fair employment policies, and as a government administrator, he hired Negroes in top slots. It wasn't the thing to do in those years, but Symington even got into an international row by insisting that one of his aides, George L. P. Weaver, a Negro, be sent to a certain country to make a study of minerals. Weaver today is the Assistant Secretary of Labor for international affairs. Senator Symington was a man who pioneered in civil rights long before that was fashionable.

The Kennedy machine that rolled through the convention, smothering those in its way, convinced me of the ineffectual role of the Negro at the king-making stage. After making pious and sometimes grandiose statements before the platform committees, our leaders retired to the stands to watch the fight. The few Negro delegates made little difference. It amused me that some Negro labor unionists jumped up on the floor of the convention and yelled against the proposal of Senator Lyndon B. Johnson of Texas as the vice-presidential nominee. "A sell-out!" one hollered. "Down with Johnson!" chanted another. "We'll bolt!" said a third. More Negroes threatened to stay home during the campaigning.

A day later, after a secret meeting with party heads, the Negroes were docile and co-operative. The Negroes in labor were told to shut up or lose their jobs. Negro politicos were threatened with loss of prestige and rank. The opposition melted like snow. What followed in the next few weeks was a political blitz, backed up by money, promises of jobs, prestige and pictures in newspapers, that virtually covered the Negro community from coast to coast. It is estimated that more than a half million dollars was spent to insure the Negro vote. Negro leaders on per diem salaries crisscrossed the country; entertainment stars flew in and out of cities; pamphlets, cards, letters and releases barraged every Negro of voting age. "It was the biggest vote hunt ever launched in a presidential campaign," a Negro said to me.

In the enthusiasm, there were the dishonesties. In our weekly news magazine, I have for years written a two-page column titled "Ticker Tape," which has a simple design of a red border and the capitol dome on the side of the banner top. Democratic promoters propositioned my publisher, seeking to "buy" the column for the campaign. Rebuffed by him, they then wanted to buy space for a column which they wanted to be identical to mine in style, make-up and typography. He again refused. Eventually, they advertised in the magazine. I boiled at the thought that a political crew could be so lacking in virtue.

On the campaign road from California to Maine, from South Carolina to Minnesota, a reporter finds himself struggling to shape news to fit the format of the Negro press. Traveling through the country—visiting four and five cities daily—one realizes the minimal position of the Negro, understands his minority status and begins to see the vastness and might of this nation. Looking from without the Negro slum is far different than from looking from within. One realizes that the strength of Negro politics is overrated and that the power of Negro politicians is skimpy in relation to the whole. Few Negroes appeared on the Kennedy speaking circuit except in the big cities, and few Negroes held any campaign jobs outside of these separate communities. Yet, in a matter of a few weeks, Kennedy transformed himself from a conservative to a man of sympathy in civil rights. His speeches were so literate and generalized that no one could take offense. Toward the end of the campaign, columnist Murray Kempton said to me, "The tragedy of a Kennedy victory will be that he has no Negroes close to him."

On Election Night in Hyannis Port, Massachusetts, Kempton's prediction began to take shape. A group of Kennedy Negroes went to the armory but were unable to gain admittance because they lacked credentials. Finally, an aide had to usher in these Negroes I had described as the elite around JFK. A few weeks after the election, the Negro politicians lined up for jobs but, except for some who were named to minor posts, most were ignored as JFK picked quality candidates for key slots—starting out with Andrew Hatcher as Associate Press Secretary, Dr. Robert C. Weaver as the Housing Administrator and George L. P. Weaver as Assistant Secretary of Labor. Thus, the most expensive Negro vote-getting organization in history collapsed suddenly and completely. Its job was done.

The day before the Inauguration, I got a telephone call informing me I had been selected as a member of the news pool to accompany the President-elect. For a Negro this was as unprecedented as JFK's earlier action, during his campaign, in sending the campaign planes on to Washington after I was refused accommodation in a Kentucky hotel. Later, he forced integration of the White House News Photographers Association, he opened his background briefing at Palm Beach, Florida to Negroes and he applied many new policies that assured our press equal status at the White House. There was little complaint from the Negro press on news managing.

It wasn't too difficult for a Negro reporter to become subjective while covering the Kennedys. That Administration was the most indomitable in history on civil rights. My people have made substantial gains under this Boston Irish family. But as a reporter, I have the job of interpreting, separating the wheat of production from the chaf of political disguise and of examining the motives for actions other than humanitarian purposes.

In the late fall of 1960, my *Ebony* article on "What Negroes Can Expect from Kennedy," concluded with the following paragraph:

> As he outlined in numerous campaign speeches, taking pains to stress the greatness of a president in making a decision based on conscience rather than popularity, Kennedy could well follow the example of his idol, Abraham Lincoln, when he signed the Emancipation Proclamation. Describing Lincoln during the critical time, Kennedy told many audiences: "His hand did not tremble. He did not hesitate. He did not equivocate. For he was the President of the United States. It is in this spirit that we must go forth in the coming months and years."

John F. Kennedy was beginning to measure up to his idol when he was tragically killed.

I said good-bye to President Kennedy on November 25, 1963, when I was assigned to the reporters' pool covering the funeral in Washington and at the Arlington National Cemetery. Sitting in St. Matthew's Roman Catholic cathedral, I saw the great leaders who had flown from across the world for this sad occasion. I thought of my experiences with John F. Kennedy, how he spoke on civil rights in every state during the 1960 campaign, how he demonstrated leadership during the crises in Birmingham and Oxford. I was very sad.

When Lyndon Baines Johnson was sworn in as the 36th President of the United States, a wave of dejection began to spread across Negro America. The new President had no civil-rights image nor wide admiration among Negroes. While Vice President, he never held a press conference for Negro reporters, his aides insisting that President Kennedy was the spokesman for the Administration.

While Carl Rowan was a deputy assistant secretary of state, he accompanied Johnson on two foreign trips and developed a close relationship with him. Rowan next became the ambassador to Finland, and in January 1964 he replaced Edward R. Murrow as director of the United States Information Agency. He was the first Negro to sit in the National Security Council.

As chairman of the Equal Opportunity Committee, Johnson spoke out on the need for increased hiring of Negroes and waged a relentless drive for improvement of Negro working conditions. But when be became President, aides realized that Johnson's weakest flank was still in the area of civil rights. With the Negro vote such a telling factor, they emphasized his responsibility for the passage of a civil-rights bill in 1957. His activity in the drive for a new civil-rights bill in 1964 was watched closely by Negroes.

A conservative from California, Richard M. Nixon became the Mr. Civil Rights during the Eisenhower Administration. As chairman of the contract compliance committee, Nixon earned newspaper space, publicity and Negro friends. To his Washington meetings came Negro leaders from throughout the country, carefully selected to include some Democrats who might change parties or votes. At such meetings, which generally were followed by receptions, a cameraman snapped the visitor with the Vice President and the picture was rushed to both the guest and the paper in the area. In the 1956 campaign, Nixon was the civil-rights workhorse, having put together the GOP's civil-rights program.

In an *Ebony* interview, I wrote:

> He [Nixon] shared credit for regaining some 22 percent of the Negro vote in 1956, after he boldly campaigned that the Eisenhower Administration had 'made the greatest advance' in Negro rights since the Emancipation Proclamation. He had even disclosed his NAACP membership at a press conference in Houston, Texas —something unheard of—and needled Democratic candidate Adlai Stevenson as being "helpless and futile" in the race-relations field. Yet 4 years later, after compiling the impressive record as a GOP civil-righter, Nixon virtually "gave up" the Negro vote by not

campaigning vigorously in the big cities and being insensitive to popular civil-rights issues.

What made Vice President Nixon decide to forego the Negro vote in 1960? Political strategists probably sold him on the theory that he would win the usual proportion of the Negro vote and that he had a chance to make greater inroads into the conservative, anti-Catholic vote of both the North and the South.

After seeing him serve in the role of a "liberal," reporters were surprised to notice the thoroughness of his campaign managers in ignoring Negro communities even in tours of cities, in keeping Negro VIPs from platforms of rallies and of failing to speak out strongly on civil rights. "I could have become President," Nixon told me in his eleventh-floor office in Los Angeles a few months after his defeat. "I needed only 5 percent more votes in the Negro areas. I could have gotten them if I had campaigned harder."

There were doubts about Nixon's sincerity. On too many occasions, he sounded like a well-rehearsed actor who played a role, sometimes not too well. After the exclusive interview in Los Angeles (granted only after he telephoned my publisher and obtained a guarantee that he could read the manuscript before publication, because he "didn't trust Booker" but "wanted Booker to do the story") the former Vice President committed a typical error. As I was leaving after the hour-long session, I said to Nixon, "Mr. Vice President, I hope you employ a Negro on your staff some day." During the eight years in the nation's capital, this man, who urged employers to hire Negroes, failed to take that step in his Capitol Hill office. Nixon smiled faintly, then grinned. "You don't have to worry anymore," he answered as if recalling something, "I've got just the man. We hired a skycap from the San Francisco airport this morning." I was flabbergasted. "Hell, Mr. Vice President," I said, "I'm talking about somebody on your executive staff." His face reddened as he probably realized his *faux pas* and my discomfort. "Give me some recommendations," he said, "I'd be interested. Don't forget."

At his home, during a reunion of the reporters who traveled

with him to Africa, a more frustrating experience took place, one which made me think the Nixon public relations system was malfunctioning. On our arriving at his house, my wife and I were given a hero's welcome (for what, I couldn't understand). I hadn't been a Nixon fan and my wife is a registered Democrat. After a maid took our coats, Nixon and his wife showed us the kitchen with its modern appliances. A Negro employee appeared and Mrs. Nixon, started the introductions but presented us as Mr. and Mrs. Louis Lautier (Lautier being a Negro White House correspondent who was a recognized Republican sympathizer). This time, I corrected Mrs. Nixon. She was apologetic, but I wondered what on earth they wanted Louis Lautier to do after such a VIP welcome.

President Eisenhower, on the other hand, was a man of conviction. He brought a moral freshness to the nation's capital along with a group of the most insensitive ex-business bureaucrats he could find. After the first years, in which Eisenhower moved to desegregate Washington and name Negroes to a few high posts, his Administration slipped into disfavor with my people. The courageous action concerning Little Rock was but a momentary flash. There was little news from Washington which had a spiritual flavor in civil rights; Ike seemed more concerned with other fields. The small coterie of Negro aides was disillusioned, disgusted or disenchanted with Eisenhower. Many had little faith in Nixon.

Coverage of Eisenhower's second term was a pathetic chore for a Negro reporter. I had stopped attending press conferences because he recognized no Negro reporters and said little on the topic of human relations. I didn't bother with the departmental or agency press conferences because compromise and retreat appeared to be the civil-rights policy. One of Eisenhower's most disastrous adventures with Negroes occurred at a summit meeting of American Negro leaders, perhaps the most distinguished assemblage of our people ever to discuss the course of race relations. At no other time had Eisenhower agreed to speak to Negroes, but he accepted this invitation. E. Frederic Morrow, the first Negro aide ever to work at the White House, helped draft his speech. For some reason, Eisenhower decided to junk the text and go it alone. The result

—the true, sincere Eisenhower spilled out, and he told the gathering to "have patience." From a "do-nothing" Administration, these were fighting words, and it took rigid courtesy for the Negroes not to boo Eisenhower off the stage. His applause was skimpy and the chairman of the meeting, Cleveland publisher William O. Walker, refrained from accompanying him from the hotel room.

After his retirement from public office, Eisenhower granted me my first interview. During the eight years he served as President, I had no contact with him or his top-level aides, especially since Press Secretary James Hagerty seemed to consider the Negro press unimportant. I felt that much of the resentment of Negroes toward the Administration could be traced to the image set forth in our press. This ill feeling could partially be blamed on Hagerty, since he had little relations with our Negro reporters and virtually excluded us from a rightful place in news gathering.

Face to face with the former President, one receives a much different impression than one does at a distance. For almost 45 minutes, the former chief executive discussed the America of tomorrow for Negroes. He predicted that segregation will disappear in America in ten years, public schools will be open to all in every state, factories and business firms will hire more qualified Negroes, there will be more housing for Negroes, Negroes will be elected to high public offices in cities and states while others will be picked for key national government jobs and that discrimination, the keystone of century-old controversy, will become a relic of the past. All of these predictions were published in *Ebony* and drew a raft of comment.

During the interview, Ike related how he and the late NAACP Secretary Walter White agreed that they didn't want their children to make interracial marriages. He made such a point of this incident that I did have the nerve to tell him that White's daughter had married a white man.

Discussing the Democratic techniques, Ike showed some knowledge of politics: "There's a lot of argument that the GOP has little appeal for Negroes because we don't advocate a welfare state. Politicians make a lot of noise in Negro areas on this subject, even to bragging that a bad Democrat is better than any Republican. This is silly, and I don't understand how Negro voters can follow such a doctrine, if it is true."

Admitting he was disappointed in 1956 at the Negro vote for him—especially in Harlem (after Representative Adam Clayton Powell took to the campaign trail for him)—Ike insisted that "Negroes should be taught to vote on the basis of the party's record and its complete platform. He felt that civil rights was an overrated issue in the quest for Negro votes and believed that the "gut" issue lay in the economic area.

In recommending ways and means for Negroes to achieve first-class citizenship, Eisenhower showed that he had little firsthand information. He took the position that "more education eventually will solve everything." He felt that no new civil-rights legislation was needed and cited the elimination of segregation in the armed forces as an illustration of executive determination. Apparently he didn't realize that Kennedy had named a committee to study discrimination problems still plaguing the military services.

As I prepared to leave, Ike flashed his famous smile, extended his hand, then said: "Tell me. You've been here 45 minutes and all you've asked me are questions about civil rights. Is that all you're interested in?" I answered, "Well, Mr. President, you spoke out on other issues while you were President, but no one knew how you really felt about the major civil-rights issues." He scratched his chin thoughtfully, then bid me farewell. But I can remember the perplexed look on his face as he asked me the question. I wish I had been able to ask some of my questions at the press conferences.

These are some of the experiences, the conclusions and the views I have gathered while covering Washington, D.C. Presidents, Vice Presidents and cabinet members are good copy for newsmen who roam Washington.

What Negroes seldom mention and what few whites realize is that the secret weapon for the increased Negro civil-rights drive is also based in the nation's capital—the twenty-odd African embassies. Because of protocol or restrictions on participation in domestic issues, African diplomats seldom are included in any discussion of the reasons for the explosive nature of American Negroes in stepping up the fight for citizenship.

The arrival of African ambassadors, together with the official visits of the heads of their countries, has awakened Negroes to the possibilities. The emergence of Africa aroused us, angered us (because many Africans dispute our freedom claims) and jarred us to quick action. When Guinea's President Sekou Touré visited North Carolina a few years ago, white state troopers appeared at the plane to hold umbrellas for the ladies in the party. This opened the eyes of many Negroes. How could a foreign Negro get such courtesy when many an American-born Negro couldn't get a job? Were Africans getting ahead of us? These are questions that have spurred arguments in the homes of educated Negroes.

At one time, Negroes boasted that we in the United States had the highest non-white literacy rate in the world. We don't brag any more. Africans said to us: "How can you feel so proud of your achievements? You've been free almost one hundred years and you still don't have your rights, even with education." The needling at this high level of Negro life has shamed many leaders and provoked them to militance.

In a *Jet* article published several years ago I wrote:

"A guest at a swank Dixie Negro home, an African dined on a five-course meal, sipped drinks on a patio overlooking a swimming pool and was driven to the airport in a big car. Passing a large public school, the African asked his host, 'Can your children go here?' 'We have our own school—just as nice,' cautiously answered the professional man. The African grinned, 'A segregationist, too.'"

Later in the article, I explained how some State Department employees obviously attempt to divide Negroes and Africans, to make them "easier to handle." One African told me: "They tell us Negroes are too sensitive, color-conscious and regard us as foreigners. Meanwhile, they tell Negroes African countries don't want them around—as ambassadors. It's all wrong. We're brothers and we want qualified people. If Negroes fit the bill, they'll get a warmer welcome than whites."

The surge of African freedom reflected in the statements of the diplomatic newcomers has caused many a Negro leader to re-evaluate the racial struggle in America. For instance, one of the major African criticisms of Negroes lies in the widespread apathy and satisfaction with segregation and discrimination. "I'm invited to many beautiful Negro homes," one of the visiting Africans told me, "and the first thought I have is whether the host has more of a materialistic value than a spiritual one. I like to know whether he shares his wealth and talent to help his brother. I don't think it unique that 'a safe Negro' acquires wealth. They did it in Africa under colonialism."

Another African visitor explains: "When I see a Negro who's ashamed to invite an African to his home, I realize that this Negro is one of the 'mental slaves' of western civilization. He's been brainwashed so long that he has given up the fight for equality for himself and merely trudges along behind the white man. He must please his master."

The exposure to "free Africans," as risky and charged with emotion as it was and is, erased the gradualism theory of Negro freedom in America. Africans sold us on the idea that "it is better to be free and makes mistakes" than "to be a slave and learn slowly."

# ★ ★ ★ 14  Challenge
## for the Future

Many white liberals have been asked to write articles on, "If I were a Negro." I have read many of these articles, which include such recommendations as taking frequent baths and smiling in the presence of whites to conceal hatred. I have grown to understand that most whites in America don't understand or know the Negro. Even the poor Southerner who made such a hit with the "I know these Nigra folk" jazz didn't really know what was happening.

Most of these writers put their thoughts down on paper as if the only difference between the two races in America is the complexion of the skin. In other words, bleach your skin and you're white. A few may suspect that a Negro occasionally runs into a cranky white personnel officer who might turn him down for a job, or an uppity apartment manager who prefers white tenants because they don't play weird jazz, or a restaurant owner who uses Negroes as dish washers and not dish samplers; but even they lack real understanding of what it is to be a Negro.

Everybody talks about Negroes but nobody wants to be one.

To most white Americans, the Negro is a cipher. He has made few contributions toward the development of this country, and his status is only a little higher than that of the slave class of a century ago. In some states, it is doubtful if Negroes receive the humane treatment accorded race horses or greyhounds. The Negro has been the common laborer, the workhorse, the toiler with brawn and strength. Generations of such practices and beliefs have made whites prejudiced; the harsh conditions have simultaneously disenchanted Negroes and withered their spirit. In the Negro community are despair and defeat, and a rising toll of crime and delinquency—so high that even civil-rights gains seems like dots on a map, when matched against the blight of human deterioration.

It is distressing sometimes to listen to pontifical white friends discuss the racial problem or write these articles of counsel for my people. I wonder sometimes whether the kids in the slums who have broken-down toilets and tubs without water can be very impressed with advice about being neat and clean, as honest as it is. Or the admonition not to steal when you are hungry and apples on a fruit stand look so appetizing. Or study hard so you can become President, when your only desk is a bed used on a shift basis, your school building is old and dilapidated, and the teachers don't particularly care whether you study or throw spitballs. If you really want to confuse the counselors, bring in some examples of Negro upper-class families who measure up to the highest standards and still cannot enjoy the fruits of democracy. The white friend begins to hem and haw and finally admits, "It's a shame."

While thousands of Negroes slip back into the slum reservation, doomed to a slow death in vice and hopelessness, white families emigrate from the metropolitan areas to escape the infection. The situation is critical.

At a downtown bar, in Washington, D.C., two whites within my hearing discussed the racial situation.

"What the hell these niggers gonna do next?" said the first, after reading headlines about a riot on the Eastern Shore of Maryland.

"They already shooting us down."

"Yeah, that's what we want them to do," said his friend. "We've got the Army, Navy, Marines, Coast Guard, the Reserves, the National Guard, all of the police departments, the arsenals, the gun manufacturers, the bullet makers, and we outnumber them ten to one. Man, just let them start something. We'll shoot the hell out of them."

"It's getting to be a hell of a condition when niggers start acting up. They ought to be glad we let them stay here."

A prominent businessman cornered me during the height of the Birmingham struggle and said, "Shameful. Your people been getting along for years and now they're losing the friendship of even those who stood up for them."

"I know," I told him, "The Negroes want to stand for themselves. They're tired of having to go through a white man to see another white man to tell another white man to help them contact another white man to give them their constitutional rights."

"Yeah, but it isn't that bad in the South," the businessmen told me, "I was born there, and my mother had a Negro maid. We always hired Negroes. We treat them fine."

"The Negroes want some maids of their own now," I said, "and they want to vote, too."

A white woman shook her head in disgust in my presence. "It's foolish. Why the idea of these Negroes conducting all of these marches and demonstrations across the country. They're just asking for trouble. Why these leaders should be telling these people to stop stealing, raping and beating people. Get rid of crime, and maybe whites wouldn't mind giving Negroes a little break."

"I just can't understand" said a white reporter," why Negroes suffer so much to eat in a white restaurant. I always thought Negro-cooked food in the South was a lot tastier than white. Why all of the commotion? I'm not a gourmet but I just can't make heads or tails of this crisis."

A white radio reporter kept prodding me to say something about Negro leadership being irresponsible, that the Muslims are acceptable to Negroes, that most Negroes go to church and would not harm a flea. "Say something that will calm down these whites. They're the ones who are getting miffed. We want to carry a broadcast saying that the Negroes are not dissatisfied with conditions. It's just these radical leaders trying to make an issue so that Negroes will give them money."

"Man, these folk got enough courage to make Paul Revere look like a Kentucky Derby entry." A correspondent, just back from Birmingham, explained, "Never seen such raw courage, such guts in a battle in which the odds were so great. Hell, I just cracked up. I felt cheap. I felt sick. Kids marching in the street. Tiny kids, who made me think of my kids, walking into police and dogs, singing about freedom. Hell, I wouldn't want my college boy to face such a danger, let alone a kid. But these Negro kids were doing it. Man, when we got people like this in America, we should never worry about democracy failing. It just can't. Bigotry melts under such a performance."

"Let me tell you about the Negro," the white politician whispered to me, "He's sick. He's been kicked in the behind for one hundred years, and all of a sudden, he gets mad and wants to kick you in the pants. Now I'm against him getting kicked in the pants. But just because he blames me for kicking him in the pants, and I ain't done it, I don't want him to level off at me. I'd say forget it and start moving out of the range of getting kicked in the pants. Don't just stand there hollering, praying and making a lot of noise. Folks might start smacking you in the mouth."

"I don't exactly understand," I said.

"Why you got to make a production out of civil rights? You been wronged. Okay, everybody knows it. Let them try to straighten it out first, and then you come in. Don't keep on knocking down doors to our churches, restaurants, hotels and everything else. Give us time to make the adjustment. We got the message."

"We're moving too fast, huh," I asked.

"No," he said. "You're not moving much. You're making more noise than you're making progress. That's the trouble. Less noise and more progress is the solution."

A white social worker said: "You Negroes raise two million dollars a year to use for civil-rights activities. What is this money used for—salaries, airplane trips, loud speakers, building rents? What more do you get from spending this money than you would get if you conducted vote registration drives, encouraged ministers whom you pay salaries or developed local leadership? Put this kind of money into education, into developing new job-retraining programs, into family service agencies, into incentive programs—and the Negro would be a lot better off. Is segregation and discrimination so great in the United States that more than two million has to be raised yearly from a poor people to fight it? Something's screwy somewhere. Even industry lobbyists don't play around with that kind of money, and they got billions."

A panorama of dissent and difference—flecked with a rich strain of prejudice—is the white man's heritage in race relations. Generations of plundering, bossing, intimidating, exploiting and robbing the Negro have given whites such a power concept that it is difficult for them to consider Negroes—first, as humans, and second, as equals. As far as the average white family in America is concerned, the Negro doesn't exist, which is all right, except that whites run this country, and a certain segment of whites like the racial supremacy kick. Enough of the poison of untruth has permeated the American scene to infect too many minds.

For the first century, race wasn't much of a problem because the Negro was so poor and tired. In the second century, we can expect agitation, unrest, division, hatred and bitterness. Americans are unaware of the realities of racial problems because, in the past, with law-enforcers looking the other way, they could do what they wanted to the Negroes. That day is over, and the Negro is fighting back. Jail or even death is no premium.

My advice to whites is: Face the fact that the day of Negro slavery, legal or otherwise, is over. The New Negro is going to fight for his rights. He carries deep scars and is bitter over mistreatment. He is sensitive, far too sensitive. He is often uneducated. He is blinded by anger at racial setbacks.

As Joe Louis once said, "You can run but you can't hide." That just about sums up the plight of whites in America. Many have escaped the Negro by living in suburbs, working in unions and firms which barred Negroes, attending all-white schools and going to all-white churches. But conditions are changing.

The Negro middle class probably advocates integration to get out of the ghettos, away from the lower classes. The movement in Negro communities would rival the run on a bank, for integration would stimulate groups to pack up and leave in the face of the horde of newcomers to the cities. But with segregation you're restricted to a ghetto, and there you stay. I knew a minister who frequently complained that, because he was a Negro, he was forced to accept as neighbors a racketeer and a bootlegger. "This was the section reserved for middle-class Negroes," he said, "The racket element was as much in the foreground as respectable families."

Bunching Negroes together in a ghetto does little to stimulate, inspire or encourage youngsters. There is crime and juvenile delinquency because houses are packed and swollen with tenants; streets teem with dropouts and unemployables. Often, and even by prominent Negroes, it is said that the presence of respectable Negro leaders in a given community gives the kids "some one to look up to." I don't doubt that it does, but to expect such a development is ludicrous. One man is not the answer. The problem is too great.

I hear my white friends say, "The Negro has got to lift himself." The most relaxed answer would be: "Friend, you are so right. But you've got to take off the chains on his legs, his hands and his mind. He knows what he's got to do, but he can't do it. That's why you've got the demonstrations." It would be inconceivable for the white to understand that a Negro family is fortunate enough in just lifting its individual members, a church is fortunate in reaching a portion of its membership and social welfare agencies are like foot soldiers moving against a fortress.

Residing in the Washington area, one hears gross accounts of Negro crime. Discussing its statistics at a meeting, a prominent businessman explained that Negro leadership had the responsibility to meet the problem head-on. Negroes who were present could have embarrassed him, but they didn't. They could have pointed out that only in the last few years had his firm hired Negroes in any capacity. If employers refuse to hire Negroes, if real estate firms refuse to rent or sell homes except in certain areas and if educators refuse to improve the caliber of training to qualify Negro kids for employment, how can a city blame its Negro leadership for a rising crime problem? Certainly they can, and certainly the daily papers can emphasize the point, and certainly white leadership in the community can wash off its past record of bigotry and wholeheartedly blame the Negroes, but those least fooled by the shenanigans are Negroes.

This same situation exists nationally. Although a citizen of a country which prides itself on its democracy, constitutional rights and religious freedom, the Negro knows that America has been a white democracy. It is foolish for the Government to spend millions on United States Information Agency attempts to persuade Africans that discrimination doesn't exist in the United States, when African officials face such conditions in the nation's capital and learn the truth from their Negro friends. Whites in America are responsible, far more than Negroes, for the state of race relations in the country today and for the pitiable plight of Negroes. How can a man who has kept you in the mudhole at the point of a gun suddenly condemn you for being dirty?

The Negro revolution demonstrates the lack of faith the average Negro has in the white man. He regards the white man as corrupt, immoral, dishonest and untruthful and no example for him. The demonstrations are protests not only against the system but against the man who tries to keep operative the system of discrimination. This is the basis for the emotionalism that is a part of the demonstrations and that instantly can be triggered into violence. It is a two-way street, of course.

Religion, idealism or sound race relations cannot soothe the intensity of the feeling—not among the masses. Whites generally ignore how Negroes think or what they believe. But Negro feelings, now coming to the fore, show the extreme bitterness and discord.

During the opening phase of the agitational period, several comments from Negroes set the pattern.

A Negro government official recently told me: "Hell, I send money to the Black Muslims. They're my boys. I pray to God they keep giving the white man holy hell. I'd give the white man hell, but I'd lose my job. So I support them, and I hope they blast hell out of him. Whites are dirty, rotten, dishonest—even in government."

"You mean you can work beside whites all day and hold such views?" I asked.

"Damn right," the government official said, "'And I don't need to apologize about swearing at those people. They're just what the Muslims say they are—devils. I would kill all of them if I ever had the opportunity and my kids had finished college."

"Then you mean you're prejudiced—just like the White Citizens Council?" I asked.

"Damn right," he said, "Only the White Citizens Council got their revenge. I haven't. I tell my kids, 'Don't trust that white bastard. Grin in his face and try to cut his heart out. They raped your grandmothers and now call you a rapist of white women.'"

"Why worry about a few kids getting killed in Birmingham?" a businessman asked me, "They'll be killed anyhow. They'll get an inadequate education and live third class all of their lives. If a few of us die, the resultant furor will make it better for all of us. I believe the time has come for the Negro to put it on the line—either he's gonna be free or he's gonna be an ass-wiping slave. Take your choice."

"What do you do to advance the race?"

"I talk bad to every white person I see. I give 'em hell. When I see young kids around, I talk even worse. I want these kids to believe the white man is lower than dirt. I deliberately do it."

"Doesn't this harm the kids?" I asked.

"What are you talking about, man?" he said, "The more we hate, the farther we can go. We get stimulated by hating."

"You don't believe in the nonviolent approach?" I asked.

"Did General Eisenhower during World War II?"

A veteran sit-in demonstrator, who had participated in many of the Dixie campaigns told me: "Serving in the antisegregation projects is more important for an American Negro than military service. I learned how to defend myself and to stand up for the first time. I was arrested and beaten, but I wasn't afraid. I felt a part of history."

"Do you have any hatred after these experiences?"

"Frankly, yes. I try to go along with the program, but it is too difficult. Some of these white people we deal with, the only way I feel we can teach them is to drive a hammer through their brains. They're the real haters. I think we're foolish trying to absorb their punishment. We should make them suffer for their stupidity."

"So really you're not nonviolent?"

"Not mentally. I guess I haven't been brainwashed enough. The more I engage in sit-ins and demonstrations, the more I find myself struggling to be nonviolent. Now I just want to fight for what I believe."

He paused, then said, "Negroes in America need a Stern gang, like there was in Israel. If we had such a secret revolutionary outfit, we could take revenge for every offense to a Negro. We could wipe out the murderer of Medgar Evers just like a lynch mob would take care of a Negro."

"What do Negroes have to fight for in America?" a Southern Negro told me, "We're poor. We're uneducated. We're weak, except in the power to embarrass the white man."

"But look at the gains we've made," I said.

"Come now," he said. "We're worse off today than when we were freed. There were no nuclear weapons, no automation, no space rockets. We could work and earn a living even though some of us couldn't write. Now we're illiterate in the most advanced technological era. We're cotton farmers in a space age. We don't have a first-rate college. We don't have enough engineers or know-how even to build a two-wing airplane."

"You're exaggerating the case," I told him.

"Maybe so, but my aim is to embarrass the white man. To hell with science. Bring him to his knees."

A prominent NAACP member once said to me, "I should have been a lawyer or doctor, made my pile, lived high on the hill, above the discrimination and frustration, developed a real shell against the color stuff. I got all mixed up in agitation and improvement. Now I'm an old man at forty. I'm shot, worked out, tired and a shell of a man from the demands of leading the agitation.

"Now when I say, 'Let's think about it,' when somebody says 'Let's give 'em hell,' they run roughshod over me, call me an 'Uncle Tom,' say I'm slow and conservative. It's rough, Jack. I've been in this business when a lot of these kids weren't born and their papas wouldn't even join me a decade or so ago.

"I say to myself, 'Who's right?' Maybe their papas had the best solution. Get an education and fight the next generation. I don't know."

A New Frontiersman told me, "The worst scolding I got from Mom was when I brought a white schoolmate home to lunch. She was emphatic. She told me never to bring any whites to her house. She didn't want them around. Mom never did outlive her intense hatred of white people. I always think about it when I get in integrated circles, and even though I now can fathom the causes, I have moments of feeling uncomfortable. I remember my Mom's words so clearly."

"How should the Negro fight his battle?" a Harvard friend asked, then continued, "By fighting to get a decent education and showing his ability. I have little respect for these street name-callers who arouse crowds, collect money and live high on the hog. The Negro, for the most part, is a dumb animal. Face it. We're damn near stupid. Sure, you can blame the white man for it. Sure, he probably wanted it that way. But hell, they know it, and the leadership has to be smart enough to lift the masses, not themselves. It's shameful the exorbitant amount of money being raised in the name of freedom. What is freedom? A hustle-buck deal to keep a few slick orators and operators in headlines and big cars. Singing songs in the street isn't a substitute for education, culture and qualification."

A newsman said to me: "If all the whites in America suddenly died, the Negro would be in a pretty poor situation. Where would we get the men and women to run industry, Wall Street, corporations, government, science and hospitals? It seems to me that the Negro should devote a generation or two to a massive education drive to develop the best minds in the race. Inspire these kids, nurture them and let them move along as fast as they can. In a generation or two, we'd have a much bigger and more profitable intellectual class. The only people in America who appreciate dumb folk are the politicians."

Mix bitterness, a sense of failure and a souped-up sense of racial nationalism—you've described the concerned Negro. Obsessed with a nightmare of his long-term suffering, the Negro fights on blindly for dignity, recognition and, finally, security. Generations of deprivation and living by wit to support his family have made the Negro suspicious, pessimistic and, occasionally, fatalistic. Many Negroes will tell you, "I ain't going anywhere." But he fights on.

In this frustrating atmosphere, racial nationalism has bound Negroes together more than any other factor. "We are all the same color," you hear, "We got to stick together." It also has provided the outlet for shoddy, second-class thinking, operations, beliefs and feelings. "He's a Negro," you hear all the time, "Don't believe no white man." Using Negro racial nationalism, an individual can quickly become a leader, a crusader, a race hero. While whites in Mississippi recognize the leader as the person who speaks loudest against the Negro, we in Harlem or Chicago quickly acclaim the Negro who shouts the loudest against the white man. "He who attacks a white man needs no defense," is the axiom in the big cities. Passion, hatreds and bigotry abound, as principles diminish.

Our communities in the metropolitan areas are dominated by the defeatist members of the lower classes, the Dixie arrivals of the last decade. Poverty is common, and an articulate speaker, politician or churchman quickly can become the leader. There is no great incentive for education, for culture or self-improvement. It is easier to lambaste conditions and blame the white man. From this turmoil have evolved the direct-action civil-rights organizations, all geared to monopolize in a field that has become as commercial as Madison Avenue. Making the correct statement, endorsing the proper demonstration or planning the proper move can mean a difference of thousands of dollars. Race relations is a profession with big salaries, handsome downtown offices and a special vocabulary. If you attend a lecture by one of the race-relations hotshots, on a subject such as, say, group dynamics, you won't know what he is talking about. They make street brawls sound like the War of 1812.

The years ahead will be eventful. There will be racial clashes and the violence and brutality that go with change. Perhaps this is the continued heritage of the Negro, but in the future the white man will suffer as well. He will feel the sting of sarcasm, rebuke and scorn, as well as the pain of gun shot, fist or jagged glass.

At the same time that the Negro has lost his fear of the white man, he also has lost much faith in his religion. He doesn't pray like he used to. He doesn't await for religion to move mountains. Even the opening of doors of opportunity somehow has embittered many Negroes, unable to take advantage of the gains. "We should have been in here a long time ago," a Negro youngster said when he joined a boys' club. He proceeded to slash a chair. "This job isn't so hot," a Negro official said when he received an important governmental appointment, "What's all the shouting about? It's just another job." The first Negroes in a certain housing project tried to throw all-night parties in retaliation for the lengthy period of discrimination. Restless, uncomfortable and demanding, the Negro today is pressing, pushing and rushing into new positions on Freedom Hill. "Damn them," he jeers, "Let's take over." There's a punitive spirit in his approach.

How long will this period of testing one another's stamina and endurance last? It is hard to say, but it would be tragic if it is long enough to embitter and disillusion both races. The Negro is a long way from his fulfillment, and if he is not satisfied after the current demonstrations have ceased, a new wave may begin. The aggressors will then be the Negro masses, who after disowning their upper-class bosses, may become their own leaders. Such a prospect worries today's Negro leadership.

Violence always hangs like a cloud over a revolution, especially a social revolution that contains such powerful ingredients as passion and hatred. The Negro has withstood the indignity of second class citizenship for a century. As barriers lower and equal opportunity develops, the tone and mood of race relations can change. America can then, and only then, be a symbol to the world. The power of love and brotherhood is the real strength of mankind.

# Index